ADVANCE PRAISE

"A sympathetic, perceptive and well researched study of one of America's most important recent religious writers. Readers of *A Severe Mercy* are in Will Vaus' debt for such an illuminating and informative study."

   Alister McGrath, author of *C. S. Lewis: A Life*

"Van was a character — a very good one as it happens, and Will Vaus catches the actuality of this intriguing man of many parts. Very illuminating reading."

   Thomas Howard, author of *On Being Catholic*

"This is a charming biography about a doubly charming man who wrote a triply charming book. It is a great way to meet the man behind *A Severe Mercy*."

   Peter Kreeft, author of *Jacob's Ladder: Ten Steps to Truth*

"Vaus has masterfully captured the spirit of Vanauken, his deep desire for beauty, his mistakes along the way, and eventually his love of God. Reading this biography takes me back to the same deep emotions I have every time I read *A Severe Mercy*."

   Jim Belcher, author of *Deep Church*

"Very well written, thoroughly researched, hard to put down despite many tears - Will Vaus captures the essence of Van in this book."

   Marion, Davy Vanauken's daughter

"Sheldon Vanauken's story of C. S. Lewis, Oxford, a passionate love, and a tragic loss captured the imagination of Evangelical Christians thirty years ago. Will Vaus' biography of the author of *A Severe Mercy* captures the same mixture of a flawed romantic quest driven by a longing for truth, goodness and beauty, that culminates in the fullness of the Catholic faith. Vaus' book is a study in divine providence and a captivating biography of a unique and noble soul."

   Fr. Dwight Longenecker, author of *The Quest for the Creed*

Sheldon Vanauken

The Man Who Received "A Severe Mercy"

Will Vaus

Sheldon Vanauken
The Man Who Received "A Severe Mercy"

Copyright © 2013 Will Vaus

Winged Lion Press
Hamden, CT

All rights reserved. Except in the case of quotations embodied in critical articles or reviews, no part of this book may be reproduced or transmitted in any form or by any means, electronic or mechanical, including photocopying, recording, or by any information storage or retrieval system, without written permission of the publisher.
For information, contact Winged Lion Press www.WingedLionPress.com

Cover photo courtesy of Lynchburg College Archives, Knight-Capron Library

The author has sought permission for quotations and illustrations where he has thought necessary. If there is any instance where he has been remiss, please inform the publisher for corrections in future editions.

Winged Lion Press titles may be purchased for business or promotional use or special sales.

10-9-8-7-6-5-4-3-2-1

WINGED LION PRESS
ISBN-13 978-1-935688-03-7

For Marion

"He has made everything beautiful in its time.
He has also set eternity in the human heart."

                    Ecclesiastes 3:11

CONTENTS

Prologue: Meeting Van   1

Part One: Intimations (1914-1934)   9

    I   Indiana Roots   11
    II   Boyhood & Glen Merle   19
    III   Culver Military Academy   29
    IV   Through the Iron Gate   35

Part Two: The Heights & The Depths (1934-1955)   41

    V   Wabash & Davy   43
    VI   Love & Marriage   51
    VII   The War Years   59
    VIII   Sailing the Keys   67
    IX   Conviction   73
    X   Ettarre   81
    XI   Oxford   87
    XII   The Leap   95
    XIII   The Other Side of the Gap   103
    XIV   C. S. Lewis & Other Friends   111
    XV   Li'l Dreary   117
    XVI   Mole End   125
    XVII   Lighten our Darkness   131

Part Three: Wandering (1955-1973)   137

    XVIII   Van's Grief Observed   139
    XIX   Flying On "Alone"   147
    XX   The Idealistic Years   155
    XXI   The Angry Years   163

Part Four: Return to the Obedience (1973-1996)   171

    XXII   Twitches Upon the Thread   173
    XXIII   The Vocation   181
    XXIV   Letters, a Novel & "Retirement"   189
    XXV   Home to Rome   195
    XXVI   Writing Away   203
    XXVII   Under the Mercy   209
    XXVIII   The Little Lost Marion and Other Mercies   215
    XXIX   A Good Correspondent   223
    XXX   The Setting of the Soul   231

Epilogue   237
Acknowledgements   239
Endnotes   245
Bibliography   281
Index   285
About the Author   293

VANCOT, LYNCHBURG, VIRGINIA

Author Photo

PROLOGUE: MEETING VAN

> Interesting? Yes, he's certainly that.
> You'll never get to the bottom of him.
>
> J. R. R. Tolkien, speaking to George Sayer about C. S. Lewis

What Tolkien said of Lewis, could also be said of Sheldon Vanauken. I doubt any biographer could ever "get to the bottom" of him. However, like many people across the United States and in England, I *began* to know Sheldon Vanauken through reading his bestselling book *A Severe Mercy* in the late 1970s. As described on the back cover of my paperback copy, *A Severe Mercy* is about Sheldon "Van" Vanauken and Jean "Davy" Vanauken, two people who...

> ... were lucky enough to discover that radiant love so often written of in books, so seldom found in real life. Van and Davy got married, crossed oceans and became inextricably bound up in a search for Christian faith. At Oxford, they met C. S. Lewis and through his influence became believers. Then Davy fell prey to a mysterious illness. What follows is an almost unbearably powerful story of hope and sorrow. Van turned to Lewis, his friend and mentor, for guidance.

That's the story of this bestseller in brief. The book has had at least a million readers to date. The synopsis almost sounds like that of a novel. However, it is a real life story.

What impressed me most about the book when I first read it? *A Severe Mercy* gave to me the same experience of joy or longing that I received from reading some of C. S. Lewis' works. The book did something to my soul I couldn't quite describe. I wanted to enter into the world that Vanauken so ably described. A few years later, when I spent time in Oxford, England on vacation, Vanauken's writing had prepared me for what I was going to see.

During my senior year in college, I read *Under the Mercy*, the sequel to Vanauken's bestseller. It tells the story of Vanauken's life after the death of his wife. In reading *Under the Mercy*, I was challenged by Vanauken's thoughts on feminism, New Testament criticism and the Church. As with *A Severe Mercy*, the words of *Under the Mercy* filled me with joy, but I also became more intrigued with the man under the mercy, Sheldon Vanauken.

Years passed after reading these books and visiting Oxford. I was attending a theological seminary on the east coast and participating in a students' group on campus. I was responsible for getting speakers for a lunchtime forum; so, I decided to write to Sheldon Vanauken in Lynchburg, Virginia to invite him to speak to our group about C. S. Lewis. In reply, I received a neatly typed postcard. Vanauken thanked me for the invitation but politely declined to speak. He said that he felt it was his business to write, since God had given him that talent. Consequently, he was in the habit of turning down all invitations to speak, except local ones. The postcard concluded with a counter invitation: "If ever you come down to the South, you will be welcome to stop by."

After graduating from seminary, I was in the South on a number of occasions. In fact, my wife and I lived in North Carolina when we were first married. I recall driving through Lynchburg on one occasion and thinking of Vanauken, but I never went to the trouble of looking him up. Still, I saved the postcard.

More years passed. We moved from North Carolina to California, then back again to South Carolina. My parents moved from Southern California to Virginia and at the same time, I started a C. S. Lewis Society in Columbia, South Carolina. Thus, my thoughts naturally drifted back to Sheldon Vanauken.

I remembered the postcard, searched and found it in a dusty box of old correspondence, and wrote to Vanauken at his old address, not even knowing whether he was still alive. I asked if we could meet when I would next be in Virginia, visiting my parents. Vanauken replied within a week, again on a postcard, this time—handwritten. He said that we could probably meet during my stay in Virginia but that I should ring him up a couple of days earlier to set a time. His phone number, interestingly enough, was VIO-LINS.

The time of my visit to Virginia, eagerly anticipated, finally arrived. I called Vanauken on the telephone as instructed. The voice on the other end was what I expected—genteel, refined, a touch of Oxford perhaps. The day was set for our meeting.

On the day of our rendezvous, I drove two hours from the tiny hamlet of Head Waters, where my parents lived, to Lynchburg. We were to meet at 2:30 that afternoon. I arrived in Lynchburg in time for lunch and a look around. I ate a quick meal at some "greasy spoon", all the while re-reading bits and pieces of *A Severe Mercy*. I strolled across the grounds of Lynchburg College where Vanauken taught English literature and history for some thirty years. I remember the dogwoods were in bloom. The stately red brick buildings and Greek columns of the school where Vanauken had spent the better part of his life left a lasting impression.

At the appointed time I drove to Vanauken's home, Vancot as he liked to call it, or the Birdhouse, so called after a tiny house in Hawaii that he and Davy had planned to live in. In fact, Vanauken and his wife had often walked by this house and wanted to have it. Therefore, although Davy had never been in it, she knew about it, and that provided Vanauken a sense of continuity after her death. He moved into the house shortly after Davy's passing, when the building was still part of the Lynchburg College campus, paying just $30 per month in rent. In the 1960s, when the college decided to build a library extension, the Birdhouse had to go, so Vanauken bought it for $200 and had the house and its garage moved down the hill. The building was said to have been a one-room schoolhouse dating to the time immediately following the War Between the States. The single storey house with wood siding painted white was only twenty feet by twenty, with an additional little bathroom wing, if you can even call it a wing. Across the street was a small park below the hill on which Lynchburg College was situated.

Parking my car astride the green, Vanauken's garden, as he liked to call it, I walked across the street and up the broken concrete steps to the bright blue front door. I reached for the knocker Vanauken had rescued from the now demolished Studio, his and Davy's 1950s Oxford flat. A man soon answered the knock, a man unlike what I anticipated. He was tall, with sandy, graying hair; I expected that. However, he was also a bit overweight and a tad unkempt. His appearance did not match the refined voice I had heard over the telephone line. I introduced myself and Vanauken invited me in. I wasn't certain until that moment whether he would wish to talk in his home or somewhere else. I was delighted to be ushered into his inner sanctum. Vanauken directed me to the left, into the main room of the house which was at once his living room, bedroom, dining room and library all in one.

"Have a seat in the blue chair," Vanauken offered.

"Thank you," I replied, as I crossed the Persian rugs covering the floor and hunted for a chair that looked even remotely blue. On the far side of the hearth was a once over-stuffed chair, threadbare after many years of use, by this time more Confederate Grey than Oxford Blue. I sat in the "blue" chair as invited, and Vanauken sat on his narrow bed—a four-poster crafted of beautiful cherry; it was Vanauken's bed from his parent's home, Glenmerle. In fact, most of the furniture was from Glenmerle. As I scanned the room I saw in the opposite corner a tall antique bookcase, filled with hardback volumes. Atop the bookcase was Vanauken's Navy cap from World War II. Beside the bookcase was a small sofa underneath three large windows trimmed with royal blue curtains. Beside the sofa was a leaded-glass Gothic floor lamp, the kind with a small table half way up the stem. Between the lamp and the bed was a table filled with numerous books, including Vanauken's current read—Colleen McCullough's *Caesar's Women*. Nearby was a wooden laptop contraption Vanauken had made for writing in bed. Above the head of the bed was a small painting by Davy. On the wall at the side of the bed were two crucifixes, one was Norman, a copy of one Vanauken had given to C. S. Lewis that had hung over the bed in which Lewis died. Along the same wall was a tiny window to which Vanauken had pasted a handmade map of Lynchburg and surrounding territory. Beneath the window was a small shelf on which he kept odds-and-ends he wanted handy. Along the wall at the foot of the bed was a small Chippendale secretary desk and chair made of the same cherry wood. The glassed cabinet at the top of the desk revealed an assortment of editions of Vanauken's own books.[1]

Shortly after we were seated, Vanauken lit a cigarette. The walls were yellowed by forty years of smoke. From time to time during our conversation, Vanauken would lift his legs on to the bed and lay on his side. Was he in some kind of pain or merely eccentric? I wasn't sure.

Vanauken opened the conversation with, "So what do you do for a living?"

"I'm a pastor in Columbia, South Carolina." I responded.

"And you drove all the way from South Carolina to see me?" Vanauken queried.

"Actually, I drove over here from my parents' home, outside of Staunton."

"I attended Staunton Military Academy in my early teens," Vanauken informed me. Despite Vanauken's outward man wasting away, to use St. Paul's expression, his inner man was certainly vital. His mind and conversation were alive to ideas, current events, to all of life. Vanauken's keen intelligence shone through his flashing blue eyes.

After we talked for a while, Vanauken stood up and asked, "Would you like a drink? Gin-and-tonic? Or whiskey?"

I hesitated for a moment leading Vanauken to query with a look of feigned horror, "You're not a teetotaler are you?"

I quickly responded, "No, I just don't drink gin or whiskey."

"How about a glass of sherry?"

"That will be fine."

While Vanauken was in his tiny yellow kitchen fixing our drinks, I further surveyed the room. In the midst of the wall behind me was a fireplace. Some of Davy's paintings and the figurehead of "Grey Goose", the Vanaukens' former sailboat, hung above the mantle. On the hearth sat an old typewriter, the one on which he had typed the manuscript of *A Severe Mercy* and which he still used to type his voluminous correspondence. On either side of the fireplace were two, floor-to-ceiling, built-in bookshelves. I quickly found Vanauken's collection of Lewis books on the right-hand side. They were all hardback, some first editions, one of *Mere Christianity* and another of *A Grief Observed* by N. W. Clerk. Newspaper clippings of some early reviews fell out of these Lewis volumes as I perused. There were also Lewis' letters to Van stuffed between some of the pages.

The Man Who Received "A Severe Mercy"

When Vanauken returned with the drinks I commented, "I love your books, especially some of the Lewis first editions."

"Well, I don't have them because they are first editions. I just happened to be living in or visiting Oxford when some of those books were first published. That's how I acquired them."

Sensing his mood I said, "It is a shame that some people love old books but never read what's in them." We both laughed.

"What about the letters tucked in some of the books? Are those the originals?" I queried.

"Heavens no! I gave the originals to the Bodleian Library in Oxford long ago."

When we had resumed our seats, I asked Vanauken about Glenmerle, his boyhood country home. "I could picture what the house and grounds were like from your description in the first chapter of *A Severe Mercy*."

"That's good. That is exactly what I intended," he responded.

"Is Glenmerle still in existence?" I asked.

"It was swallowed up by the growth of the city," Vanauken answered with a wary look of sadness on his face.

"What city swallowed it up?" I pursued.

"I'll leave you to figure that out," Vanauken countered.

"I always thought of Glenmerle being in Virginia." I said.

At this Vanauken smiled. He always wanted people to think he was born and bred in the South. However, later on in the conversation he gave me a clue as to Glenmerle's location.

Changing the subject I asked, "What was C. S. Lewis like?"

"He was a hearty man with a booming voice. When we walked into a pub together, he would call out to the publican, 'Any pies today?' When I was at Oxford in the 50's there would be three or four hundred students attending Lewis' lectures. They would sit spell-bound by that great voice."

"What about Lewis' home, The Kilns? You visited there?" I asked.

"Yes, on more than one occasion. I met his wife Joy there, shortly after one of her hospital stays. She was in bed in the common room and Jack left us alone together for the first half hour of our visit, just so we could get acquainted without him interrupting us."

"What was Joy Davidman like?"

"She was very courteous to me. I did not see anything of the brash, New York, Jewess that some of Jack's Oxford friends didn't care for."

"Did you ever spend the night in Lewis' home?"

"No, but I did stay overnight with Jack when he was a professor at Magdalene College, Cambridge. We stayed up very late one night talking about all manner of things. I wish now that I had kept notes on the conversation."

"Tell me about your last visit with C. S. Lewis. What was that like?"

"I saw Jack at The Kilns a couple of weeks before his death in November 1963. We were alone in the house. Jack warned me that he might doze off during our visit and not to worry. I still got concerned when he actually did nod off in the middle of our conversation and he didn't wake up for a couple of minutes! Later he perked up and we moved from the common room to the kitchen where he served me a cup of tea. We planned to meet again a couple of weeks later."

"But you didn't?"

"No, we weren't able to. I was having breakfast with a friend in Oxford one morning. Reading the *Oxford Mail* I saw Jack's obituary. The day of his funeral was the day we were supposed to meet again. Instead of attending the funeral, I went to the Eastgate Hotel, had a drink, and reminisced about our friendship."

"Do you have any photos from your time in Oxford?"

"Very few. I had given up photography by that time of my life. I much prefer to draw pictures with words. Mind you, I once took a photo of Jack that was later published in a book somewhere. There are some photos in that burgundy colored book on the shelf behind you. You are welcome to take a look."

I reached behind me and pulled a book off the shelf entitled *A Severe Mercy: Davy's Edition*. Vanauken told me, "There are only ten thousand copies of that edition. It was printed mostly as a gift for friends and *Severe Mercy* enthusiasts."

On the frontispiece of *Davy's Edition* is a color print of Davy's "Sin Picture" which is mentioned in the book. There are also eight pages of pictures in the middle. Later that year my wife and my mother got together to buy me a copy of *Davy's Edition* from a rare book dealer. On my next visit to see Vanauken, he signed the title page: "To Will Vaus—a good correspondent. Sheldon Vanauken."

After perusing the book, we continued our conversation. "Did you see the movie *Shadowlands* with Anthony Hopkins and Debra Winger?" I queried.

"Yes, I saw it in the theater."

"What did you think?"

"Hopkins was not at all like Jack. Debra Winger was a good Joy Davidman. And the actor who played Warnie was perfect for the part."

"What about the BBC version of *Shadowlands*?"

"I don't own a television but some friends showed it to me on their set. Joss Acland gave a much more accurate portrayal of Jack. However, both Acland and Hopkins were too sentimental. When it came to handling grief, Jack had a rod of steel down his spine, at least when it came to talking about his grief with outsiders."

Vanauken and I plumbed some spiritual depths in our first meeting. We talked about the reality of the spiritual realm—both the good and evil sides. We shared with one another experiences we both had with people involved in the occult.

After an hour or so of conversation, I asked Vanauken if I could use his bathroom. He pointed the way. In the bathroom, I noticed a photo of Pope John Paul II propped up on a table. When I returned to the main room I used the photo as an opportunity to ask Vanauken yet another question.

"I noticed the picture of the Pope. Obviously, you admire him greatly. But why did you join the Catholic Church after living for so many years as an Anglican?"

Vanauken responded with keen interest, "Because of apostolic succession. I came to the point where I realized that the only true apostolic succession is through the Catholic Church because the Bishop of Rome is the successor of Peter. Therefore, the Catholic Church is the only true church. Protestants talk about the Bible being the Christian's ultimate authority, but 1 Timothy 3:15 says that the Church is the pillar and bulwark of the truth."

"What about the relationship between faith and works in justification?"

"You need both. I am skeptical of the 'born again' experience and assurance of salvation claimed by many evangelicals. We Catholics believe we must be 'born again,' or have many conversions throughout our lives."

From there the conversation meandered through all the Catholic/Protestant hot buttons: the presence of Christ in the Eucharist, the role of Mary in the Church, the tension between being true to the teachings of Scripture vs. unity with other believers in Christ. With regard to this last point Vanauken said, "In the tension between truth and unity one must trust the Church."

I glanced at my watch and was surprised to discover we had been talking for three hours. It was dinnertime and my stomach was growling but I certainly did not want the conversation to end. I asked, "Would you like to go out to dinner?"

"No, I don't go out to dinner anymore, though I often do go out to a restaurant for lunch."

"Well then, I'd better be going."

"You don't have to rush off." Vanauken encouraged.

"No, I better go. I have a long drive ahead."

As Vanauken walked me to the door I paused by the shelf with the C. S. Lewis books and said, "I've felt very close to Lewis while visiting you. I might have to come back and visit these books again."

Vanauken smiled and said, "You'll be welcome anytime."

Sheldon Vanauken

We covered an amazing amount of ground in our first conversation on that April day in 1996. However, I felt like I had only begun to paddle on the surface of Vanauken's amazing life, a life that spanned most of the twentieth century, a life that witnessed events as diverse as the bombing of Pearl Harbor and the March on the Pentagon. Indeed, I was soon to wade deeper into the life of this unusual man, discovering through our correspondence and through subsequent research, that there was a lot more to Sheldon Vanauken than being the author of one bestselling book.

PART ONE
INTIMATIONS
1914-1934

There was a time when meadow, grove, and stream,
The earth, and every common sight,
To me did seem
Appareled in celestial light,
The glory and the freshness of a dream.

William Wordsworth, *Ode: Intimations of Immortality*

Indianapolis Star Newspaper
Sketch of Van's Father

I
INDIANA ROOTS

> I have always been a wand'rer
> Over land and sea
> Yet a moonbeam on the water
> Casts a spell o'er me
> A vision fair I see
> Again I seem to be
> Back home again in Indiana.
>
> Ballard MacDonald

Sheldon Frank Van Auken was born August 4, 1914. As Van[2] once pointed out, he was born the same day that England declared war on the German Kaiser.

However, what Van didn't like to point out was the place of his birth. Why was he so secretive about it? As one colleague said, "Indiana was not where he wanted to be from."[3] This "looking down upon" the place of his upbringing can be traced fairly far back in Van's life. In 1951, he wrote to Dr. Osborne of Wabash College in Indiana about a possible return to teach at his alma mater. In that letter Van wrote, "It's hardly necessary to expand on why I should like to return to Wabash. I am, after all, Indiana born (which is more important than I once thought)."[4]

Van was a lover of the Old South from very early on in his life, as indicated in *A Severe Mercy* by the tiny Confederate battle flag pinned to the wall in his Glenmerle bedroom.[5] Perhaps Van's love of Virginia can be dated to his brief time at Staunton Military Academy in Virginia during the school year of 1928 to 1929. At any rate, it is clear that Van came to wish, at some point in his life, that he had been born and raised in Virginia. He wanted so much to be from the South that he once wrote to a correspondent pointing out that Indiana was part of the territory of Old Virginia.[6] This statement is historically true (in 1803 part of Virginia became Ohio and Indiana territory) but it also reveals much about Van's *desired* birthplace.

For some reason, Van also chose to change the spelling of his family name from Van Auken to Vanauken.[7] No one knows why. When I lived in Irmo, South Carolina Van wrote to me and said that he wished he dwelt, like me, in a four-letter town and had a four-letter first name and last name. Maybe that's why he chose to be called Van, at least as early as his time in the Navy; it was, simply, a shorter first name. Moreover, perhaps Vanauken sounds more Anglicized; Van was a lover of England as much as he was a lover of the Old South, a love that was born in him, perhaps as early as the year he spent in England as a small boy.[8] He never showed much interest, that I know of, in his Dutch heritage.

The name "Van Auken" means "from Auken." Auken may be an alternate spelling of Aachen, the favored residence of Charlemagne and the place of coronation for the medieval kings of Germany. Going further back, Aken was the Egyptian custodian of the ferryboat carrying the souls of the dead to the Underworld. It seems an appropriate family name for a man who would come to love boats and a man who would write a bestselling book chronicling not only a great love and a unique conversion, but also a tremendous grief.

Van's family tree can be traced back at least as far as Marinus Van Aken who emigrated from Holland to Ulster County, New York sometime before 11 April 1683 when he married his wife in Kingston.[9] Marinus' great great-grandson was Jacob Hornbeck Van Auken, born in Machackemack (Deerpark near Port Jervis), Orange County, New York on 13 August 1810.[10] This Jacob was Van's great-grandfather, the one whom he describes in *A Severe Mercy* as the owner of "the great farm called Magic Grove, a grove planted in a mathematical figure."[11] The *History of Steuben County Indiana*, published in 1885, refers to Jacob's birthplace as being Pike County, Pennsylvania, whereas the US Census of 1870 indicates Jacob's birthplace as New Jersey. All of these, in a sense, may be correct. Machackemack was located in what is now known as the Tri-State area, the place where Pennsylvania, New Jersey and New York states all meet. According to the *History of Steuben County*:

> [Jacob] attended the country schools of Sussex County, N. J., his feet clad in rags, later to be exchanged for leather shoes purchased with quails which he had entrapped. The lad's perception and memory were bright and, accordingly, at sixteen he graduated from the college of the common people with the degree of master of the three R's, reading, 'righting and 'rithmetic. Shortly thereafter we find him the leading schoolmaster of Peter's Valley, and studying also logarithms and surveying under a private tutor. Among his pupils was Nancy Strawway, nearly five years his junior, to whom in March, 1831, he was married, a relationship which lasted nearly fifty years, to her death July 19, 1878. Four years later, Oct. 6, 1882, he also died from the gradual bursting of the heart.[12]

Soon after Jacob's marriage to Nancy, they decided to try their fortunes in what was then known as "the far West." They settled in Deerfield, Portage County, Ohio, which was, many years later, coincidentally, the birthplace of Van's mother. In Deerfield, Jacob and Nancy had three children born to them. Jacob divided his time between farming and teaching in the village school where one of the patrons was Jesse Grant, the father of Ulysses S. Grant.

The Man Who Received "A Severe Mercy"

From Deerfield, it was on to Chagrin Falls, Cuyahoga County, where Nancy gave birth to twelve more children, including Frank Buckle Van Auken, Van's grandfather.

During Jacob's time of residence in Ohio, he also labored in surveying parts of northern Michigan. This was a trade in which he trained several of his sons, including Frank. On one occasion Jacob had as his assistant a rough and tumble, young lad named Jim who attracted his interest. The young man was the son of a widow in the area. Seeing the boy's intelligence and aptitude for learning, Jacob encouraged him to attend the school of his friend, Dr. Harlowe. Years later Jacob met up with Jim once again and this time the latter urged Jacob to attend with him his inauguration, as President of the United States, for Jim was none other than James Garfield.[13]

Jacob Van Auken attributed both his political and religious views to the influence of Thomas Jefferson. Jacob was raised a Presbyterian, in which church he remained until he became convinced that the main articles of the Christian religion were contrary to the laws of nature. He came to believe in the "God of Nature" whose only revelation could come to human beings through the study of natural law.[14] In this, we see a pattern similar to the religious wanderings of his great-grandson's early life.

In the fall of 1860 Jacob's family moved yet again, this time to a place of greater permanence: Pleasant Lake, Steuben County, Indiana. It was here that Jacob "purchased the homestead now known, by the arrangement of nineteen stately evergreens in nine straight rows which they planted, as Magic Grove Farm."[15] Jacob died in Pleasant Lake on October 6, 1882, one year before the birth of his grandson, Robert Glenn Van Auken. On the Sunday following his death, approximately one thousand people attended Jacob's burial service at the Pleasant Lake Cemetery where he was laid to rest beside his beloved wife Nancy.[16] A friend and work associate, A. V. Ball, remembered Jacob as a man well able to defend himself with his tongue, a gift Jacob apparently passed on to his descendants.[17]

Jacob's son, Frank B. Van Auken was born 13 November, 1850 in Chagrin Falls, Ohio but grew up on the Magic Grove Farm in Indiana, of which farm he became the proprietor in 1882. From 1867 to 1870, Frank studied in the Angola Academy, receiving a teacher's license at the age of seventeen. Concurrent with his studies, and by the age of eighteen, Frank was teaching school at Pleasant Lake. A year later, he was engaged as an itinerant teacher of writing. (Again, one can't help but discern a gift that Frank must have passed on genetically to his grandson.) In addition, at the age of twenty Mr. Van Auken organized the first graded school at Orland. That same year he began attending Hillsdale College along with his brother J. J., from which school Frank graduated in 1874 with a Bachelor of Science degree.

During his years in college, Frank found sufficient time to court and wed Rheumina H. Sanders on November 23, 1873 in Otsego, Indiana. His new wife assisted him from the start in his teaching endeavors as principal of the school at Pleasant Lake.

One year after the two brothers graduated from Hillsdale, they were elected surveyors of Steuben and DeKalb counties, following their father's example. This task, however, did not keep Frank from continuing in the teaching profession. He spent five years as Superintendent of the Waterloo City Schools, graduating the first class from there in 1878.[18]

When Frank Van Auken died on December 1, 1915, it made the front page of the Steuben County Republican newspaper. According to his obituary, he was one of the most widely known citizens of northeastern Indiana. Frank was survived by his wife, Mina, and by his children: Nannie Van Auken Ladd of Chicago, Sanders Van Auken of Newport News, Virginia, Frank Verne Van Auken of Denver, Colorado and Robert Glenn Van Auken of Auburn, Indiana, all of whom were at his side when he died. Amazingly, for he could have been at the most a year or so old at the time, Sheldon Vanauken later remembered sitting on his grandfather Frank's knee and being given a tiny gold dollar.[19]

Van's father, Robert Glenn Van Auken, was born 8 November 1883 on the Magic Grove Farm. Glenn attended the common, or public, schools that his father was so instrumental in starting.[20] And, like his father, he attended college, but Glenn's was the Tri-State Normal College close by in Angola where he took classes for two years.[21] After college, Glenn entered the National Guard in 1902, serving for fifteen years and rising to the rank of Captain in the third Regiment. For two of those years, 1906-1907, he was in the Panama Canal Service.

Upon his return to Indiana Glenn met and married Grace Merle Hanselman, a young woman in her mid twenties, with family connections in Steuben County, who was most attractive to Glenn because of her lovely auburn hair which she wore piled high atop her head. They were married on February 1, 1909 in Ravenna, Portage County, Ohio—Grace's hometown.

Grace was born October 12, 1882 in Deerfield, Ohio to Sheldon Fitch and Laurie Slack Hanselman. Grace's father Sheldon was born in Angola, the county seat of Steuben, Indiana on April 11, 1858. He was the son of David C. Hanselman, a man belonging to one of the pioneer families of Ohio who became a renowned preacher in the Christian Church, Disciples of Christ. David and Lucy had three children, the only survivor being Sheldon Fitch. Sheldon gained his early education in the public schools of Indiana and when he was twelve he moved with his parents to Ohio. Later Sheldon attended school in Bethany, West Virginia and Butler University in Indiana (a college

The Man Who Received "A Severe Mercy"

which will enter our story more than once). After his schooling Sheldon was employed in various jobs including managing his father's homestead in Steuben County, working as a shoe clerk in Canton, Ohio, as well as spending a year as a traveling glove salesman. In 1878, Sheldon married Miss Laurie R. Slack of Deerfield, Ohio and began managing the farm and flourmill belonging to his father-in-law. It was during this time that Sheldon began reading law. He was admitted to the bar in June 1888.

Sheldon and Laurie moved to the town of Ravenna where Sheldon entered into practice with Philo B. Conant until Conant's death in 1889. After that time Sheldon worked with I. T. Siddall. Sheldon became known as an "able trial lawyer and well fortified and conservative counselor."[22]

Sheldon, like Van's other grandfather Frank, became associated with the Republican Party. He served for six years as prosecuting attorney of Portage County and was appointed a member of the Ohio state board of pardons by Governor Bushnell. As Sheldon Vanauken alludes to in *A Severe Mercy*, his grandfather Sheldon was elected mayor of Ravenna for two years beginning in 1899. Then starting in 1905, he served as city solicitor for several years.

Van certainly knew his Grandpa Sheldon much better than his Grandpa Frank since the former lived until 1922. Thus, the Hanselman's home at 120 North Freedom in Ravenna receives a half paragraph of description in *A Severe Mercy*. Van recalled his grandparents' Ohio home as a Victorian house with many verandas, set in a wide expanse of tree-shaded lawns. Inside the house, there were a number of unique features: a stained-glass staircase window and a huge bathroom with a long tin bathtub. In the bathroom, (as was common in those days) there was a vent in the floor to bring heat up from the kitchen. Thus, Van long-remembered taking morning baths at his grandparents' house while hearing his family talking away in the kitchen and smelling bacon frying in the pan. Van would always recall his Grandpa Sheldon as white-bearded and jovial, the seemingly permanent mayor of Ravenna.[23]

When Glenn Van Auken and Grace Hanselman were first married, they lived in Angola, Indiana in a nondescript house at 115 North West Street.[24] Grace quickly became pregnant and gave birth, prematurely, to a baby boy on October 2, 1909. They named the baby Robert Glenn, after his father. However, the child only lived for one day and was soon buried in the Pleasant Lake Cemetery beside his forbears.

While Grace handled her grief by focusing on the care of her new husband and home, Glenn plunged himself into his work. He began serving as a Court Reporter for the 35th Judicial Circuit of Indiana. At the same time, he began to study law, perhaps influenced by his father-in-law. In those days, a degree was not necessary to practice. Glenn was admitted to the bar in 1914. By this time, Glenn and Grace had moved to Auburn, the seat of neighboring

DeKalb County. They lived at 905 North Main Street in an attractive and spacious one-and-a-half storey wood-frame bungalow. It was in that house that Sheldon Frank Van Auken entered this life and was named after his two grandfathers.

Two years before Van's entrance into this world, a very important event took place in his father's life. On August 16, 1912, Glenn Van Auken received the Democratic nomination to be the next joint state senator representing Steuben and Dekalb counties.[25] Since Glenn's father was a Republican, one wonders how that went over.[26] However, the public received Glenn's nomination with much acclaim. As the Auburn Courier stated, "The applause which followed the announcement of Mr. Van Auken's name clearly indicated the state of mind of the majority of the delegates." Van Auken was nominated unanimously. In the following months Van Auken's newspaper advertisements presented him as: "Clean, able, honorable. A man who has the qualifications and the knowledge necessary to represent all the people." Many years later Glenn's son Sheldon would also describe his father as a man of honor and a gentleman. Both Glenn and Grace instilled in their son that which was honorable without having to say much about it.[27]

Returning to 1912, by the time the November election rolled around Glenn Van Auken had won by a large margin, riding into office on the coattails of Woodrow Wilson. It was a Democratic sweep statewide.

Glenn was re-elected to a second term in 1916, the same year that his third son was born (Paul Slack Van Auken came into this world on August 29, 1916). During his second term as a state senator, Glenn was chosen as Democratic floor leader.[28] However, Glenn's service in the Indiana General Assembly was interrupted by a larger event on the world scene: The Great War. Thus, from 1918 to 1919 Glenn served in the United States Army. He was a major in the infantry and worked in several large camps in Oklahoma, Louisiana and Georgia as an instructor in gunnery. He was known as the best shot in the entire army. Glenn's love of guns and of the military was something he would seek to pass on to his sons, though at first somewhat unsuccessfully with Sheldon.

Van's Birthplace, Auburn, Indiana

Author Photo

GLEN MERLE

Photo Courtesy of Barbara Lee McCormick

II

BOYHOOD & GLEN MERLE

> Home, for my heart still calls me;
> Home, through the danger zone;
> Home, whatever befalls me,
> I will sail again to my own!
>
> Henry Van Dyke, *Homeward Bound*

In 1919, Glenn Van Auken was appointed by Governor James P. Goodrich to be a member of the Indiana Public Service Commission.[29] This appointment led to the Van Auken family move to Indianapolis.[30] The Van Auken's first home in Indianapolis was a rather ordinary two-and-a-half storey wood-frame house at 3830 Carrolton Avenue on the north side of the city near the Indiana State Fairgrounds.[31]

Glenn and Grace were on the Charter Roll of Northwood Christian Church, at 4550 Central Avenue, when the congregation was officially established on Sunday, May 1, 1921. Thus the Christian Church, Disciples of Christ, was the Protestant denomination in which Sheldon Van Auken received his early spiritual formation.

The Disciples of Christ grew out of two movements seeking Christian unity that sprang up almost simultaneously in western Pennsylvania and Kentucky in the early 19th century. Thomas and Alexander Campbell, a Scottish Presbyterian father and son in Pennsylvania, were increasingly disturbed by the sectarianism which kept members of different denominations, and even members of the same denomination, from partaking of Holy Communion together. At the same time, Barton W. Stone in Kentucky, who was also a Presbyterian, objected to the use of creeds as tests of fellowship within the church. Campbell and Stone were seeking a sort of "mere Christianity" long before C. S. Lewis ever wrote on the subject. Campbell and Stone's aims and aspirations being similar, the two movements united in 1832 after about a quarter century of separate development.

This was the first new Christian movement to spring up on American soil. The founders of the Disciples of Christ hoped to restore Christian unity by returning to New Testament faith and practices, much like their earlier Protestant forbears. The Disciples believed and still believe in a personal relationship with Christ as more important than doctrinal precision; they practice baptism of believers by immersion, and weekly, open Communion. In their weekly worship services, they emphasize the preaching of the Gospel.

Given their roots, it is understandable that the Disciples of Christ have had a long history of openness to other Christian traditions. Both locally and internationally, the Disciples have frequently been involved in ecumenism. Thus in the mid twentieth century the Disciples helped organize the National and World Council of Churches. In keeping with their ecumenical mission, the Disciples have approximately 270 international church partners in close to 70 countries. Their membership at the beginning of the twenty-first century was nearly a million people in the United States and Canada. Interestingly enough, the Disciples of Christ headquarters today is in Indianapolis.[32]

Of his early religious upbringing, Van later wrote in a letter to C. S. Lewis that his family was devout and so was he, up to the age of 14. Indeed, Van told Lewis he was ardent in his love of Jesus, or perhaps ardent in his love of himself for being so noble.[33]

As much as he may have loved Jesus as a child, there were a number of things missing in Van's childhood experience of Christianity. He wrote about this in a booklet entitled *Encounter with Light*. First, Christianity as Van knew it in childhood was not exciting enough. The Greeks he was learning about in history, with their deep desire for truth and beauty, and their sunlit temples, they were exciting.

Astronomy was another interest that was thrilling, with its burning stars and the vast distances of outer space. One time when Van was very young, he stood outside on a winter's night and stared up through bare, black branches at the glittering stars. All of a sudden, he felt overwhelmed by the beauty of it all.[34] As he looked intently at the blazing stars, millions of miles away, it filled him with a longing for eternity. In nature, there were many hints of the eternal, countless traces of incredible beauty, but he saw very little that was beautiful in the religion of his childhood, and therefore nothing that evoked a sense of awe, or longing for heaven.

In addition to beauty in nature, Van was discovering poetry; as a young man, he reached out for beauty through words, and felt the exhilaration of their touch. However, Christianity, with its seemingly fractured tales of dark and strange happenings in Palestine, along with the solemn, humorless voices he heard in church, all of this was too boring for words as far as he was concerned.

The faith he was learning about in Sunday school was not positive enough. At least the Christians dying in the Coliseum had died *for* something. Furthermore, the crusader knights, they were positive, as they rode out under their gold crosses; they fought *for* something. However, at Van's local church they did not talk about the crusades. Rather, the Christian life was more about attaining respectability. The main message was that you were evil if you said: "Damn!" or missed church or drank alcohol. Never mind that

The Man Who Received "A Severe Mercy"

Jesus changed water into wine at Cana; if Jesus had actually shown up at Northwood Christian Church in the 1920s, the church members would have preferred he perform the miracle the other way around. It seemed the only things Northwood Christian Church was working *for* was new chairs for the Sunday school and, perhaps, a rather dull heaven.

The Christianity of Van's childhood was, also, not big enough. How could it be large enough to take in all the planets revolving around a million suns in the vast expanse of outer space? How could a seemingly local religion like Christianity, born and bred in a tiny Middle Eastern nation in the first century have any connection to the far-flung galaxies? Christianity was just too darn small to be true, or so Van came to think.

Finally, the Christian faith preached at Van's childhood church was not related to life. Outside the church doors, in downtown Indianapolis, there seemed to be the throbbing pulse of real life: business, education, entertainment, and so much more. However, Van's pastor never talked about life outside the church. Sure, the church was against sin, but the businessmen who disregarded Christian ethics six days a week seemed to be welcome at the altar rail and at the collection plate. Van had a hard time believing that his church, in all its stuffiness, had a corner on the truth market, not when all the beauty and laughter and pain of life was kept outside the church doors.[35] Nevertheless, as much as Van didn't like it, his parents took him regularly to church, and life went on, with Van's father trying to make a living in that "dog-eat-dog" world outside the church.

In 1923, Glenn Van Auken was re-appointed by Governor Warren T. McCray to the Indiana Public Service Commission. However, Glenn only served for a few more months in that position, resigning in the fall of 1923 to enter the practice of law in Indianapolis.[36] Glenn made his office in the Continental National Bank Building.

On the home front, Glenn and Grace were concerned, not only for the spiritual development of their two sons, but also for their intellectual, emotional, social and physical growth. With these concerns in mind, in the summer of 1925, when Van turned eleven years old, his parents enrolled him in the summer Woodcraft School of Culver Military Academy, 115 miles almost directly north of Indianapolis. After his son's acceptance to the school, Glenn wrote the following about Van to General L. R. Gignilliat at Culver:

> He is clean minded and I think about the normal boy. During his early years he was ill a great deal and so lost time in school and time at play. As suggested in his application, for that reason he is somewhat backward in athletics of all kinds and somewhat backward in his school work, although he is about up with the proper grade in school.[37]

Perhaps inspired by the military discipline he experienced at Culver, Van

came up with a code of ethics for himself. He was about twelve at the time. His code had just three points:
1. Never betray a friend.
2. Never betray beauty.
3. Never betray the sword.

By this last point, he meant acting out of bravery even when he was scared. His father had a fancy dress sword from his days in the army. As a boy, he often enjoyed taking the sword down from the wall in his father's study and holding it in his hands. He dreamed of what it would be like to use such a sword in battle, like Sir Lancelot.[38] Soon he would have the opportunity, not simply to dream about military exploits, but to actually receive training, and not just for a summer.

Up until the fall of 1928, Van attended various public schools in Indiana. However, in the autumn of that year his parents sent him far away, to Staunton Military Academy in Staunton, Virginia. One thing Van remembered for the rest of his life from his experience at Staunton was meeting an elderly man who had been one of the brave Virginia Military Institute cadets who fought for the Confederacy in the battle of New Market. Van and the other cadets at SMA thrilled to hear the old war-horse's tales of adventure and battle.[39]

William Hartman Kable founded Staunton Military Academy in September 1860 at Charlestown, Jefferson County, Virginia (now West Virginia). At the time, the school was known as the Charlestown Male Academy. Its founder was a graduate of the University of Virginia. His goal was to teach and train young men to become good citizens. Shortly after the school's founding, the War Between the States broke out. William H. Kable joined the Confederate Army and served with distinction as a Captain in the 10th Virginia Cavalry.

After the war, Captain Kable re-established his school at its original location, and conducted it most successfully in that place. However, Captain Kable's love for the South being what it was, he moved the school to Staunton, Virginia in 1883 and renamed it Staunton Male Academy. The original grounds were much smaller than the present campus, now occupied by Mary Baldwin College. The relocation to Staunton provided the school with a much more desirable location and surroundings.

In its early years at Staunton, the founder of the school and his family lived in the building now known as the Kable House. Kable's students lived upstairs. In 1886, the school became a military academy. Then in 1900, Captain Kable turned over the management of the school to his son William. Colonel William G. Kable was a genius when it came to leading SMA as an institution. The Academy grew, prospered, and was placed by William Kable in an outstanding position among educational institutions of its type.

The Man Who Received "A Severe Mercy"

SMA survived the Great Depression and even prospered, becoming one of the country's most prestigious military preparatory schools. By the time Van went there in 1928 he would have seen not only the original Kable House but the new South Barracks rebuilt after a fire in 1905, the Mess Hall constructed in 1913, and the North Barracks, built in 1918.

Van entered SMA on September 12, 1928. He was a private in Company B. According to his student record card, he took classes in European History, English, French and Algebra. While his IQ was 121, his grades were, overall, average.

In his first letter to C. S. Lewis, written on December 12, 1950, Van revealed that he was fourteen years old when he lost the Christian faith of his childhood. Therefore, it was during his year at Staunton that he ceased to be a Christian. In his letter to Lewis, Van attributed his turn to atheism to his wide reading, especially of science fiction. Books like those of Olaf Stapledon brought doubt and disbelief.[40]

However, Van's reading also had a more positive effect on his life. Inspired by some of the great authors of the day, Van took up his own pen and began to set it to paper. According to Van's later bibliography of his own works, sometime during this period of his life he wrote a tale entitled *The Story of Man*. It was a chronicle of the Coming of Man, the Pinnacle of Man and the Fall of Man. Unfortunately the story was never published and now is lost.[41]

Sadly, Van wasn't just writing about the Fall of Man. He was about to experience a "fall" of sorts for himself. Away from home and parents for the first time in his life, doubting the faith in which he had been raised: Van reacted to his inner pain in a way not unlike other young teens sent away to boarding school. He went absent without leave for four days. Where did he go? Did he hop on the train that came through Staunton and head west to Chicago? Lonely for family and friends, did he run home? Alternatively, did he take off with a fellow cadet for unknown points local? We do not know.

Even more serious than his going AWOL, Van was in hospital for 28 days that year. In the end, he withdrew from SMA because of "physical disability." His withdrawal took place on May 23, 1929, during final exams. He never returned to Staunton, but always remembered fondly his first boarding school, even including mention of it in his self-composed obituary over sixty-seven years later.

As Van wrote in *A Severe Mercy*, Glenmerle was a place to come home to, and come home to Glenmerle he did in May 1929. Glenn Van Auken was experienced in the buying and selling of real estate, having done so already in Steuben County. In the mid-1920s, Glenn purchased some thirty-five acres on the south side of Carmel Township, Hamilton County, Indiana from a Maurice Donnelly. The large plot of land was situated on the east side of

South Range Line Road near the intersection of 111th Street, not far from the Monon Railway that would take Glenn into his office in Indianapolis. Glenn and Grace named the house Glen Merle, a combination of their two middle names. In fact, on Grace's personal stationary from the time they lived in Carmel, the separate words "GLEN MERLE" appeared in art deco lettering at the top of the page. If you lived in Carmel at the time and wanted to reach the Van Auken family by phone you would have dialed Carmel 247.

Even as I write this more than eighty years after the Van Auken family bought the property, the remnants of the Van Auken's white board fence, and the long X's formed by the diagonal boards, are still visible along South Range Line Road where it now becomes Westfield Road. The last time I visited the spot, one could even see the remains of the stone gateposts of Glen Merle. The driveway still is there, though along one side are the logs of the many trees felled from the property which now belongs to the Woodland Country Club. When the land was purchased by the golf course the house had already fallen into a state of almost complete ruin. The country club allowed the house to remain standing for a time and even made efforts to salvage it. However, in the end, it had to be demolished. One can see the bridge over the stream and the lily pond beside it. Moreover, one can imagine the white and green, three-storey, Craftsman Foursquare style house sitting atop the hill where now sits hole number twelve.

As Van so well describes in the opening chapter of *A Severe Mercy*, one would enter the property by a gravel driveway off South Range Line Road. The beginning of the drive was lined with maple trees. To the right there was pastureland and a little hill on which wild strawberries grew. To one's left was a stream running through the property from north to south. As the road wound its way down the hill, taking a sharp bend to the right, one would come to a one-lane wooden bridge over the stream with the lily pond on the right. After the bridge, the driveway took a sharp left, uphill to the house, and here the drive was lined with purple irises in the springtime. The driveway circled around to the east of the house with a large elm tree in the center. At the far end of the drive was a large two-car garage with white wood siding. To the north of the garage was a little outbuilding Van called: "the cottage." Then beyond the cottage was the grape arbor, and further afield was the apple orchard with "Van's acre" in the far northeast corner along with his little cabin for "sleeping out."

Returning to the driveway one would approach the front entrance to the house by a path that ran between two large blue spruce trees. It was these spruce trees, among many others on the heavily wooded lot, which obscured the view of the front of the house. Of course, if one was a good friend of the Van Auken family one might enter the house by the kitchen door on the east side.

The Man Who Received "A Severe Mercy"

Since this house is almost a character in and of itself in *A Severe Mercy*, let's imagine what a visit to Glen Merle would have been like. Assuming this is our first visit, we will enter by the front door. To do so we must climb a few steps on to the front porch and then enter through the main door into what Van called "the drawing room." What strikes us at first upon entering Glen Merle is that it is not an average house. There are many windows and so the drawing room seems light and airy. There is also beautiful woodwork throughout, such as the crown molding around the ceiling.

However, more important than the setting are the people who live in it. Grace Van Auken, true to her name, graciously greets us and invites us to have a seat on the Duncan Phyfe sofa just inside the door, while the cook prepares dinner. Gazing about the room we cannot help but notice the Chippendale chair and behind it the wood railing of the staircase ascending to the second floor. Directly ahead of us, beside the white-columned mantelpiece surrounding the roaring fire in the fireplace, we see a grand piano. If we are lucky, Grace will play for us some of the light opera songs she loves.

Before long, we hear Glenn Van Auken's deep voice in greeting, along with the creaking of the wood floors as he emerges through the French doors from his book-lined study on the north side of the house. Glenn stands over six feet tall, a trim man with graying hair and richly tanned skin. After a brief chat with the Van Aukens, the cook beckons and so we all get up and go through another set of French doors to the east of the house and sit down to a lovely candlelit supper in the dining room.

After dinner, Van takes us on a tour of the rest of the house. We pop our heads into the kitchen where the cook and the maid are washing up. Just beyond the kitchen, at the very back of the house, we can see the breakfast nook, with window looking out onto the woods to the north.

Van then leads us back into the drawing room and up the staircase, first to a large landing, then around to our right and up to the second floor. At the top of the stairs we reach a corridor, where Van leads us, to the left, to his L-shaped bedroom in the "stubby wing" at the east end of the house, with windows facing the sunrise. Van's room, with its floor to ceiling bookcases and cherry wood furniture, is just above the kitchen where he often breathes the aroma of his mother baking bread, or perhaps the cook preparing one of her delicious meals.[42]

Continuing our tour of the second floor, Van leads us back out into the hallway past a bathroom on our left. On the front, east corner of the house, Van points out his father's small bedroom, and next to it, also on the front, to the west, a larger bedroom belonging to his mother. Brother Paul's bedroom is at the west end of the house. From Paul's bedroom, we walk through a doorway onto a sun porch at the back of the house above the study. The windows are open to the cool night breezes and we can smell the sweet scent of Glenn's pipe tobacco from below.

As we head back out into the hallway, we notice a smaller stairway leading to the third floor servants' rooms. However, Van leads us back downstairs where we say farewell to Glenn and Grace. Van walks with us outside. To our right through the trees and down a small hill we can just glimpse the glint of moonlight on the rippling waters of the swimming pool. We stop and breathe in the "immemorial peace" of Glen Merle before saying farewell.

Van's Company, Staunton Military Academy, 1928

Photo Courtesy of Staunton Military Academy Museum

Author Photo

III

CULVER MILITARY ACADEMY

> Back, back to Culver days,
> The song my heart sings ever,
> No matter where I roam,
> 'Tis Culver! Culver! Culver!
> To hear the bugle call,
> Old mem'ries how they thrill me,
> And proud am I of Culver,
> And to be a Culver man!
>
> The Culver Song

September 1929 was the continuation of what can, at best, be called a "checkered" high school career for Sheldon Van Auken. After a difficult year at Staunton Military Academy, Van's parents enrolled him at Carmel High School, only a few miles away from Glen Merle. His time at Carmel during the 1929-1930 school year was brief, and it is unclear from the record whether he gained any credits there.

However, Van must certainly have enjoyed living at home. One important experience from this time in his life happened not too far from Glen Merle. He was walking his dog Polly through the woods and meadows one day when he got to thinking about the great brains in their towers in Olaf Stapledon's *Last and First Men*. How horrible that would be, Van thought. If one was just a brain in a tower that would mean no dog to love, no beauty to enjoy, no feelings at all. He suddenly realized that what made life worth living was emotion. However, girls were certainly more emotional than boys. Maybe this meant that girls were experiencing more of life. If one wanted to get the most out of life then one needed to experience the highest emotions, and the highest of all was joy. "But how did one acquire joy?" he asked himself. In the books he had read, joy always came through a great love. Thus, if *he* wanted to experience the highest that life had to offer he needed to discover just such a great love. However, he had also read that great love was often accompanied by extreme suffering. Still, if that was the only way to joy, it might be worth it. There and then, standing in the meadow with Polly, meditating on all this, fifteen-year-old Sheldon Van Auken chose the heights and the depths. He was going to seek joy through love, no matter the cost.[43]

Unfortunately, Van was not to know the joy of living at home for much longer. Despite his difficult time at SMA, his parents decided to send him to military school once again. By the spring of 1930, Van found himself attending

Miami Military Academy in Miami, Florida.[44] He took Chemistry, Ancient History, tenth grade English, ninth grade Algebra and ninth grade Latin but, once again, as at Staunton, he did not complete his course work.

Though Van failed to complete tenth grade, the summer of 1930 must have been a happy one for him; it was during this summer that he encountered one of the great pleasures of his life: sailing. Rather than allow him to lounge around Glen Merle all summer with no structured activities, Glenn and Grace arranged for Van to return to summer school at Culver Military Academy where he had participated in the Woodcrafter's School five years previously. This time it was the Summer Naval School. There, Van learned to sail for the first time, on Lake Maxinkuckee.

Van's application to summer school reveals that his father had, by this time, moved his law office from the Continental Bank Building to 820 Illinois Building, Indianapolis. Van's height at almost age sixteen was five feet eleven inches. His weight was 169 pounds. Van's references included: J.R. Williams, President of Miami Military Academy, Basil Middleton Lieutenant Colonel at Culver (who acted as his "Patron"), and Bailey Hawkins a well-known banker in Carmel with whom Glenn Van Auken must have had dealings.

Learning sailing wasn't the only thing Van would have done at the Culver Summer School. The academy showed concern for all aspects of its students' development, including their physical growth and health. On July 5, 1930, Dr. Paul Campbell of CMA wrote to Mrs. Glenn Van Auken at Carmel, regarding Sheldon's physical exam. His only abnormal finding: a slight visual deficiency to be corrected with proper glasses. Dr. Campbell also mentioned a head cold, which had subsided.

After summer school, Van, his mother, and his brother vacationed in Florida. The 1930 census found them living at 928 Michigan Avenue, Miami Beach. During that summer, Van's parents must have concluded that Culver Military Academy was better able to stimulate their son's interest in learning than Miami Military. Perhaps Van liked being at school closer to Glen Merle. Whatever the reason, the Van Aukens enrolled Van in the Culver winter school in the fall of that year.

There is one revealing note from Van's application to CMA winter school. Thomas Boardman, principal of Carmel High School, filled out a reference form for Van. When asked on that form if Van was "a boy with whom you would wish your son to be intimately associated; for instance as a roommate", Boardman wrote briefly: "Yes, if his parents would keep out." Apparently, Boardman, as a principal, found Glenn and Grace Van Auken to be too interfering in the life and education of their son.

Though Van must have looked forward to attending boarding school closer to Glen Merle, at a place where he enjoyed sailing and other activities, a serious bout with health issues delayed his start at the CMA winter school. Though Van's parents had applied and gotten him accepted to CMA, they chose to send him south, presumably back to their vacation home in Miami, for health reasons. In particular, a telegram from Glenn Van Auken to CMA dated 9/15/1930 states: "Son Sheldon Vanauken very ill and unable to report for duty today. Physician advises may be two to four weeks. Hope you can accept him when able. Will keep you informed."

What was the health problem that kept Van out of school for the first several weeks of the 1930 to 1931 school year? A CMA memo dated October 8 reveals that Mrs. Van Auken called the academy by telephone to inform the school that Van was taken ill with Small Pox on September 10. Afterwards Van developed a kidney condition that required bed rest.

Under these conditions, Glenn and Grace chose alternative means for the education of their son. A letter from Emmerich Manual Training High School to CMA on April 13, 1931 introduced Mrs. Edith Rose Badger who was tutoring both Van Auken boys at the time. So apparently for the 1930-1931 school year both Sheldon and Paul were privately tutored. While having their sons tutored, Glenn and Grace kept in touch with CMA in hopes that Van could enter as a student there, once he was physically able. However, Van's schoolwork certainly continued to suffer during this time. A letter from the Headmaster of CMA to Mrs. Van Auken on May 1, 1931, indicated that the only credits Van had up to that time were for two units of English, one half in Algebra, one in Early European History, one in American History, and one in Chemistry (the last was completed in summer school 1930 at CMA). He also had one year of French from Staunton. Despite all of these setbacks, Van finally entered the winter school of Culver Military Academy in the fall of 1931.

CMA was in Van's day, and now, a place with the air of an exclusive prep school for the children of the wealthy. Situated in the midst of rural, northwestern Indiana and its seemingly endless cornfields, Culver's location is definitely out of the main stream, and would have seemed even more remote from civilization during Van's time there. Similar to Staunton Military Academy, Culver was the vision of one man, Henry Harrison Culver, who founded CMA in 1894 "for the purpose of thoroughly preparing young men for the best colleges, scientific schools and businesses of America." In 1896, a fire at Missouri Military Academy brought about its consolidation with Culver. Missouri's headmaster, Colonel Alexander Fleet, enabled the new joint Academy to get off the ground. By the 1930s, under the leadership of General Leigh Gignilliat, the Superintendent during Van's time, Culver achieved national and international prominence.

However, one of Culver's students in 1931 was prominent for only one thing: illness. Van's medical report at CMA on September 9 of that year indicated that he was wearing glasses, he had already had his tonsils removed, and in addition to his previous bouts with small pox and kidney trouble, Van had endured measles, diphtheria, influenza, whooping cough, pneumonia, bronchitis and eczema. He also had dental problems requiring two fillings in his front teeth.

Problematic as his illnesses were, health was not Van's only problem at school. It becomes clear when reading his record at CMA that Van began to use his health problems as an excuse for not doing his work. Correspondence from the school to Van's parents in October 1931 indicated "Sheldon is not working hard enough." Moreover, from that fall through the winter, Van had one minor illness after another. On January 9, 1932 a letter to CMA from the Van Auken family doctor in Carmel, Dr. Cooper, indicated Van was ill and would be unable to return to school for ten days. A subsequent letter from Dr. Cooper later that same month revealed that he had to treat Van for pneumonia. It was Dr. Cooper's recommendation that Van should be relieved of military drill and athletics until deemed physically able to participate.

Van returned to school at the end of January. However, he immediately caught another cold and was confined to the school infirmary for one week. He had barely recovered when this was followed by another trip to the infirmary and then three weeks on leave during which Van saw a specialist in Indianapolis. Obviously, by this time, Glenn and Grace were sufficiently concerned about their son's health that they felt the need to seek more help than what could be provided either at CMA or in Carmel.

Finally, by mid March, Van was ready to return to school. However, it was at this point that tragedy struck. By this time Van was seventeen years old and already accustomed to driving himself to various locations. On March 23, 1932, on his way back to Culver, Van was in an auto accident and suffered a skull fracture. He was immediately hospitalized in the closest medical care facility—Dukes Miami County Memorial Hospital in Peru, Indiana. The hospital immediately notified A. S. Stoutenburgh, Aide to the Superintendent at CMA that Cadet Van Auken had met with an accident and that it was of such a serious nature he would probably not be back to school for at least six or eight weeks. Twelve days later Van was still not out of danger. As if having her son in the hospital, hanging between life and death, was not enough of a burden for Grace Van Auken to bear, it was in the midst of this horrendous ordeal that Grace's mother died.

Fortunately, by the middle of April, Grace had better news to celebrate. Her son was finally well enough to receive visitors from CMA. The bad news was that Van didn't recover quickly enough to return to CMA at all during the spring of 1932.

The Man Who Received "A Severe Mercy"

By the end of April Glenn Van Auken was turning his mind to slightly more mundane matters. On April 26, he wrote to CMA saying he hoped to be able to send Van back to Culver in the fall if the finances could be arranged. There seemed to be a bit of a dispute over money owed for Van's incomplete spring semester. In the end Van's father and the authorities at CMA were able to come to a mutually satisfying agreement and Van returned to the military academy in the fall, albeit with some caveats. The school doctor, Paul Campbell, informed Colonel Miller of CMA that due to Cadet Van Auken's skull fracture in the spring he should not be allowed to do any activities which might lead to "over-heating." In particular, Dr. Campbell barred Van from boxing and football, and did not permit him to participate in drill on hot days.

These restrictions, however, did not keep Van from resuming some of his physical activities. In mid-October, he engaged in a scuffle with another cadet that resulted in Van injuring a finger that had experienced two previous bone fractures. Dr. Campbell recommended that Van see a specialist. In addition, the visit to the specialist required, once again, that Van miss some school.

As if Van's accident in the spring of 1932 and his continual round of physical problems were not enough, Van created some serious problems of his own in January 1933.

Van in his Cadet Uniform at Culver, 1933

Photo Courtesty of Culver Military Academy

IV

THROUGH THE IRON GATE

> Let us roll all our strength and all
> Our sweetness up into one ball,
> And tear our pleasures with rough strife
> Through the iron gates of life:
> Thus, though we cannot make our sun
> Stand still, yet we will make him run.
>
> Andrew Marvell, *To His Coy Mistress*

At the beginning of 1933, Van and two other Culver cadets decided to visit a speakeasy about five miles from the grounds of CMA. According to one cadet, they did this because they were "discouraged and unhappy." Then, on January 19, Van and another cadet, Johnny King, went A.W.O.L.

Johnny was a "soft-speaking Georgian." He and Van dreamed together of high adventure. Sometimes they shared musings of military adventure in the distant past, fighting for the Old South. One afternoon, excited after a cavalry charge on the school horses, Van and Johnny talked about how great it would have been to ride with Jeb Stuart and the Virginian cavalry. However, not having a time machine to travel back to the 19th century, the two boys settled on the pursuit of an adventure slightly more attainable. As they laid their plans, a broad grin spread over Johnny's face, followed by a deep laugh that Van would remember for years to come. After talking over many possibilities, the two boys decided to run away from school. Their plan was to steal rides on freight trains and trucks and make their way to Mexico.[45]

About the ensuing escapade, the records of CMA reveal much. What happened next was this: Van and Johnny made contact with a local taxi driver who had provided liquor to minors in the past. They passed messages to this cab driver through a woman working in the canteen at the Academy. The driver agreed to help Van and his friend desert to Indianapolis. The messages arranged for a meeting at Palmer House, a local establishment.

However, the staff of CMA overheard one of Van's telephone conversations with the taxi driver. As a result, the Acting Superintendent, Robert Rossow, deliberately set a trap to catch Van and Johnny in the act of deserting. Rossow organized twelve to fifteen Academy officers to surround the point of the cadets' rendezvous with the cab driver. Rossow also recruited the town marshal, Mr. Buffington, to stand at the point of meeting.

A few minutes before the arranged time, Van and Johnny appeared, walking along the shore of Lake Maxinkuckee in the darkness and the mist.

It was, according to Rossow's later report, "a terrible night." Van and Johnny continued walking along the lakeshore past the point of rendezvous and so Buffington and Rossow followed in pursuit, fearing all the while that they would lose the cadets in the darkness. Rossow directed Buffington to cut across the ball field to the northeast, just in case Van and Johnny decided to make a break for it. Rossow continued to follow, under cover of the trees along the lake. Rossow was the first to make contact with the cadets. Van and his friend each carried a laundry bag with their belongings slung over a shoulder.

Rossow asked, "What exactly are you two gentlemen doing?"

"We are deserting, sir."

"Stand fast where you are," ordered Rossow.

Van and Johnny stood at attention in the middle of the road. At this point Rossow signaled by flashlight one of his assistants who was waiting in a car fifty yards away. This assistant (Mr. Friend) started to drive his car toward the two cadets. The cadets were sure that the man in the car was the cab driver coming to take them to freedom.

Van ran away from Superintendent Rossow toward the approaching vehicle, shrieking at the top of his voice, "Go back! Go back! You're trapped!"

Rossow barked, "Cease and desist this tomfoolery, Cadet Van Auken!"

Van sheepishly returned to Rossow's side when he realized he had been yelling to no avail and that the person in the automobile was not who he thought it was.

After several minutes, another car passed them on the highway, blinking its lights several times and turning into the Academy grounds. Buffington and Friend caught up with the car and found the occupant to be another young man from town, conspiring with the taxi driver. The man was immediately arrested and taken to the town jail.

Despite being caught in the act, Van and Johnny pleaded with Rossow, "Please let us desert, we cannot go back to the Academy now. It will be too embarrassing." Rossow, needless to say, did not comply with their request but rather accompanied them back to the grounds of CMA where he put them under guard.

The next day the matter was brought before the Executive Board of the school in some detail. The board immediately decided to dismiss Van and Johnny. Both cadets were sent down from school—and Johnny went to his own death. Some time after returning home, he dove into icy water to save a small boy. As Van later put it, it would have been better if Johnny had gone adventuring with him.[46]

The bootlegger who arranged for Van and Johnny's escape from CMA was sent to the Indiana Penal Farm and the woman in the CMA canteen who assisted him was dismissed from her post. Naturally, Glenn and Grace

The Man Who Received "A Severe Mercy"

Van Auken were both heartbroken when they received the news of their son's obvious downward spiral. What could they do? They immediately arranged for Van to attend Shortridge High School in Indianapolis.

Shortridge, started in 1864, was the oldest free high school in Indiana. The school eventually became known for its academic excellence, being rated by *Time Magazine* in 1957 as one of the top 38 high schools in the United States. Shortridge also had a number of students who became famous in the wider world over the years. Among them were: author Kurt Vonnegut (Class of 1940), Senator Richard Lugar (Class of 1950), author Booth Tarkington and Madelyn Pugh, writer for *I Love Lucy* and *The Lucy Show*.

However, once again, an academically excellent school did not seem to have any positive effect on Sheldon Van Auken. He was a student there in the spring of 1933 but his record shows only a few subjects undertaken (English, Math, French and History). Before he could complete any of these classes, however, his parents moved him, yet again, to a school in Florida, perhaps for health reasons. The good news in all of this was that Van completed three subjects satisfactorily under the instruction of a Mr. Coborm in Miami.

During this whole period of what Van later called "rustication", he used any free time he had to secretly learn how to fly an airplane. He had saved tips on flying from various relatives. Thus, Van became a pilot, using a highly maneuverable Waco F biplane for his lessons.[47] He "slipped the surly bonds of earth and danced the skies on laughter-silvered wings."[48]

While Van viewed his time away from Culver as an opportunity for various sorts of "naughtiness", his parents had other plans in mind. The senior Van Aukens had their sights set on getting Van readmitted to Culver.

No doubt led by his parents, Frank Van Auken, as Van chose to be called at the time, met with General Gignilliat regarding readmission to CMA on June 14. He also wrote to the general on his own Glen Merle stationary. Van said he would "rather graduate from Culver than any other school. In fact, I believe I would value a Culver Diploma more than a college degree. I respectfully beg of you to receive my application, and promise there will be no further occurrence of those acts which brought disgrace upon me and upon the school."

Apparently Van's respectful but pleading tone worked. He was allowed to return to the CMA summer school in 1933 on probation, with his readmission to the winter school to be determined by the Executive Board, based upon his summer performance. The Executive Board even waived two $350 payments that were due on Van's previous winter school account for the schooling that he actually missed due to his dismissal. It seems that the Superintendent of CMA was anxious to help Van as much as he could and maintain a good relationship with an important Indianapolis lawyer such as Van's father.

Despite Van's protestations to the contrary, his behavior during the Summer Naval School at CMA was a mixed bag. On the positive side, he made sufficient improvement in order to be appointed as an aide to Commandant Rossow, his old nemesis. Upon receiving the news, Van's mother was so proud that she had one of Van's Indianapolis friends drive up to Culver to deliver to him his father's dress saber, the same one he loved to handle when he was younger. However, Van used this occasion as an opportunity to take his Culver friends for a joyride in his parents' car. Major Fleet apprehended the cadets one-half mile west of the Academy grounds, clearly outside of appropriate boundaries. As a punishment, Van was reduced to ranks, assigned fifty demerits and confined to Academy grounds for two weeks. This event took place just before the decision being made regarding Van's reinstatement to the CMA winter school.

When the Executive Board met to consider Van's case in early August much concern was expressed about Van's behavior. One faculty member said, "He impresses me as a boy who enjoys poor health. He will use a great many clever ideas to get out of doing work and it is mostly on a health basis. He will work for several days and then drop out of class for health reasons." Another teacher commented, "Unless an immediate and complete transformation and reformation take place in Van Auken, he cannot hope to pass his French this summer. He has not prepared a third of his work and insists he has no more time to spend on French. He is very slow, and worse than that, he seems to expect special privileges, that is, credit for little or no work."

Despite these concerns voiced by some on the Executive Board, Van was reinstated and continued with the winter school in the fall of 1933, with the understanding that he would need to spend two more years at CMA in order to complete his secondary education and be ready for college. That fall, Van made a concerted effort to improve his grades and this was recognized by all of his teachers. As a result, he ranked 18 in a class of 105 and was third from the top in the Artillery.

Given their son's considerable improvement, Glenn and Grace Van Auken requested that CMA transfer him to the first class, allowing him to "walk through the Iron Gate" and graduate in June. However, the faculty ruled against this request because Van would be one and a half units short of the requirement for graduation. The Van Aukens renewed their request in May, asking that Van be allowed to pass through the Iron Gate at Commencement with a dummy diploma. However, this request was also denied.

In the end, Van completed the additional one and a half units necessary to graduate in the summer of 1934. In addition, he graduated with honors in English, a harbinger of even greater things to come in that field of study.[49] Twenty-two years later Van would write to Culver to thank his former English

The Man Who Received "A Severe Mercy"

teacher, J. Harry Smith, whom he said was perhaps the most influential teacher of his school days, the man who taught him to love poetry and Shakespeare.[50]

Van in CMA Naval Summer School

Photo Courtesty of Culver Military Academy

PART TWO
THE HEIGHTS & THE DEPTHS
1934-1955

I said—Then, dearest, since 'tis so,
Since now at length my fate I know,
Since nothing all my love avails,
Since all, my life seem'd meant for, fails,
Since this was written and needs must be--
My whole heart rises up to bless
Your name in pride and thankfulness!

Robert Browning, *The Last Ride Together*

Van's Fraternity at Wabash (he is the furthest left)

Photo Courtesy of Wabash College

V

WABASH & DAVY

> Oh, the moonlight's fair tonight along the Wabash,
> From the fields there comes the breath of newmown hay.
> Through the sycamores the candle lights are gleaming,
> On the banks of the Wabash, far away.
>
> Paul Dresser, *On the Banks of the Wabash*

In the fall of 1934, at the age of 20, Sheldon Van Auken, or Frank as he was called at the time, entered Wabash College in Crawfordsville, Indiana as a freshman. As Van describes it in *A Severe Mercy*, Wabash was a "small, academically excellent men's college."[51] The school was about fifty miles from Glen Merle to the northwest of Indianapolis. Van chose Wabash because of reading a novel about the place—*In Freshman Year: The Story of a Real Boy and His Dad* by John G. Coulter, published in 1934.[52]

Presbyterian ministers founded Wabash College in 1832. The goal of the institution was to "be at first a classical and English high school, rising into a college as soon as the wants of the country demand."[53] The first teacher at Wabash was Caleb Mills, a graduate of Dartmouth College and Andover Seminary, who arrived in 1833. Mills later became one of the founders of the Indiana public school system. The school took as its model the conservative liberal arts colleges of New England. Mills set out the college aims: "learning, virtue, and service." One of the teachers at Wabash in the early 1900s, the poet Ezra Pound, didn't last long there because he was considered to be "lacking in virtue." Wabash is one of the few remaining all-male colleges in the United States and has appeared as one of the top forty schools in Loren Pope's *Colleges that Change Lives*. Today the 60-acre wooded campus contains 25 buildings predominantly of Georgian architecture, in red brick.

Van joined the Phi Gamma Delta fraternity. His fraternity brothers thought of him as "set apart" both in bearing and intellect, though he was always friendly.[54] The House, as Van called it in *A Severe Mercy*, was right across the street from the college, on the corner of Grant Avenue and Jefferson Street. I was able to see the old House just before it was torn down in 2009.

When Van arrived at Wabash, he only planned to stay for a year. He hoped to transfer to either Princeton or Yale as a sophomore.[55] However, he apparently fell in love with the place and decided to stay.

In addition to his participation in a fraternity, Van also took part in a number of other activities on campus. During his first year, he worked on honing his writing skills by contributing regular articles to *The Caveman*, a somewhat humorous magazine produced by the students. He also wrote for the *Bachelor*. Van's senior yearbook reflects his participation in the International Relations Club and the Scarlet Masque drama club. However, there is only record of him performing in one courtroom drama entitled *Libel* during his junior year.

At first Van continued some of the sloppy academic habits developed in his younger years. As a freshman at Wabash, he apparently decided that he didn't like his zoology class. He dropped the course and therefore took a failing grade. The Dean wrote to Glenn Van Auken with some concern about his son's behavior. Van's father wrote back saying "there is no reason for anyone carrying him along unless he delivers. It is a hard world, and the sooner he finds it out the better it will be for him."[56] It seems Glenn had decided by this time not to interfere in his son's academic career any longer; it was sink or swim and Van learned how to swim. His grades at Wabash were never the greatest; he got by with a B-minus average. However, in the end he must have surprised his professors by handing in a "brilliant" final examination paper in his major, English, thus earning a "first."[57]

One might say that the most important event of Van's college years was not academic in nature. In December of 1936, Van met Jean Palmer Davis. Davy (as she was known to family and friends) was working in the photographic studio of the L. S. Ayres Department Store in Indianapolis. Van went to the studio to have a tinted miniature photograph made of Johnny King, his former roommate at Culver who had drowned. When he went to pick up his order, an argument ensued between he and Davy over the miniature, which had been badly done by some other employee.[58] Despite that argument, Van was smitten with Davy from the first and arranged for a date with her that very night, along with two other young men from his fraternity and their dates.

Who was this Jean Davis, who so immediately conquered Van with her beautiful brown eyes and charming manner? Jean Palmer Davis was born in Hackensack, New Jersey on July 24, 1914. She was the daughter of the Rev. Staley Franklin Davis and Helen Larter Fredericks Davis.

Staley Davis was born in Pataskala, Ohio on April 8, 1877. He was a member of Phi Beta Kappa, a graduate of Ohio Wesleyan in 1902 and Drew Seminary in New Jersey in 1904. He married Helen Larter Fredericks on November 4, 1907. Helen was a New Jersey native, having been born in Newark on May 17, 1885. Apparently, Staley Davis' education at Drew Seminary and marriage to Helen anchored the Ohio native in New Jersey. Staley Davis eventually became an instructor in pedagogy at Drew Seminary from 1920-1922.

The Man Who Received "A Severe Mercy"

Davy's father was a Methodist Episcopal clergyman.[59] The Methodist Episcopal Church grew out of the first efforts of Methodist evangelists in North America. The M. E. Church officially began at the Baltimore Christmas Conference in 1784; Francis Asbury and Thomas Coke were the first bishops. Through a series of divisions and mergers, the M.E. Church eventually became a major part of the United Methodist Church.[60]

Rev. Davis became a rather well known Methodist Episcopal minister who served several churches in New Jersey and often spoke at Sunday school conventions and other events outside his own parish. Davis was at one time President of the Newark Conference Board of Sunday Schools and later Director of the Eastern Division of Sunday Schools based in New York City. Davy's father was a teetotaler, strict observer of the Sunday Sabbath, and supporter of evangelist Billy Sunday. He was also the author of *Methods of Bible Study*, published by the Correspondence School of Theology at Drew Seminary in 1912, and *Christian Neighborliness: An Elective Course for Young People*, published by The Methodist Book Concern in 1924.

Staley and Helen Davis had three children. Davy's older sister, Helen Marjorie Davis, was born on October 8, 1908 in Elizabeth, New Jersey. Her younger brother, Donald F Davis, was also born in New Jersey, circa 1917.[61] At the time of Davy's birth, her father was serving the Methodist Church in Hackensack.

Sadly, Davy's father died in 1926 when she was but twelve years old. Two years later, as a freshman in high school, Davy, who was apparently running a bit wild without fatherly supervision, got pregnant. She told her mother and sister about the pregnancy and they supported her. Thus, Davy gave birth to a child whom she named Marion and she gave up the child for adoption to a Reformed minister and his wife who were childless.[62]

In the 1930 census, Davy appeared with her mother and siblings as a resident of an apartment house in Nutley, New Jersey. Though Davy was able to finish high school, due to her father's death she had to give up college plans for a time.[63] Instead, she went to work in the photographic studio of a large New York department store.

Eventually, Davy saved enough money to enter college. At first, she attended Troy Conference Academy in Poultney, Vermont,[64] a Methodist Episcopal school founded in 1834.[65] However, in the fall of 1936, Davy transferred to Butler University in Indianapolis. What drew Davy to move from Vermont to Indiana for college? Davy's mother certainly would have been encouraged by the fact that Butler was a Christian school. The Christian Church (Disciples of Christ) founded Butler in 1855 as North Western Christian University. The school was eventually renamed after its founder, Ovid Butler, a prominent abolitionist.[66] While the Christian foundation of

Butler would have been a selling point to Davy's mother, it certainly offered no better a Christian education than Troy Academy.

Perhaps Davy was drawn to Butler by its excellent music program. At the time, Butler had a close working relationship with the Arthur Jordan Conservatory of Music.[67] Davy chose music as her major and she lived in the white columned Pi Delta Psi Sorority House on the Butler campus, though she was not a member. Apparently, Davy did not have very many, if any, transferable credits from Troy Academy. Therefore, she entered Butler as a freshman and engaged in part-time work at the photographic studio to support herself.[68]

Van and Davy's first date took place on a mid-December night in 1936, in front of a roaring fire at Van's fraternity house at Wabash College.[69] The others in attendance were Van's fraternity friends: Don Purdy, Bob Trimble, and their dates: Margery and Mary. That night Van and Davy found that they shared a love for ships and the sea, poetry, dogs and the country.[70] Perhaps what knit Van and Davy's hearts together that first night, more than anything else, was their discovery of a common experience: the pain of beauty. The two were so eager to know each other better that they talked late into the night, and all the way home, while their friends fell asleep in the back of the Van Auken family car.

They went on two more dates before the month was out. Their first kiss, improbably, took place after their car slid on the ice across a busy intersection in Indianapolis. Then Van brought Davy to Glen Merle to meet his parents on New Year's Day 1937. Already a pattern was set, for Glen Merle was to be the scene for the deepening of their love.

Van later said that from that New Year's Day on there was to be no one else for either him or Davy. They did, however, each have to face a somewhat difficult choice. Davy was already scheduled to go out with a West Point cadet whom she had previously dated. He was flying in specifically to see Davy and their date was on the same day as a Wabash College dance. Under the influence of Van's gentle persuasion, Davy changed her plans and went to the college dance with Van instead.

Van too had a difficult choice to make. Bob Trimble, who was a flying companion as well as frat brother, urged Van to join him on an aerial adventure in Arizona. It would have required Van to take a break from college for a year. It also would have meant being away from Davy for the same length of time. Thus, Van turned down the friend and chose Davy instead.[71]

Once Van and Davy were both back in school after the Christmas break of 1936-37, they had less time available for one another. Their dates were confined to weekends and an occasional mid-week evening together. With so little time available, they chose to focus on each other rather than spend much time with friends or family. They would have quiet dinners together at one restaurant or another in Indianapolis. Some of those old restaurants from the 1930s are still in existence, like St. Elmo's Steakhouse that has had an uninterrupted history, or Iozzo's Garden of Italy that was reopened in recent years after a long hiatus. During one of these dinner meetings Van had a violinist come to their table and play Dvorak's *Humoresque*. While the gypsy girl played, Van whispered in Davy's ear, "Now and always: *The Humoresque* means I love you."[72] This was the first of many classical pieces of music that would come to have a special meaning for the couple.

However, the place Van and Davy met most often was his father's club. This was the Indianapolis Athletic Club, also the setting for Indiana Democratic Club meetings, of which Glenn Van Auken was also a member. The club was founded in 1920 and a nine-storey structure built for it at the corner of Meridian and Vermont streets, completed in 1924. Members of the club at one time included *Indianapolis Star and News* publisher Eugene C. Pulliam and Governor Paul McNutt whom Glenn Van Auken supported in his run for the presidency in 1940. Many years later, in 1992, the club made national headlines when a faulty refrigerator wire caused a fatal fire; this made the national news because jury members for Mike Tyson's rape trial were sequestered there at the time.[73] Glenn Van Auken and family appeared on the 1930 census at this location so they apparently had an apartment there as well.

As Van later recounted, one of the bars in the club was open to ladies. One can still see the ladies' entrance marked in stone on the outside of the Athletic Club. Van and Davy would sit in this wood-paneled bar on one of two red leather sofas in front of the stone fireplace. On the mantelpiece these words were inscribed:

> Fires, Friends, and Books Decree
> Wisdom, Strength, and Courtesy.[74]

These words summed up much of what Van and Davy's courtship was all about. They were friends as well as lovers. Literature as well as music was very important to both. They joined each other from the start in a pursuit of wisdom. In one another's arms, they discovered strength, and they showed to each other, from the beginning, a type of courtesy that has, since their time, largely been forgotten in our culture.

The great poetry of the ages became part of Van and Davy's love language. There were the Sonnets of Shakespeare and even more, the poetry of the Romantics like Shelley and the Victorians like Browning. These poets, and many others, inspired Van to write his own poetry for Davy, as well as a small, unpublished book entitled *The Loveliest Lamp*, which contained both prose and poetry.[75] It is interesting to reflect on how, from the first, there was the hint of warning about death in the lines of Van and Davy's favorite poems. For example, here is one favorite, Richard Le Gallienne's *A Ballade-Catalogue of Lovely Things:*

>I WOULD make a list against the evil days
>   Of lovely things to hold in memory:
>First, I set down my lady's lovely face,
>   For earth has no such lovely thing as she;
>   And next I add, to bear her company,
>The great-eyed virgin star that morning brings;
>   Then the wild-rose upon its little tree—
>   So runs my catalogue of lovely things.
>
>The enchanted dogwood, with its ivory trays,
>   The water-lily in its sanctuary
>Of reeded pools, and dew-drenched lilac sprays,
>   For these, of all fair flowers, the fairest be;
>   Next write I down the great name of the sea,
>Lonely in greatness as the names of kings;
>   Then the young moon that hath us all in fee—
>   So runs my catalogue of lovely things.
>
>Imperial sunsets that in crimson blaze
>   Along the hills, and, fairer still to me,
>The fireflies dancing in a netted maze
>   Woven of twilight and tranquility;
>   Shakespeare and Virgil, their high poesy;
>Then a great ship, splendid with snowy wings,
>   Voyaging on into eternity—
>   So runs my catalogue of lovely things.
>
>ENVOI
>Prince, not the gold bars of thy treasury,
>Not all thy jeweled scepters, crowns and rings,
>Are worth the honeycomb of the wild bee—
>   So runs my catalogue of lovely things.[76]

In this one poem, there is so much that typifies Van and Davy—their love of poetry, of nature, treasuring thoughts of one another against "the evil days", a great ship voyaging on into eternity.

April by William Morris was another favorite. Here too was the warning

The Man Who Received "A Severe Mercy"

of death, the alert that springtime inloveness could not last:

> When summer brings the lily and the rose,
> She brings us fear; her very death she brings
> Hid in her anxious heart, the forge of woes.[77]

The Rev. Staley Franklin Davis

Helen Larter Fredericks Davis

Photos Courtesy of Elizabeth Rose

Jean Palmer Davis

Photo Courtesy of Elizabeth Rose

VI

LOVE & MARRIAGE

> And to dream fondly of the delightful, irrevocable past,
> on the very spot of all where I and mine were always happiest.
>
> George du Maurier, *Peter Ibbetson*

Popular films of the day inspired Van and Davy's love no less than poetry and music. One such film was *Maytime* with Jeanette MacDonald and Nelson Eddy. It debuted in March of 1937, as Van and Davy were caught up in their own springtime love. Van overheard Davy one day by the lily pond at Glen Merle, singing the famous lines from the title song:

> Sweetheart, sweetheart, sweetheart,
> Will you love me ever?[78]

The film and the song may have inspired Van's own poem of the same title with its own foreshadowing of death …

> Until the lilacs close
> Beneath the deathly snows[79]

Then there was Gary Cooper and Ida Lupino in *Peter Ibbetson*. The film debuted in 1935, before Van and Davy met. However, George du Maurier's book about a deathless love, upon which the film was based, was another beloved piece of literature shared by Van and Davy. Therefore, Van arranged for a special, private showing of the movie that they both enjoyed greatly.

In University Park across the street from The Athletic Club in Indianapolis are several bronze statues. One of these, Syrinx the wood nymph, standing east of the fountain, listens to the music that Pan the satyr is playing on the west side.[80] Syrinx is the one Van refers to as a small bronze fairy on a stone tree stump. Van and Davy dubbed her "la fée Tarapatapoum" after one of the invisible beings in du Maurier's story.[81]

Peter Ibbetson is the story of a love that transcends all obstacles. The tale is about two children who fall in love, become separated by circumstance, and then, by fate, meet up again years later. Though the couple are again separated, due to the man being in prison, they come together in their dreams, until one day the girl does not appear any more because of her own death.

How striking it is that this story of a transcendent and all-consuming love, broken by death, should be a favorite of Van and Davy's. What a foreshadowing in this story there is of Van's own heartbreak over Davy's death, which would take place some eighteen years in the future.

The truly amazing thing about Van and Davy's relationship was not that they fell hopelessly in love; that has happened to countless people down the ages. What was unique about Van and Davy's experience was what they did with it. They made a conscious decision to erect a protective wall around their love, what they came to call "The Shining Barrier."

Van and Davy's first argument, over the keeping of secrets from one another, led to a discussion of justice between lovers and what might make love endure. Their conclusion was that the secret of enduring love had to be sharing. Therefore, they decided they would share everything; this total sharing became the cornerstone of The Shining Barrier. If one of them liked something, then there must be something for the other to like in it, and so it must be shared. They decided to read all the books the other had read, even stories from childhood.[82] Davy was certainly stretched by the effort to acquaint herself with all of Van's reading, while Van extended himself to learn about all the music Davy knew. Each had special gifts and areas of interest, but they purposely chose to share those gifts and interests with one another. This total sharing involved Van in trying to understand life from a female perspective, and Davy sought to see life from a male vantage point. By this effort at total sharing, they drew thousands of bonds of connection between one another, thus making it almost impossible for their relationship to be severed.

Some readers of *A Severe Mercy* have criticized Van and Davy for what may appear to some, on the surface, to be an act of selfishness. However, to be just, one must recognize that the relationship Van and Davy constructed for themselves was not precisely self-centered, but rather "us-centered." Furthermore, their relationship did not exclude the importance of other relationships in life, namely that of family and friends. What Van and Davy did was simply to give priority to their love-relationship and do things to protect it. In fact, I think, it is possible to get the idea that Van and Davy were more focused on themselves than they really were. Van admits from the start that *A Severe Mercy* is the autobiography of their love, not of the lovers. Therefore, we are not told quite a few things about their mutual lives. Van and Davy may have spent far more time with family and friends, even in their days of courtship, than *A Severe Mercy* suggests. Nevertheless, the reader must also keep in mind something Van later admits in his book, that there *was* something excessive and obsessive about his relationship with Davy, something that eventually had to end.

The Man Who Received "A Severe Mercy"

There were other principles that became part of the construction of The Shining Barrier. One of these was total trust. Another was that possessions could become an unnecessary burden, separating lovers from one another. Thus, Van and Davy made a conscious decision to live simply, with few possessions. This was a decision that Van was to live out for the rest of his life, even after Davy's death.

A third idea that was very much a part of The Shining Barrier was that of spontaneity. If one had an idea to do something on "the spur of the moment", the other would immediately "plump" to do it. As Van admits in *A Severe Mercy*, this involved both he and Davy in cutting college classes on a number of occasions. Years later Van wrote to the Dean of Wabash explaining that his courtship with Davy was the reason for many of his absences during his junior and senior years in college.[83]

One key to the success of The Shining Barrier was communication. Van and Davy conducted what they called "Navigator Councils." Once or twice a month they would sit down and talk about the state of their relationship. All decisions reached were based upon the answer to the question: "What would be best for our love?" They became so expert at communicating with one another, both verbally and non-verbally, that it led one friend to say, "It almost scared me. It was too perfect."[84] While some readers of *A Severe Mercy* might be in hearty agreement with this sentiment, others might say, "Yes, but wasn't Van and Davy's relationship a realization of the biblical idea of a man and a woman becoming 'one flesh' in marriage?"

One thing is certain, Van and Davy became "one flesh" in the physical sense, rather early on. In *A Severe Mercy*, Van says that they "knew each other" in the spring of 1937, and that "without guilt."[85] Apparently, since both he and Davy had, by this time, abandoned the faith of their childhoods, they saw nothing wrong with sex outside of marriage. Of course, for them the important thing was that sex was part of a much larger whole—the wholeness of inloveness.

However, Van and Davy both realized early in their courtship that their love was vulnerable to at least one thing: death. They were, perhaps, haunted by the words of Walter de la Mare's poem, *Fare Well*....

> Look thy last on all things lovely,
> Every hour.[86]

Neither Van nor Davy could bear the idea of one dying before the other. Therefore, they resolved that if one were to die the other would follow, or if possible, they would go together.[87]

Due to Van's love of flying, one way they imagined dying together was to go up in a plane, just the two of them, and then purposely crash it. They called it "the last long dive."[88] Somber as this idea sounds, most of Van's flying experiences were much more happy.

On a May morning in the first year of their acquaintance, Van arranged to take Davy up in an open cockpit biplane. Before dawn, he picked her up from the sorority house at Butler and drove her out to an abandoned airfield near Indianapolis.[89] There he placed her in the forward cockpit, along with a bunch of lilacs. As the plane rose above the clouds into the dawn, the lilac petals scattered in the wind. Davy sang loudly and smiled; it was her first flight. Van even dared a loop and they hung suspended upside-down for a few seconds. When Van returned Davy to the sorority house, and he stood by the door in his leather flight jacket, helmet and goggles in hand, a ray of sunlight touched his light brown hair and Davy said, "My golden one."[90] Indeed, they had made a golden memory together on that May morning.

One of Van's later flights was a bit more mischievous. He and his flying companion, Bob Trimble, of the Phi Gamma Delta fraternity, engaged in various acts of aerial derring-do. During football season the frat brothers got together before a Wabash-Butler weekend game and made cards which read: "Wabash Always Fights." Then Bob and Van went up in the open cockpit biplane and, diving deep into the Butler Bowl on a cloudy game day, dropped these cards on to the unsuspecting fans. After Monday morning chapel at Wabash, Dean Kendall called Van and Bob into his office. Kendall informed the young men in no uncertain terms: "You can break your necks flying if you want to, but if you ever do it again in the name of Wabash you will be dismissed." As things turned out Kendall didn't need to dismiss them, federal agents soon appeared on campus and took Bob and Van's pilot licenses away.[91]

Van's life flew on, even without a plane. In the summer of 1937, he did head off to Arizona, but not for an aerial adventure, rather to be a ranger at Grand Canyon. This had been arranged before he and Davy met. Davy despaired at being parted from her new love for the entire summer. Therefore, she persuaded her mother and brother to journey with her to Arizona. She and Van had the summer together after all.[92]

Upon their return to Indiana for the beginning of the fall semester at their respective schools, the couple decided to marry. However, they took this important step under a cloak of secrecy because Van knew his father wouldn't approve of him marrying while still a student. On Saturday, September 25, 1937,[93] with their marriage license in hand, Van and Davy set out in search of a clergyman to marry them. The elopement took place in a village far from their usual haunts. Afterwards, Van and Davy even disagreed about which village they had wed in. This seems quite believable since I have yet to find their marriage license in any county in Indiana where they were resident at the time.[94] After the impromptu wedding, the couple honeymooned for the weekend at a hotel in a wooded park.[95]

The Man Who Received "A Severe Mercy"

The fall of 1937 was Davy's last semester at Butler; she never received a degree. Nevertheless, Van continued with school and graduated from Wabash College in the spring of 1938. According to *A Severe Mercy*, Davy spent the summer of '38 at Glen Merle.[96] One wonders what Van's parents thought of this arrangement since they presumably did not know that Van and Davy were married. Be that as it may, every morning Van and Davy went for a long walk or a bicycle ride together. It was on one of these walks that they ended up buying a collie from a litter of puppies at a nearby farm. They named the dog Laddie; she was to be an important companion for the next couple of years.

Some of their most valued reading from this time included the poetry of Welshman W. H. Davies, in particular, his poem, *Leisure:*

> What is this life if, full of care,
> We have no time to stand and stare.
>
> No time to stand beneath the boughs
> And stare as long as sheep or cows.
>
> No time to see, when woods we pass,
> Where squirrels hide their nuts in grass.
>
> No time to see, in broad daylight,
> Streams full of stars, like stars at night.
>
> No time to turn at Beauty's glance,
> And watch her feet, how they can dance.
>
> No time to wait till her mouth can
> Enrich that smile her eyes began.
>
> A poor life this if, full of care,
> We have no time to stand and stare.[97]

Poems like this, as well as Lin Yutang's words on the necessity of leisure to the good life, led Van and Davy to question how they might create a life with room to "stand and stare." The dream that was born in their hearts one summer day in '38, as they sat by the pool at Glen Merle, was that of living on a sailboat, eating what they could catch from the sea, and writing books. They began to read everything they could about boats and sailing. Based upon his sailing experience at Culver, Van applied for and received a naval-reserve probationary commission to learn navigation. Together, Van and Davy took correspondence courses, but their actual experience on the water was confined to navigating a canoe on one of the rivers in Indiana, probably the White River that flows through Hamilton County near Glen Merle.

From the beginning, Van and Davy planned to name their yacht *Grey Goose*. They chose this bird as their symbol because of its wild nature and being a water bird, but also because the grey goose, if its mate dies, flies on alone for the rest of its life. They even had a jeweler design and fashion grey-goose signet rings, gold with a small sapphire star.

After the summer of '38, Van went to work, briefly, for Westinghouse. He performed rather unpleasant shop work on electrical engines, and soon realized that he had less than no future with the company, since he had no electrical training.[98] This was followed by a longer stint as a radio announcer at his father's station, WIBC, which then operated out of the Athletic Club. WIBC had its first broadcast on October 31, 1938. The station was owned by Glenn Van Auken's Indiana Broadcasting Company and managed by C. A. McLaughlin.[99] According to the Indianapolis City Directory of 1940, Van was still working as a radio announcer at WIBC and living at Glen Merle. Why Van continued to keep his marriage to Davy a secret from his parents remains a mystery.

It is also a mystery to me why Davy put up with this arrangement of living apart from her husband. However, put up with it she did, perhaps because she was so deeply in love. Davy worked at a series of odd jobs and lived in rented accommodations in Indianapolis. According to the Indianapolis City Directories for these years, in 1938 she was living at 3532 Washington Boulevard and working as a receptionist. The next year she had relocated to 3327 Central Avenue and was employed, again as a receptionist, at the Holland Studio. According to the 1940 Census, Davy was working as a teller for the telephone company and living at 2222 Central Avenue. By 1941, she was employed as a clerk at L. S. Ayres & Company where she and Van first met.

While Davy was working at these various jobs and living in rented accommodations under her maiden name in order to keep their marriage a secret, Van had his sights set on leaving Indianapolis. He applied to Columbia and Duke Universities for their post-grad programs. However, World War II interrupted his plans for further education.

Syrinx the Wood Nymph
whom Van dubbed "la fée Tarapatapoum"
after a character in *Peter Ibbetson*

Author Photo

Van & Davy

VII

THE WAR YEARS

> This is the way the world ends
> This is the way the world ends
> This is the way the world ends
> Not with a bang but a whimper.
>
> T. S. Eliot, *The Hollow Men*

At the beginning of 1941, it must have seemed the world *was* ending, with war raging in Europe, and conflict with Japan imminent in the Pacific. Against this backdrop of world cataclysm, Van and Davy finally decided to announce their marriage.[100] As Van says in *A Severe Mercy*, the secret marriage had already become a rather open secret.[101] How could it not when Davy was living at Glen Merle, at least for the summer of 1938? Van's mother was aware of the marriage and approving. Van's father must have had his suspicions. Still, for whatever reason, the official announcement did not come until the beginning of 1941.

At that time, Van's mother offered to pay for a honeymoon in Florida. It also fell to Grace to make the official announcement to Van's father before news of the marriage appeared in the paper.[102] Van and Davy took off for Florida, stopping at the home of Van's aunt, Marie Reese, in Winchester, Kentucky along the way.[103] They never got any farther. Van's mother phoned the next evening to let Van know that the Navy was ordering him to sea.

Back again at Glen Merle, Van said goodbye to his mother and then to his brother Paul on the bridge by the lily pond. Van's father drove him to the train station to board the Monon Railway. As the train pulled out Van could still see his father waving and grinning as he stood on the station platform, "tall and bronzed and young-looking."[104] Van didn't know it then, but it was to be their last goodbye.

By special arrangement, the train was flagged down at the Carmel station and Davy got aboard. She rode with Van all the way to Chicago then took another train back to Glen Merle. For Van, it was on to Long Beach, California, from whence he sailed aboard the U. S. S. Kanawha to Pearl Harbor on March 15.[105] Two days earlier, an announcement appeared in the Indianapolis News beside a photo of Davy saying that she was the bride of Ensign Sheldon Frank Van Auken who had already departed for active duty with the United States Navy.

Van was part of the United States Naval Reserve and had requested reassignment to active duty.[106] When he was actually called up, he was assigned to the four-stacker destroyer Perry.[107] Van joined the Perry at Pearl Harbor in March of '41.[108] It was less than three months before he and Davy were reunited in the islands. On May 20, Davy sailed on the SS President Coolidge from San Francisco, arriving in Honolulu on the 25th.[109] Van didn't know exactly when Davy was coming; furthermore, he was out at sea when she arrived.

Friends from Indianapolis, Jack and Allene Ford, met Davy as she got off the ship. Davy had known Allene as a fellow student at Butler University[110] and Van had known her as staff pianist at WIBC.[111] Like Davy, Allene had a father who was a preacher.[112] Jack and Allene were new to Honolulu just like the Van Aukens. They had sailed from New York on the United States Army transport *Republic* on February 6 that year.[113] Lieutenant Ford was assigned to two years' duty at the Hawaiian department air corps and had recently trained at Langley Field, Virginia. Allene worked in the United States Army Women's Air Raid Defense[114] attached to the Seventh Interceptor Command.[115]

As soon as Davy settled in, Jack, Allene, and some other army friends arranged to take her on a tour of the islands. Their boat was the cruiser Ebbtide and they just happened to meet up with the commodore of Van's destroyer squadron in Kaunakakai on the island of Molokai on the last day of May.[116] Thus, Davy in the Ebbtide was able to cruise out to see Van aboard the Perry that day, off the coast of Molokai.

An unusual thing happened on the day of their reunion that was to stay in Van's memory for a long time. As the cruiser Ebbtide came alongside the Perry, the shadow of the destroyer's mast and yardarm fell across the white motorboat, making the shape of an X. Though Van was caught up, at that moment, in greeting his wife across the water, the shadow of the X struck Van as faintly ominous. Upon later reflection, during a mid-watch on the Perry from midnight to four o'clock in the morning, it occurred to Van that the X he had seen fall across Ebbtide was really more like a cross. This got him thinking that perhaps, some day, he ought to have a second look at Christianity. He told Davy about this later; they laughed it off and tried to put it out of their minds, but the idea never really disappeared.[117]

After Van and Davy's all-too-brief meeting at sea, Van had shipboard duty for another week. He had such duty aboard ship every other four-week period.[118] Upon his return, they settled in together at a Navy apartment in Waikiki. However, it wasn't long before Van was back at sea. In the late spring, the Perry sailed back to San Diego. Then, on July 1, the Perry escorted the battleship Arizona back to Pearl Harbor. Van later recalled seeing a flotilla of Japanese sampans fishing off the coast of Point Loma on a misty morning as

The Man Who Received "A Severe Mercy"

they departed San Diego Harbor with the Arizona. The sampans quickly got out of the way as the battleship bore down upon them.[119]

There are two days out of their four and a half years in Hawaii that Van later recalled vividly. The first was December 6, 1941. Van was on leave from the Perry for the weekend because his ship was in port.[120] He and Davy took the opportunity to drive around Oahu in their 1931 Ford Roadster convertible. They spent time at various windward beaches opposite Honolulu on the eastern shoreline of the island.[121] Today, the drive from Waikiki over to the windward side of Oahu could take an hour or less depending on where you were headed. Van and Davy may have followed the coastal route east out of Honolulu and around. A leisurely drive in this direction, in an old car like they had, could take hours, but they had plenty of time with over eleven hours of daylight.

As Van suggests in *A Severe Mercy* they may have visited several beaches. Perhaps they drove all the way to Kahana Bay, a location with one of the most secluded beaches on the island. The sandy shoreline provides a great place for sunbathing and one can hike up the Koolau Mountains from the beach.[122] The weather that day was warm and clear, reaching into the 80s, but it would have felt a little cooler on the breezy windward side of the island, a perfect day for swimming.[123]

In the late afternoon, Van and Davy returned to their apartment in Waikiki. After showering and dressing for an evening out, they drove to Hickam Field, the army air force base near Pearl Harbor, for dinner with Allene and Jack. Van and Davy noticed as they drove along that the Christmas lights had been put up along the streets of Honolulu, but were not yet lit. Allene had asked Van and Davy to bring their record of Tchaikovsky's Sixth Symphony, the *Pathétique*. Allene was, apparently, still haunted by the memory of a man with whom she had listened to it years before. After dinner, the couples chatted and Jack played the violin. The two men talked about the possibility of war but concluded that the Japanese would never dare to attack. Then Jack said, "How about flying with me in the morning?" Van replied, "No, I have some Navy work to do." At the conclusion of their evening, the couples listened to Tchaikovsky's symphony. As the last mournful notes died away, Allene said, almost prophetically, "It sounds like the dirge of a dying world."[124]

Van's appointment the next morning was at the Red Hill Underground Fuel Depot, a storage facility that served the United States Armed Forces during World War II and continues to serve the military up to the present time.[125] This facility, operated by the Navy, was under construction from 1940 to 1943 and remained secret until many years after the war. The Red Hill facility is on a small knoll overlooking Pearl Harbor from the northeast.

As Van left Davy reading at their apartment in Waikiki and drove to Red Hill he saw few signs of life; it was a sleepy, Sunday morning in Honolulu.

After arriving at Red Hill, while waiting for the man he was to see, Van read the Honolulu Advertiser. The Sunday supplement feature had an article entitled *Uncle Sam's Mighty Arm in the Pacific*. From Red Hill Van had a clear view of the harbor; he noted that both battle forces of the Pacific fleet were in port; the scouting force was the only one at sea.

Van continued reading the newspaper until he heard an enlisted man talking through the open window of the building where he was sitting. "Look at that big fire down at the sub base! That's sabotage, I bet."[126] Van decided to stroll outside and see what was happening. The fire was not at the sub base but rather at the Naval Air Station on Ford Island in the middle of Pearl Harbor. As Van surveyed the scene, he could see the Perry moored in the northwest part of the harbor next to the other minesweepers (USS Trever, Wasmuth & Zane) and a light minelayer (the USS Breese). The time was 7:55 AM.

Then Van saw fighter planes, with the telltale "red sun" emblem on their bodies and on their wings, heading toward battleship row. He ran out to his old Ford Roadster where he had binoculars and a .45 automatic. The first thing he saw as he focused the binoculars on the harbor was a red flicker of flame on the West Virginia. Just as he set his sights on the Arizona, the front magazines exploded. On the edge of the blast Van saw a white-clad sailor flying through the sky, arms outstretched. At the same moment, the Oklahoma was in the process of capsizing. Van realized he was watching history in the making.

Looking south, Van could see that Hickam, where he and Davy had been the night before, was being bombed heavily. He asked another officer, "Why aren't the fighter planes from Wheeler doing anything?" The officer turned him around and pointed to a huge column of smoke ascending from Wheeler Field to the northwest. One Japanese plane flew low enough over Red Hill for Van to see a grin on the pilot's face. Van fired six shots from his automatic without any noticeable results.

When the attack slowed, Van drove back to the apartment to check on Davy and get into uniform. As he passed Fort Shafter, an army post, he saw countless bodies of men killed in the first wave of the attack. However, when Van reached the heart of Honolulu, it seemed like an ordinary Sunday morning. Civilians were walking around, oblivious to what was happening a few miles away. The only sign that anything unusual was going on were the many Navy vehicles he saw heading quickly to the harbor.

When Van arrived back at the apartment, he found Davy still reading her book. She was completely unaware of the attack. Van explained what was happening and Davy replied, "I thought the noise was just the usual Sunday morning coast artillery practice." Van said, "I've got to get to my ship. I don't know when I'll get back." Davy assured him, "I'll be alright."

Next, Van went to fetch another officer who lived nearby. He found the

The Man Who Received "A Severe Mercy"

officer asleep and was unable to convince him that a raid was really happening. The fellow officer refused to believe Van until he listened to the radio broadcasts confirming the report. The time was 8:40.

Together, they made a mad dash back toward the harbor in the Roadster with the top down. At certain points, shell fragments were flying all around them[127] but only one small fragment bounced off the radiator with no detrimental effect.[128] Traffic was heavy; they arrived at their ship's base just as the second wave of Japanese planes was attacking. The time was 9:00 AM and the Perry had already gone to sea sometime before they arrived. Having already downed one Japanese fighter plane, the Perry took up patrol and sweeping duties near the harbor entrance.[129]

Van and his companion were disappointed, no doubt, to have missed getting aboard their ship. However, there was plenty of work for them to do on land. At the end of day, a large rainbow arched over the burning ships in the harbor. That night, Davy huddled with a dozen other Navy wives in one of the blacked-out rooms of the apartment complex.[130] Van didn't get home to see Davy until Christmas night, and even that visit was brief, three or four hours at the most. In the midst of the blackout, they made eggnog by the light of the refrigerator and drank it by the light of the radio dial.[131]

Davy was not evacuated with the other Navy wives because she obtained a sensitive Naval job.[132] In the months that followed, Van and Davy both became accustomed to blackouts, air raid alarms, military law, curfews, seeing each other rarely, and the countless other inconveniences of wartime. They also became used to losing good friends; Jack Ford went down at the controls of his bomber somewhere near Midway.

The Van Aukens tried to get on with their lives as best they could. Davy performed her daily work in the naval yard where some of the ships damaged on December 7 were salvaged and the Pacific Fleet was rebuilt. Van was reassigned to a small yacht converted to service as a patrol boat.[133] He also served, for a time, as a communications officer. In that capacity, he learned "touch-typing" in order to type code into a cipher machine.[134]

On one occasion, when Van's boat was lying off the coast of one of the islands he caught a 13-foot-long shark. It required almost the entire crew to drag the shark aboard. In the end, Van made a necklace of shark teeth for Davy and kept one tooth for himself as good luck.[135]

On another occasion, Van's patrol boat was off the coast of the island of Niihau, the smallest of the Hawaiian chain, southwest of Kauai.[136] When Van visited it was the summer of 1942 and far to the west of his location, the Battle of Midway was beginning.

The Navy was considering Niihau for a watching station. Thus, Van volunteered to swim ashore from his patrol boat and inspect the situation, planning to rejoin his ship on the other side of the island. Supervised by a small group of native Hawaiians (Kanakas) Van swam toward a shoreline consisting of sharp-edged lava. Once ashore, one of the men greeted Van with "Aloha!" Another climbed a palm tree, retrieving a large green nut to quench Van's thirst.

As Van made his way across the island with the natives, one of them, who spoke English, led him deep into a jungle area. There he showed him the wreck of a Japanese fighter plane, partially covered with vines. Undoubtedly, this was one of the enemy planes that had attacked Pearl Harbor months before. Van wondered: could this be the plane I shot with my .45 automatic?

He looked over the plane and noticed that some of the instruments had been manufactured in Detroit of all places. Van took one of the instruments to pass on to Naval Intelligence. As he walked on to the other side of the island, one of the natives told him the story of the downed Japanese pilot.

Unhurt in the crash landing, the well-armed pilot shot one or two of the native men and proclaimed himself king of the island. He demanded food from the natives and chose one of the girls as his mistress. The girl's Kanaka boyfriend soon arrived and was informed of the situation. He approached the Japanese pilot who in turn fired a warning shot over the Kanaka's head. The big Hawaiian continued coming on. So then, the pilot shot him. Still the brawny Kanaka approached the pilot. The Japanese bully shot him again. The Kanaka continued staggering toward the pilot and grabbed the gun. The Japanese man shrieked just before the Kanaka broke his neck. In a matter of moments, two men lay dead in the sand; the brief reign of terror was over.[137]

Soon, Van was back in Honolulu after his adventure on the island of Niihau. During the war years, Van and Davy were never separated for long. When they were together, they listened to music and read poetry as they had always done. Furthermore, they continued to enjoy the sun, surf and green mountains of Oahu.

Sadly, on August 31, 1943, Van received a cablegram telling him his father had just died. He had been in the Methodist Hospital in Indianapolis after a weeklong illness. Now, due to a doctor's blunder, he was gone. Glenn was only 59 years old. During the last year of his life, he had been appointed as special assistant to the United States attorney general to hear appeals of conscientious objectors to military service.[138]

Van flew home to Indianapolis for the funeral and to help settle his father's estate. By this time, Glenn and Grace had a house in Indianapolis at 6059 Carrollton Avenue in addition to their home in Carmel. Sadly, Glen Merle had to be sold. Grace continued to live in the city. Glenn was buried at Arlington Cemetery.

After a month at home, Van returned to San Francisco by train and then

The Man Who Received "A Severe Mercy"

sailed from San Francisco to Hawaii on a Navy cruiser.[139] It was, perhaps, during this trip that Van had an experience that would prove very important to his own personal and social development. He was on a troop train. At lunchtime, white and black military personnel were seated on opposite sides of the train. There were spaces available for someone to sit on the black side while there were none for Van on the white side. Rather than wait for the white side to open up, Van realized how silly the whole thing was and approached a black naval quartermaster who was sitting alone. Van asked if he could sit with him and the quartermaster obliged. They had a good discussion together about the stupidity of segregation. From that moment on Van rejected segregation for himself, while not objecting to the chosen segregation of others (for example: a black or white men's club). Van came to this conclusion despite his upbringing; at Glen Merle, black servants were the norm and segregation was taken for granted.[140]

After Van returned to Hawaii, and sometime during the last two years of the war, he and Davy were able to revive their Grey Goose dream. They bought a tiny sloop and began to hang around the Honolulu Yacht Club. Partly through Van's efforts, the club was allowed to resume ocean racing. As a reward, Van and Davy received a membership. Thus, they began to crew some of the larger yachts.

On one occasion, while sailing aboard a forty-foot sloop, a flap of the sail knocked Van's Navy cap into the ocean. Davy reached over the side to retrieve it and accidentally fell in. Before long, Van realized that the boat was pulling farther and farther away from his wife. Davy's head was a small dot in a big expanse of blue. Thus, Van kicked off his shoes and dove into the water. Once he reached his wife, they had to tread water, several miles off Diamond Head, for some time before the boat was able to return and pick them up.[141]

Early in 1945, Van and Davy rejoiced in their first and only leave from the Navy. They were granted ten days off and they began it with an extended "Navigator's Council", a pleasant review of their eight years together. They concluded that they were still "on course", as much in love, if not more, than they had ever been.[142]

A few months later, Van received orders to report to the Naval Station Great Lakes, in North Chicago, Illinois, pending reassignment.[143] However, soon after Van and Davy arrived in Illinois, the United States dropped an atomic bomb on the Japanese city of Hiroshima. The date was August 6, 1945. Three days later, a similar bomb leveled Nagasaki. The next day Emperor Hirohito made the "sacred decision" to surrender.[144] Soon thereafter, Van was released from Naval duty, having achieved the rank of lieutenant commander. He and Davy decided to pick up where they had left off, four and a half years before. They headed for Florida to take up his mother's offer of a long-promised honeymoon.

A SKETCH OF THE VAN AUKENS' BOAT FROM YACHTING MAGAZINE

VIII

SAILING THE KEYS

> Wither, O Splended Ship, thy white sails crowding,
> Leaning across the bosom of the urgent West,
> That fearest not seas rising, nor sky clouding,
> Wither away, fair rover, and what thy quest?
>
> Robert Bridges, *A Passer-by*

In the fall of 1945, Van and Davy began to fulfill the dream that was born poolside at Glen Merle. They moved to Miami, Florida and looked for a boat to buy, one that would be the forerunner of the long-planned schooner, Grey Goose. They wanted something small and easy to sail, while still big enough to live aboard. They originally planned to purchase a boat perhaps twenty-six to thirty feet in length. In the midst of their search, they met an old salt of the sea by the name of Frank Watson. Cap (as Frank was known to friends) had fifty-years sailing experience. He it was who told Van and Davy that a particular eighteen-foot sloop was the one for them. The couple talked it over.

"There may not be much room," Van said.

"But we'll still have sitting headroom," responded Davy with a smile.

"As long as we don't sit up straight," added Van.

"It will be a good boat to learn in," Davy offered.

"And just think how roomy a 40-foot schooner will feel after this."

"We'll buy it!"[145]

Van and Davy named their new boat *Gull*. Then they set about re-rigging her, scraping, sanding, painting and varnishing. Once they had their new sailboat in shape, they spent four or five afternoons messing about close to home, learning to sail by chart and compass. Finally, Van and Davy decided it was time to put all their book knowledge to a real test. They bought canned food, charts, filled their tanks with gasoline and prepared to depart for a month-long trip exploring the Florida Keys.

The day of embarkation dawned brilliant. One hour out of Miami, *Gull* passed the old lighthouse on Cape Florida. Ahead there was no beacon, no land in sight, just the vast expanse of Biscayne Bay. By sunset, *Gull* made it to the other side of the Bay and anchored in a tranquil spot at Sands Key.

The next day *Gull* cruised ten miles further south to Pumpkin Key. The day after, the wind seemed too strong and so the novice sailors decided to lie at anchor for another night. However, next day Van was determined to push on, no matter what.

"Are you sure?" asked Davy uncertainly.

"No," Van replied, but tied in the reefs anyway.[146]

Gull handled the strong winds well, but Van and Davy were still a bit jittery about the whole experience. Thus, they took down the sails, started the engine and proceeded under power through Card Sound into Barnes Sound.

Van and Davy's goal was to reach Tavernier where lay the twenty-six-foot sloop, *Beachcomber*, and their new friend, Captain Frank Watson. The entire voyage took about a week. *Gull* went rather unceremoniously aground on Tavernier Bar. Once Cap had finished laughing he said, "Everyone goes aground on Tavernier." It was little consolation to the embarrassed Van Aukens. However, things were looking up; Cap invited the couple to sail along with him.

The first night after departing from Tavernier the two boats anchored at Cotton Key. That evening they enjoyed a dinner of crawfish speared in the shallows and discussed the day's sailing. Thus, the pattern was set for the rest of Van and Davy's time with Cap. During the day they sailed and by night they talked. Actually, Cap talked while Van and Davy listened, and learned. Cap led them westward into the many keys and sandbars of Florida Bay. In time, under Cap's tutelage, the strong winds lost their terror for Van and Davy and they learned to trust what *Gull* could handle. This was, perhaps, the most enjoyable part of the Van Auken's first sailing cruise. They circled through the keys, stopping every so often to fish, or swim or explore. Then, every evening they would enjoy chowder or a lobster salad. After dinner, they would sit back and watch birds overhead or porpoises in the clear blue water below.

After a month of learning and leisure in the Keys, it was time to head back to Miami. As *Gull* crossed the rough waters of Biscayne Bay once again, the skyline of Miami rose in the hazy distance. A worn out *Gull* and her crew entered their home slip just as a blinding rain started pelting down. That night Van and Davy sent a postcard to Cap saying they would see him in another month. At their mooring in the Miami River, Van typed out the story of their adventure and sent it off to *Yachting* magazine. With the money earned from freelance writing, Van and Davy would be able to purchase more supplies needed for *Gull*, some food, and soon they would be off again.[147]

Van's next tale of adventure in the Florida Keys published by *Yachting* magazine took place in the following summer of 1946.[148] This time Van and Davy went cruising in *Gull* for seven weeks. Again, they went south from Miami to Tavernier, where Captain Frank Watson joined them on their journey. This time they had overnight stays near Key Largo and Pelican Key en route to meeting up with Cap. Van and Davy, having grown much more confident in their sailing abilities by this time, made it to Tavernier in half the time.

The Man Who Received "A Severe Mercy"

It was a joyful reunion celebrated all round with a glass of Red Heart Rum. Soon, the three sailors had charts spread out in the cockpit of the *Beachcomber* planning their voyage southward where Van and Davy had never been before.

The next day Cap filled his two-hundred-pound icebox, while Van and Davy stocked up on groceries. The Van Aukens used their ten-foot double-ended dinghy, the *Ilikea Moana*,[149] brought with them from Hawaii, to haul countless pounds of supplies from shore to ship. The next morning *Beachcomber* sailed out of the channel followed by *Gull* with her dinghy in tow. They sailed an easy fifteen miles south to Lignumvitae Key. There, where the northern stretch of the Florida Keys ends, they spent the night.

The two sailing vessels continued south, another fifteen miles to Channel Key. There, Van experienced one of the most unnerving events of the entire trip. As he, and Cap and Davy were swimming in the warm, shallow water off the coast of Channel Key, Van decided to try spearing one of the mangrove snappers common to the area. He went snorkeling along, lightweight spear in hand, his eyes trained on the sandy bottom. Suddenly, he glanced up and saw a three-foot-wide stingray only ten inches from his face. He tried to keep his cool and swim gently backwards. Thankfully, the stingray turned and proceeded in the other direction.

The next morning, after a chilly swim at dawn (without any stingray meetings) and a breakfast of lobster and eggs, *Gull* led the way through the sandbars southward. Most of that day, *Gull* and *Beachcomber* sailed almost soundlessly, side by side. That evening the two sailboats anchored in the lee of Bamboo Key. The three sailors followed their usual routine of dinner aboard the *Beachcomber* followed by discussion of the day's sail and the next day's plan. However, after dinner Davy was the first to return to *Gull*. Van came later after chatting with Cap for a while. He found Davy in the cabin of *Gull*, her eager face studying the shells she had collected that day from the island. The only illumination came from the Van Auken's oil lamp in the cabin below and the starlit sky above. For Van, the sight was another "moment made eternity."

From Bamboo Key it was on to Vaca Key and the town of Marathon where the two ships filled up on their supplies. From Vaca they made the long trek to East Bahia Honda. This was the first time during their entire trip together that land completely disappeared. However, East Bahia Honda soon rose out of the misty distance.

The next day the two sailboats made their way across Big Spanish Channel. On this leg of the trip, they were met by a squall. Suddenly there was wind, driving rain and white, frothy waves all around. They were lucky to see one hundred yards in any direction. However, almost as quickly as the storm stirred up, it died down. Still, the two sailboats had to put down anchor in the shelter of Porpoise Key and wait out the strong winds for a few days. True to its name, there were a number of porpoises to be seen swimming around this Key. The three sailors explored the south side of the Key and discovered a channel replete with starfish and snapper. Van and Davy explored a deserted island on foot and found a clearing in the middle where they were surrounded by many bright red wasps and a single, six-inch, blue butterfly, the largest they had ever seen. There was no indication anywhere on the island that any human being had ever explored there before. When Van and Davy found their way back to the dinghy they lay down in the water, exhausted. As they soaked up the rays of the sun and the caresses of the water, the only thing sticking above the surface were their heads clad in straw hats. Occasionally they would see a dorsal fin penetrating the surface of the water, but the sharks were too small to do much harm. At the end of the afternoon, the Van Aukens made their way back to *Gull* and *Beachcomber* where they found Cap sound asleep.

Once the strong winds died down, Cap, and Van and Davy continued their cruise along the coast of Big Pine Key. Their next anchorage was near Big Torch Key where Van was able to spear two, three-pound snapper.

By eleven o'clock the next morning, *Gull* and *Beachcomber* had navigated the shallowest stretch of the Inner Narrows, between Snipe and Saddlebunch Keys. Since the wind was picking up again they decided to lie at anchor five miles distant from Key West. It had been seventeen days since the Van Aukens had left Miami and the winds had been strong most of the time.

The next morning they sailed on a fresh wind into Key West Bight where they were able to tie up, without charge, for a weeklong stay. Van and Davy found the town to be a charming mixture of Spanish flavor and the Old South. Everywhere they wandered, they found galleried houses, bright bougainvillea and towering palm trees, along with happy children playing in the sunny streets. Each evening they would dine on things like turtle or conch steak, then trudge back to the harbor for a night of rest.

Over the course of the next month, *Gull* and *Beachcomber* sailed gradually back in a northeasterly direction. Along the way, they explored beaches, swam in the shallows, fished, talked and read. As delightfully full of leisure as this trip sounds, it wasn't without its irritating aspects. At night, they would have to get under netting for protection from mosquitoes, and even this was not always successful. In addition, on the return trip they were hunted by deerflies that could inflict a vicious bite. One afternoon Van counted fifty-eight kills with the slap of a hand, but ten of them had bit him in the process of dying. Despite these little annoyances, Van and Davy found joy in their own companionship, in the wild beauty that spanned around them, and in the peace of being away from the noise and hurry of the city. Thus, it was with some reluctance that the Van Aukens left Cap once again in Tavernier and made their way back to the civilization of Miami, but not without one, last, horrendous storm on Biscayne Bay.

After almost a year of basking in the sun and playing in the surf of the Florida Keys, Van and Davy were ready to move on. Despite the joys of sailing without schedule or other commitments, the Van Aukens had grown tired of the cramped lifestyle aboard *Gull*. Besides, *Gull* was only one step toward realizing the *Grey Goose* dream. They were hoping for a post-war drop in boat prices to enable them to purchase the larger, planned-for, schooner, but it didn't happen. While waiting for the right time to buy *Grey Goose*, Van and Davy decided to turn to the university life once again. Perhaps a further degree would help Van to pick up the odd job here or there while he and Davy sailed the world alone together. They looked into the possibility of Oxford, but the way was barred, due to all the former soldiers flooding that institution following the war.

Thus, Van set his sights on one of the Ivy League schools he had dreamed of attending so many years before when he was first a student at Wabash. In the end, Yale was the one to open its hallowed doors to Sheldon Van Auken.

YALE UNIVERSITY

Author Photo

IX

CONVICTION

> All the powers of nature call so earnestly for the confession of sin, that these black weeds have sprung up out of a buried heart to make manifest an unspoken crime.
>
> Nathaniel Hawthorne, *The Scarlet Letter*

Van and Davy found themselves at Yale in the fall of 1946 where Van began a Master of Arts course in General Studies; this degree included classes and research in English (American Literature and the English Novel) and History (English historians and American Intellectual History).[150]

Yale University was, at the time, made up of several residential colleges. This distinctive system, of smaller colleges within one grand university, was modeled on the example of Oxford and Cambridge. The college dining halls, with their hammer-beam ceilings, leaded glass windows with gothic tracery, and exquisite portraiture, are reminiscent of the dining halls at the great universities in England. The Hall of Graduate Studies, built in the 1930s, was the place, other than the library, where Van would have spent most of his time while on campus. Once again, the Gothic style has a hint of Englishness about it, with its leaded glass windows, stone arches, whimsical carvings, and gracious courtyards.

Yale's Sterling Memorial Library was a place Van would have visited often during his two years at the university. The library has numerous architectural features similar to the great cathedrals of Europe; as well as its intellectual resources, Van would have appreciated the beauty of the library with its many carvings, ironwork and stained glass windows.

Located midway between New York and Boston, the city of New Haven offered to Van and Davy many cultural and recreational opportunities —great restaurants, theater, musical performances, museums, hiking trails, parks, beaches and much more. New Haven was a city of moderate size in 1946; contained in twenty square miles, the city boasted a population of 160,000.

Whenever Van and Davy wanted to get away from the city, they always had Davy's family cottage on Culver Lake in New Jersey. In those days, it would have been a relatively easy drive of maybe three or four hours. There, Van and Davy could indulge their love of the outdoors with a peaceful walk or canoe ride by day and the hooting of owls by night.[151]

In New Haven, Van and Davy lived in a large, old house with other graduate students. All they had was a single ground floor room, the former dining or drawing room of the house, with a small but elegant fireplace in which they burned walnut gunstocks from a local arms factory.[152] Van and Davy sometimes used the ground floor communal kitchen; at other times, they cooked on a hot plate in their own room. It was while they were living in this house that the Van Aukens adopted a stray dog they named Gypsy. She was a black and tan mixed breed, part collie and perhaps part husky.

Although Van and Davy enjoyed the bare branch beauty of winter during their first year in New Haven, they missed the leisurely, sunny, warm days of life aboard *Gull*. Van often wondered what he was doing in New Haven when somewhere beyond Yale's gothic grandeur trade winds were blowing. However, he continued with his studies, and kept his nose in the books. Most importantly, during these years of study, Van and Davy's love for one another held true.

One winter evening when Van came home, Davy already had wood burning in the fireplace, candles glowing on the mantle, and a delicious meal on the table in their one-room apartment. The Bruch violin concerto was playing on their gramophone; the beauty, joy and loveliness of the scene overcame Van; he took Davy in his arms and whispered his love to her. The springtime Eros of Glen Merle was still beating in their hearts through the seeming desolation of an icy Connecticut winter.[153]

Perhaps one of the most significant events that took place for Davy during their time in New Haven happened one spring afternoon when she visited a local park. This may have been the expansive Eagle Rock Park in the northern part of town, or the smaller, more intimate, New Haven Green, closer to the university. Davy was reading and occasionally looking up at children playing. The hours drifted on and soon Davy was alone, or so she thought. Suddenly there came a hoarse cry behind her. There it was again. She turned around and saw: a man exposing himself. Before she knew what was happening, the man was running toward her. Davy quickly got up and ran out of the park, eventually proving too fast for the man chasing her. She returned home along the busy New Haven streets, glad to be around other people again where she could cry out for help if necessary. Later that evening, Davy told Van about the event. He was greatly angered by it, but she, by now, was taking it all a bit more lightly, at least, for the time being.[154]

There were three pieces of literature among many that touched Van and Davy's souls at this time. Living in New England, and reading widely in both English and American literature for his M. A., it is natural that Van would read Nathaniel Hawthorne. Apparently, Hawthorne's twin themes of guilt and sin, as expressed especially in *The Scarlet Letter*, haunted Davy, if not

The Man Who Received "A Severe Mercy"

Van. Then there was William Blake's poem, "The Sick Rose" from *Songs of Experience:*

> O Rose thou art sick.
> The invisible worm
> That flies in the night,
> In the howling storm:
>
> Has found out thy bed
> Of crimson joy:
> And his dark secret love
> Does thy life destroy.[155]

Perhaps W. H. Auden's poem, written at the outbreak of World War II, captured best what Van and Davy were feeling during their years in New Haven:

> Faces along the bar
> Cling to their average day:
> The lights must never go out,
> The music must always play,
> All the conventions conspire
> To make this fort assume
> The furniture of home;
> Lest we should see where we are,
> Lost in a haunted wood,
> Children afraid of the night
> who have never been happy or good.

Whether Van realized it then or not, Davy certainly did: she was a child afraid of the night who had never really been happy or good. One evening, Van came home from the library to find Davy dissolved in tears. When Van was finally able to extract from her the cause of this flood of emotion, she said that her sins had come out and paraded before her. Van found himself scarcely able to think of his wife as a "sinner." However, Davy knew better. Was it a sense of guilt about conceiving a child out of wedlock so many years before, and giving that child up for adoption? Had the evil of the man in the park made Davy recognize a stain upon her own soul? One thing was certain: Van either couldn't or wouldn't understand it.[156]

Thus, Van plunged himself into his work and tried to forget, or explain away, Davy's conviction of sin. During his two years at Yale, he wrote at least two essays subsequently published in various journals and magazines. If any reader or student of Van Auken's life should question whether Van, by this time, had truly become a historian of some academic weight, even a casual perusal of the following, lengthy essays, should lay all such doubts to rest. Van's article on "The Southern Historical Novel" was published in *The Journal of Southern History*, May 1948. Another essay on "A Century of the Southern Plantation" was published in *The Virginia Magazine of History & Biography*, July 1950.

Soon it was time to leave New Haven. Van earned his Master of Arts degree from Yale in the spring of 1948 and obtained a position teaching English and history at Lynchburg College in Lynchburg, Virginia, starting in the fall.[157]

Dr. Josephus Hopwood, a pioneer in Christian co-education, started Lynchburg College in 1903. From the beginning, the school was associated with the Christian Church (Disciples of Christ), the same denomination in which Van was raised. The school began on the site of a failed resort—the Westover Hotel—that was available for sale. The property was bought for $13,500 and the school was first established under the name, Virginia Christian College.[158]

When Van arrived on campus, Dr. Riley B. Montgomery was President. Riley had served in a number of leadership positions in The Disciples of Christ before coming to Lynchburg. He had been a pastor and president of the International Convention of the Disciples. Riley presided over the school during the difficult years of the depression and saw a large influx of students after World War II, straining the college's limited facilities.[159]

The chair of the English department was a man after Van's own heart. Dr. John Turner graduated from the University of Michigan with a Master of Arts degree and from Harvard with a Ph.D. He began teaching English at Lynchburg in 1933. Like Van, Turner was not only a good teacher, but a poet as well. Furthermore, he conducted his classes in an almost courtly manner.[160]

In Lynchburg Van and Davy found an old farmhouse to rent. A horse at the farm gently "nipped" Davy during their first visit, so the Van Aukens christened their new home: "Horsebite Hall." The farm was a couple miles away from Lynchburg College on Wards Road but sadly no longer exists. It was replaced long ago with a shopping center.

Van's first two years at Lynchburg College must have been rather uneventful, for Van says little about his work there in *A Severe Mercy*, and there is little mention of him in the college's publications from that period. During his first two years at the college, he taught courses in Freshman English, American Literature, the English Novel and World History.[161] In addition, Van became the Faculty Adviser to *The Prism*, a student journal, in the fall of 1949. In the February 1950 issue of *The Prism*, there was a somewhat interesting letter from an alumna to Van Auken. The alumna, Winnie Deatt Fitzgerald, from the class of 1919 and the mother of a freshman, complained

The Man Who Received "A Severe Mercy"

to Van Auken about the November issue:

> I found eleven pages of so-called literary prose; of these, nine and one-half are taken up with maudlin and indecent chatterings of drunken men, sprinkled rather generously with a vile sort of profanity not permitted in our homes, and certainly not acceptable for our girls to hear or read—or boys either. If this is "a correlative cross-section of student thought" ... at Lynchburg College, I do not feel we can conscientiously encourage our young people to go there. And if this "represents the best of Lynchburg College's creative endeavors" ... they might better stop creating. To be frank, I felt a bit of nausea, as I read them.[162]

Van responded courteously by saying that he agreed with much that Mrs. Fitzgerald had to say. However, he pointed out that it was not his job to censor a student-run publication. Furthermore, Van said he did not look at the students of the college as "boys and girls" but rather as young adults. Van noted it would not be right to speak reverently about "freedom of the press" and, at the same time, deny such liberty to a publication produced by college students. Certainly, if Mrs. Fitzgerald could have seen into the future she would have recognized how tame these indecent scribbles were in *The Prism* when compared to what would follow in the much more radical 1960s and early 70s. It is also interesting to note how Van, in a way, took the side of the students in his polite response to this alumna. Such a response would become characteristic of Van throughout his career as a teacher at Lynchburg College.

As intriguing as this little sidelight is into the beginning of Van's time at Lynchburg, what was much more important to Van, at the time, was life on the home front. At Horsebite Hall, Van and Davy maintained a rather rural lifestyle in the midst of the city. They kept chickens, stoked the wood stove, drank pure spring water, even rode the farm horse bareback. Van and Davy especially enthused over walking together in the more rural, outlying areas near Lynchburg.

Down one of those country roads, the Van Aukens discovered St Stephen's Episcopal Church in Forest, Bedford County, Virginia. The Reverend Nicholas Hamner Cobbs established St. Stephen's around the year 1824. The land on which the church was situated was originally part of Thomas Jefferson's Poplar Forest tract. The present red brick church was built in 1844. Sadly, the church closed in regard to regular services for a period of time beginning in 1911. It wasn't until 1941 that St. Stephen's was officially re-opened and the building renovated.[163] The Van Aukens were attracted by the loveliness of this hundred year old church with its view of the Blue Ridge, and so decided to attend services at St. Stephen's, if only occasionally; this decision did not arise out of any Christian belief, but because Van and Davy found great beauty in the language of the ancient Anglican liturgy. On one Sunday, they even took Communion; again, this was not because of any upsurge of faith, but because everyone else was doing it.[164]

It was during this time that Davy took up art. She enjoyed painting scenes of rural Virginia, especially the rolling hills along the St. Stephen's road or even the flora and fauna surrounding Horsebite Hall. Davy did a couple versions of the meadow on their farm which had a large, walnut tree standing alone in its midst. Her second attempt at painting this scene evolved into a sort of religious statement. The ghostly looking bare branches of the walnut tree predominate, and the shadow cast by the branches forms the shape of a cross. To the right of the tree a wraith-like figure is reaching out one arm in the direction of the over-towering tree. Van, somewhat mockingly, called the painting: Davy's Sin Picture. He knew that the painting of it grew out of his wife's experience at Yale, and he regarded her continuing preoccupation with Christianity with no small amount of discomfort.[165]

Davy's "Sin Picture"

Photo Courtesy of Elizabeth Rose

Sketch of Ettarre from Yachting Magazine

X

ETTARRE

> There is no woman like you in my country, Ettarre.
> I can find no woman anywhere resembling you
> whom dreams alone may win to.
>
> James Branch Cabell, *The Cream of the Jest*

What was far more enjoyable for Van, than thinking about Davy's growing interest in Christianity, was the continuing pursuit of their Grey Goose dream. On January 1, 1949, the Van Aukens made a new year's resolution: that not another summer should pass without them being on the water again. Thus in March, Van and Davy took a trip from Virginia out to the Eastern Shore of Maryland to look at boats.[166] The Van Aukens sold *Gull* before leaving Florida. Now they wanted to take a further step toward realizing their schooner vision. They had seen a picture of the perfect ship in an advertisement sent to them by a yacht broker—a 36-foot, dead-rise, centerboard, gaff-rigged, schooner.[167] Then in Maryland, they got a look at the very boat, the *Sabra*. However, Van and Davy had many questions that needed answering. Thus, they decided to take a drive to Cambridge, Maryland and talk to the builder, William C. Dickerson, who had started making sailboats in 1946 on nearby Church Creek.[168] The builder informed the Van Aukens that his neighbor, Howard Chapelle, had designed the ship in which they were interested. Now they were certain, this was the schooner for them, for they had long regarded Chapelle as a designer who expressed the ultimate in nautical wisdom.[169]

The next day, Van and Davy visited with Chapelle himself in the old salt's book-lined study. After extensive discussion back and forth, Chapelle all the while puffing on his pipe, the Van Aukens were satisfied. "We're going to have a schooner!" they said to one another with glee. They returned to Dickerson and asked him to begin construction. Business was concluded with a handshake, and Van entrusted to the builder a sliver of wood from the Confederate ironclad ship *Virginia* to be embedded underneath the mainmast.[170] Dickerson promised to have the ship ready to sail in two months.

While the Van Aukens waited for their schooner to be completed, their crew was born; their New Haven mutt, Gypsy, gave birth to puppies to which Van and Davy gave sailing names: Jib, Tops'l, Spinnaker and Flurry. The latter was the one they chose to keep, the dog who would sail with them aboard their new ship.

The writings of Richmond author, James Branch Cabell, gave to Van and Davy an idea for a name for their schooner. In his fantasy, *The Cream of the Jest*, Cabell has a character named Ettarre, an unattainable witch-woman who lures dreamers out of the set ways of life. With Ettarre in mind, the Van Aukens had an appropriate figurehead made for their new ship. Davy drew sketches and Chapelle's neighbor, Earl Geoghegan, made clay models from Davy's drawings. Finally, Geoghegan patiently carved the figurehead out of mahogany and there appeared the mysterious face and beautiful bosom of the witch-woman. To Van's mind the figurehead represented perfectly the soul of their new schooner.

As the completion of the schooner drew near, a flurry of messages went back and forth between Lynchburg and Cambridge. One by one, each of the Van Aukens' questions were answered satisfactorily: the decks of the schooner would be tan, the cabin trunk was made a little longer, and they bought a new six-horsepower engine for auxiliary power.

In June, with dogs and an assortment of friends in tow, Van and Davy alighted at the Dickerson Boat Yard. At high tide, the Chapelles, Geoghegans, Dickersons, Van Aukens, additional friends, workers, and others from the Church Creek community gathered around the bow of the newly crafted ship. Davy held a bottle containing a concoction of various liquors. As she smashed it against the bow of the schooner she said, "I name thee *Ettarre*! Keep us out of the set ways of life!"[171]

The gathered assembly pushed and shoved, and finally got the boat into the water. However, Van's prideful look was soon replaced by a face of panic. *Ettarre* suddenly sank to the bottom of Church Creek. Dickerson quickly reassured Van and Davy, "Don't worry. We'll have her sealed up tighter than a drum by morning. The hot sun must have opened her up."

It actually took a few days to pump *Ettarre* dry. One night during this period, Van and Davy rowed out to the schooner in their dinghy, *Ilikea Moana*. However, it was so dark that night they couldn't seem to find *Ettarre* in the tidal pool. After awhile, Van stopped rowing long enough to light a cigarette. Suddenly, the Van Aukens saw towering immediately above them the bow of the schooner. They made their way aft and clambered aboard. It was all, in a way, the fulfillment of a dream, one written about in a poem at Glen Merle, all about rowing out to *Grey Goose*.[172]

Soon an engine was installed on *Ettarre* and the Van Aukens were able to motor about Church Creek. Once all their gear was moved aboard, the schooner was ready for her maiden sailing voyage. The appointed day having arrived Van and Davy made a trial run from Church Creek to Cambridge, a distance of thirty miles by water. The Van Aukens got a late start and so did not make it all the way to Cambridge. That evening they celebrated nonetheless over dinner with other Chesapeake friends, the Brewingtons.

The Man Who Received "A Severe Mercy"

The next morning dawned grey, damp and windy, but Van and Davy were determined to sail anyway. They were less sure of their decision once they reached the wide mouth of the Great Choptank. The Van Aukens spied only one other ship as they made their way against the wind and the tide up the Choptank to Cambridge. After sailing several miles upriver, they decided to seek shelter for the night in a small cove. The next day was brighter as the sun glinted off the much tamer waters of the Choptank. *Ettarre* sailed into a happy welcome at the Cambridge Yacht Club. The Chapelles even joined Van and Davy on the return leg of their trip to Church Creek. As *Ettarre* pulled up in front of the Chapelles' home, Tolland, after a fast sail before a fresh breeze, the naval expert made a fitting pronouncement on the Van Aukens new schooner: "She'll do!"

Van and Davy spent the summers of 1949 and 1950 exploring the Chesapeake; in particular, they surveyed the ports of the Eastern Shore of Maryland. Sometimes they took friends along. At other times, it was just the two of them with their dogs Gypsy and Flurry in tow; that is, until Gypsy ran away and never returned.[173]

On at least one occasion, Van and Davy took a cruise aboard *Ettarre* with Van's brother, Paul.[174] The voyage began, as usual, from the schooner's anchorage in Church Creek. The three Van Aukens, and Flurry, sailed down the Little Choptank to the Sandy Roads, in between James Island and Oyster Cove. However, the Van Aukens hearkened to the wisdom of a man named Uncle Sol whom they met that day. Sol had lived in the area for 75 years; he warned them they wouldn't make it over the Sandy Roads that day due to the tide going out. Therefore, they spent their first night in Oyster Cove. The next day they made their way into the Chesapeake proper and south to the Honga River. They made the outer beacon of Hooper's Island by five o'clock that day and sailed under what was then a swinging bridge crossing Fishing Creek. They stopped at the town of Honga on Hooper's Island to get some help with their ship's engine that wasn't working too well. They received the generous assistance of a man named Cap'n Travers; he worked the whole of the next day trying to fix the engine, all for no charge.

The day after that, the Van Aukens sailed south around Asquith Island and anchored in Fox Creek. A brief swim followed, but it was an unpleasant one due to stinging sea nettles. The Van Aukens went to bed that evening gasping for breath because of the heat and humidity. They fell asleep that night to the sound of mosquitoes close by and Navy gunfire in the distance; Patuxent River Naval Air Station was just across the bay.

At three o'clock in the morning, the Van Aukens were awakened by a gale of wind pouring through the hatch. On deck, they discovered a brilliant night with a million stars twinkling overhead, but dark thunderclouds and lightening in the distance. The most beautiful thing was the water, alight with phosphorescence. Paul, and Van and Davy sat for an hour, awed and full of wonder at the whitecaps that were a cream of cold fire. Eventually they returned to bed, but Van would remember the experience for years to come as another eternal moment in time.

The next day *Ettarre* sailed south to Hooper Straits; the Van Aukens took their breakfast of ham and eggs while underway. They waved at the lighthouse keeper as they went through the Straits and he waved back from the lighthouse gallery. *Ettarre* set a course for the southern tip of Deal Island ten miles distant. As the schooner drew near to the island, the Van Aukens could see a cluster of red roofs. Wenona Harbor was very picturesque with its skipjacks and bugeyes, two types of sailboats used for oyster dredging on the Chesapeake.

The Van Aukens went ashore and paid a visit to Albert E. Brown & Brothers, the family-run business that had made the sails for *Ettarre*. Inside the brown shingled sail loft, the schooner's crew breathed in the air of canvas and tar as Mr. Brown revealed some of the intricate skills involved in the ancient craft of hand-sewn sails. As the Van Aukens walked back to the pier that day a kind and generous stranger gave them four ripe tomatoes and a dozen soft shell crabs, as well as one hard crab for Flurry.

Ettarre sailed on to Teague Creek where Van spent a lazy afternoon reading *Walden* by Henry David Thoreau while Davy and Paul napped. That evening they dined deliciously on crabs, but the night brought a storm with wind gusts of forty or fifty knots and stinging rain. The only event the next day was Flurry trying to eat the Van Aukens' copy of *Two Years Before the Mast* while the humans were out exploring in the dinghy.

On the way to Tangier Island, the day after Flurry's indigestible meal, the Van Aukens came upon *Ettarre's* sister ship, the *Sabra*. The Robinsons, owners of the *Sabra*, and the Van Aukens exchanged admiring looks, as well as a wave, and then went their separate ways.

The Van Auken's first sight of Tangier Island included a church spire as well as a cluster of whitewashed houses with red roofs. After anchoring in the harbor, the Van Aukens rowed the dinghy ashore and Van went in search of his friend, Henry Jander, the man who brought electricity to the island. That evening the Van Aukens dined at *Crab's Hole*, the home of Henry and Anne Jander, followed by a Haydn symphony on the Janders' record player and much talk about Tangier. The Van Aukens especially enjoyed the accents of the natives who, when pronouncing words like "nybors" (neighbors), sounded faintly Cockney.

After a couple days' stay on Tangier, the witch-woman, *Ettarre*, pointed north once more. The return trip was not without its challenges; the Van

The Man Who Received "A Severe Mercy"

Aukens faced a squall near Asquith Island. However, in the end *Ettarre* sailed up the Little Choptank once more to her home harbor in Church Creek.

Soon Van and Davy would set sail, without Paul or Flurry, on a much greater adventure.

Sketch of Flurry aboard Ettarre from Yachting Magazine

THE PERCH PUB, BINSEY, OXFORDSHIRE

Author Photo

XI

OXFORD

> This winter-eve is warm
> Humid the air! leafless, yet soft as spring,
> The tender purple spray on copse and briers!
> And that sweet city with her dreaming spires,
> She needs not June for beauty's heightening
>
> Matthew Arnold, *Thyrsis*

On August 13, 1950, the *Lynchburg News & Advance* announced that Sheldon Van Auken, Assistant Professor of History and English at Lynchburg College, had been granted a leave of absence by the school's new president, Orville W. Wake, to study at the University of Oxford, England. By the time this announcement appeared, Van and Davy were already in Indiana visiting Van's brother and mother before their departure.

On August 26, the Van Aukens "set sail" out of New York harbor on the Cunard liner Stratheden.[175] During the voyage, they grew accustomed to eating Indian curries and using English money. They wondered if the England they had known through books, the country Van had known directly, albeit briefly as a child, would seem foreign or familiar once they arrived. Sometime during the trip, Van and Davy performed the kind deed of taking up a collection for a woman who had lost her purse. The Van Aukens found it surprising when they were asked *why* they were doing this good turn for a woman they didn't even know: "Are you Christians?" Van and Davy wondered why so many people should think that only Christian faith could account for their actions. The Van Aukens were certainly not Christians; they were just doing what they thought to be the right thing to do under the circumstances.[176]

Before departing for England, Van and Davy planned to spend a month in London. However, they must have been anxious to get on to Oxford for they ended up spending only two weeks in the capital. Thus, they made their way to Paddington Station and took the train to Oxford. Just before their arrival at Oxford station, they had their first brief vision of "that sweet city with her dreaming spires."[177] Van would later urge anyone visiting Oxford for the first time to be sure to sit on the right side of the train to catch that first breathtaking glimpse.

Lew and Mary Ann Salter welcomed Van and Davy to Oxford. Van had known a relative of Lew's in Virginia. Lew was in Oxford on a Rhodes scholarship and was attached to Jesus College doing a master's degree, followed by a doctorate in theoretical physics. He was later assistant professor, then President and finally Chancellor of Van's alma mater: Wabash College.[178]

Van entered Jesus College, Oxford, at the beginning of Michaelmas Term, October 7, 1950.[179] He was a candidate for the B.Litt. (Bachelor of Letters) degree[180], working in English history and literature. His plan was to remain at Oxford for at least three terms, the equivalent of one school year at an American university.[181]

Early in his time at Oxford, while he was still casting about for a subject for his thesis, Van worked on an essay for *History Today* that paid twenty pounds.[182] The subject was the English historian, James Anthony Froude, in particular, his book, *History of England*. A. L. Rowse of All Souls College, Oxford, assisted Van with his research. "Froude: A Collision of Principles" was published in *History Today*, July 1951 and subsequently included in *Histories and Historians*, edited by A P Fell, published by Oliver & Boyd, London, 1968.[183] In his essay, Van sought to answer the question whether Froude's writing of the history of the Reformation had relevance to the twentieth century. His conclusion was that Froude's insight into the human mind and his philosophy of the dignity of human beings was definitely of value in a century when human beings were standing in fear and awe before the great machines that dwarfed them. Van found the central theme of Froude's writing to be very significant: the battle between the proud aggressive intellect and enslaving superstition—the collision of principles.[184]

It is interesting that Van, at this time in his life, would write about the great 19th century historian. Froude was brought up in the midst of the Anglo-Catholic Oxford Movement and intended to become a clergyman. However, doubts about the doctrines of the Church of England, published in Froude's scandalous 1849 novel *The Nemesis of Faith*, eventually led him to abandon his religious career. Thus, Froude turned to writing history. Van did not suspect it right at that moment, but he was about to make the opposite journey—from writing history to living out his own story of faith. In addition, like Froude in his work on Thomas Carlyle, Van too would write a somewhat polemical dissertation on a different subject: English sympathy for the Southern Confederacy, later published under the title, *The Glittering Illusion*.[185]

However, of far more interest to Van than working on his thesis were all the cultural amenities of Oxford. He and Davy found a three-room, ground floor, furnished flat, in North Oxford. It was in a red brick Victorian house at 224 Woodstock Road, on the corner of Thorncliffe, about two miles from Jesus College. The flat came complete with piano and fireplace, the latter a necessity in the damp days of an Oxford winter.[186] From their flat, Van and Davy could set out on the bicycles they purchased and have easy access to all the riches of perhaps the most wonderful university town in the world. Oxford's foggy autumn days reminded Van of the words of Reginald Fanshawe,

The Man Who Received "A Severe Mercy"

> Calm, cold and sad, the soft mists brooding bathe
> In ghostlier glamour chapel, tower, and hall,
> Dome, pinnacle, spire; they clasp and subtly swathe
> Oxford's grey magic.[187]

There were of course, countless pubs to be discovered. Some of Van and Davy's favorites were: The Victoria Arms in Marston[188] (accessible by ferry in those days), The Trout in Godstowe (Schubert's quintet "The Trout" thus became a favorite reminder of their many happy times in Godstowe), and The Perch in Binsey. All of these were only about two miles distant, in different directions, from the Woodstock flat.

Perhaps Binsey was, and is, the most magical place of all. Van was taken there first by a fellow Jesus College student he met in the dining hall, Edmund Dews. In the 1950s, the seating arrangement in the dining halls of Oxford colleges was very hierarchical. However, Edmund held court at a table that welcomed everyone. No doubt, Van as the "new boy" was directed to Edmund's table and introduced to him as a fellow American. The two took to each other immediately. Van presented himself, in a way, as a Virginian of long standing, and Edmund shared sympathy with Van for "the Old South." Edmund, like Van, had studied history, only at Stanford instead of Yale. Edmund also appreciated the youthful vigor of his new American table companion, even though Van was seven years his senior. Edmund offered to take Van on a tour to some of the "out of the way places" surrounding Oxford. Thus, their first enchanting walk to Binsey came about.[189]

Van loved Binsey so much that he often took Davy there. They would walk or bicycle across Port Meadow, as countless people still do. Then they would make their way over what Van called "the humpbacked bridge", actually called the Rainbow Bridge. After lunch in the garden behind the Perch, Van and Davy would walk down the lane to St. Margaret of Antioch Church, a tiny building dating from the 12th century. There is a well in the churchyard associated with St. Frideswide, made famous in Lewis Carroll's *Alice's Adventures in Wonderland*.[190]

In addition to pubs, walks, and bicycle rides to the surrounding countryside, there were musical productions like the annual visit of the D'Oyly Carte Opera Company performing Gilbert and Sullivan. There were London plays doing trial runs in Oxford. Then, in the springtime there were the bump races of the college eights that Van and Davy were able to watch from the Jesus College barge on the Isis (known as the Thames River to those outside Oxford).[191]

However, Van was bothered by some of the things he couldn't experience with Davy because she was not, and could not be, a member of his all-male college, things like dining on hall.[192] Davy urged Van to take in all he could and then come back to the flat and tell her about it, just as Peter Ibbetson did for Mimsey in their shared dreams. Thus, Van chose to dine in college two or three times per week and frequent the Junior Common Room of Jesus College where he made a number of friends. He also joined a college dining society called the Antler; the society had dinner twice per term somewhere in Oxfordshire such as the ivy-clad Bear Hotel at Woodstock (north of Oxford) or the former 16th century Benedictine nunnery, Studley Priory, in Horton-cum-Studley (east of the city).[193]

Van and Davy did share, during their time at Oxford, a growing circle of friends. Among these were Lew and Mary Ann Salter, who welcomed them to the university. Through the Salters, the Van Aukens met their English friends, Peter Campion (another physicist)[194] and his wife, Beryl.[195] Another friend was Thad Marsh, who was reading English at Worcester College. As it turned out, these first friends at Oxford were all Christians. Van and Davy liked them all so much that it caused them, imperceptibly at first, to revise their opinion of Christians in general.[196] These, and many other acquaintances, would often visit Van and Davy at their flat on the Woodstock Road. There would always be talk: about books, about the research each was doing, and about Christianity.

The very atmosphere of Oxford itself also got the Van Aukens thinking about Christianity in a wholly new way. Wherever they went there seemed to be the change-ringing church bells. There were the towers and spires pointing heavenward. Furthermore, there were the colleges themselves, with names like All Souls, Blackfriars, Christ Church, Corpus Christi, Jesus, Magdalen, Trinity, Wycliffe, and all the Saints: Anne, Benet, Edmund, Hilda, Hugh, John and Peter.

At last, it was too much for Van; he simply had to have that "second look" at Christianity which he had promised he would do "someday", a promise made way back when he stood aboard his destroyer in Hawaiian waters and the "shadow of a cross" was cast upon the Ebbtide. The point of decision came upon him one day during his first Michaelmas term at Oxford. One afternoon, after strolling with a friend across Port Meadow, he returned to central Oxford, noticing once again the ever-present sound of bells. As Van made his way through the streets to pick up his bicycle from Jesus College, he happened to look up at the thirteenth century spire of The University Church of St Mary the Virgin on the High Street.[197] At that moment, he decided to take "the second look." He immediately turned around and walked a few hundred feet over to Blackwell's Bookshop on Broad Street, where he purchased "an armload of books" about Christianity.

Later that afternoon, arriving at the Woodstock flat with a pile of books, Van told Davy of his decision to have that "second look." She, agreeing with him, was quite pleased. Among the books that Van had amassed were some by C. S. Lewis, then a Fellow in English Literature at Magdalen College. Lewis' books were quite popular among the Van Aukens' Christian friends, so Van and Davy decided to begin their "second look" with Lewis. Davy read *The Screwtape Letters* because she had heard it was funny. Van chose Lewis' science fiction trilogy, beginning with *Out of the Silent Planet*, due to his love of that genre.

Van found Lewis' trilogy to be both beautiful and enthralling.[198] The series helped him to see that the Christian God might, quite reasonably, be big enough for the whole galaxy. Lewis helped him to get over the seemingly insuperable difficulty of Christianity being only a local religion, one of many.

Van went on to read some fifty books on Christianity during that autumn and winter of 1950-1951. Among them were the works of Charles Williams, Graham Greene, Dorothy Sayers, T. S. Eliot (whom Van had read and loved previously but now understood in a whole new way), St. Augustine, John Henry Newman, G. K. Chesterton and, of course, C. S. Lewis. By mid-December, Van had read the following Lewis works in addition to his sci-fi trilogy: *The Problem of Pain*, *The Screwtape Letters*, *The Great Divorce*, and *The Abolition of Man*.[199] Before long, Van was consumed by what was at first, just an interesting study. Eventually, he neglected everything else, including work on his B.Litt.[200]

On the night of December 12, 1950, Van and Davy were continuing their discussion of Christian faith. On that evening, they noted the fact that Christianity claimed to provide a consistent answer, so said their friends, to all of the eternal questions of life.[201] They admitted to one another that they desperately wanted an answer to the ultimate questions. Van's trouble was he simply couldn't believe the Christian answer. He suggested to Davy that they take a walk, but she was feeling a headache coming on and so went to bed. Van went for a stroll along Woodstock Road and began thinking of what he would ask C. S. Lewis if the author were there with him. He returned to the flat and immediately wrote a letter to Lewis at Magdalen College.

Van began by telling Lewis that as he read the end of chapter five of *The Problem of Pain* he felt a strong conviction that he was beginning a voyage that would some day lead him to God.[202] However, after laying the book down, he was inclined to add a qualifying "maybe." I find it intriguing that what pushed Van over the edge and caused him to write to Lewis was this chapter on "The Fall of Man" from *The Problem of Pain*.[203] However, Van was still hesitant; he was not certain that Christianity was true. Furthermore, faith seemed an impossible leap.

Van went on to tell Lewis a bit about himself: that he was American, nominally Anglican, and from a devout family. He told Lewis that he had been ardent in his love of Jesus (or of himself for being so noble) up to the age of fourteen. It was his wide reading, including science fiction, like that of Olaf Stapledon, that brought about his turn to atheism. However, this was only temporary. Soon he returned to belief in something—a power—an intelligence, but such a being was remote, unknowable. He pointed out to Lewis that no conviction of anything beyond death accompanied this belief, but he had experiences of awe at the Numinous.

Van also noted for Lewis how he had devised or retained for himself, purely on rational grounds, a code of ethics. Words like honor and courage were very important to him. He told Lewis that he agreed with what he had to say about the Tao, or Natural Law, in *The Abolition of Man*. Van found Lewis' use of the word "axioms" to be very illuminating. However, he saw no bridge between a code of ethics and God.

Van wrote about his contempt for some aspects of the church; certain hymns and Christian phrases like "fruitful fellowship" and "washed in the blood of the lamb" he found particularly distasteful. Despite this, he found himself drawn to Christianity, not because of its truth but because of beauty. First, it was simply an aesthetic joy in certain church music, architecture and stained glass windows. Then the stately ritual of the service of Morning Prayer in the Anglican Church drew him deeper, despite the way the sermon would often spoil the affect.

He explained to Lewis how he had come to Oxford to do a B.Litt., not to find God. However, now more than ever Van was feeling the beauty and nobility of the Christian story. He said he wanted to know God; he would like to believe, but when he attempted to pray he had no conviction that anyone was listening to him.

Van said that if the accounts of Jesus were true then he was a noble fellow, even if he suffered from an illusion. However, he could *not* accept Lewis' contention that either Jesus "was a raving lunatic of an unusually abominable type, or else He was, and is, precisely what He said."[204]

What Van *could* accept was that Something made the universe and that all people must know this and must feel awe at the Something's might and infiniteness. According to Van, human beings went on to elaborate this simple belief, thus the various religions arose: Judaism, Christianity, Buddhism, Islam and others. "How can one believe that only one of these religions is the true one?" he asked Lewis.

Van confessed to Lewis that he wanted to believe that Jesus was the Son of God. However, he wondered whether his *wanting* to believe was the way to self-deception. Belief seemed easy for the disciple John who could talk to Jesus. Faith seemed simple even for Lewis' character Ransom in his cosmic trilogy. However, Van bemoaned the fact that *he* lived in a "real world" of busses, lorries, and blue sky, with only the record of *other* people's experience with deity ... and nothing else. That is, nothing else but living Christians. Somehow, Lewis, in this same world, had made the leap of faith. Could he help Van to make the same leap?

ST. MARGARET'S CHURCH, BINSEY

AUTHOR PHOTO

The Woodstock Flat

Photo Courtesy of Jason Lepojärvi

XII

THE LEAP

> "Alas," said he, "I have never learned to dive."
> "There is nothing to learn," said she. "The art of diving is not to do anything new but simply to cease doing something. You have only to let yourself go."
>
> C. S. Lewis, *The Pilgrim's Regress*

Lewis wrote back two days later, December 14, 1950....

Dear Mr. Van Auken,

My own position at the threshold of Xtianity was exactly the opposite of yours. You wish it were true; I strongly hoped it was <u>not</u>. At least, that was my conscious wish: you may suspect that I had unconscious wishes of quite a different sort and that it was these which finally shoved me in. True: but then I equally may suspect that under your conscious wish that it were true, there lurks a strong unconscious wish that it were not. What this works out to be is that all that modern stuff about concealed wishes and wishful thinking, however useful it may be for explaining the origin of an error which you already know to be an error, is perfectly useless in deciding which of two beliefs is the error and which is the truth. For (a) One never knows all one's wishes, and (b) In very big questions, such as this, even one's conscious wishes are nearly always engaged on both sides.

What I think one can say with certainty is this: the notion that everyone <u>would like</u> Xtianity to be true, and that therefore all atheists are brave men who have accepted the defeat of all their deepest desires, is simply impudent nonsense. Do you think people like Stalin, Hitler, Haldane, Stapledon (a corking good writer, by the way) wd. be pleased on waking up one morning to find that they were not their own masters, that they had a Master and a Judge, that there was nothing even in the deepest recesses of their thoughts about which they cd. say to Him "Keep out. Private, This is <u>my business</u>."? Do you? <u>Rats</u>! Their first reaction wd. be (as mine was) rage and terror. And I've much doubt whether even you wd. find it simply pleasant. Isn't the truth this: that it wd. gratify some of our desires (ones we feel in fact pretty seldom) and outrage a great many others? So let's wash out all the wish business. It never helped anyone to solve any problem yet.

Sheldon Vanauken

I don't agree with your picture of the history of religion—Christ, Buddha, Mohammed and others elaborating an original simplicity. I believe Buddhism to be a simplification of Hinduism and Islam to be a simplification of Xtianity. Clear, lucid, transparent, simple religion (Tao <u>plus</u> a shadowy, ethical god in the background) is a late development, usually arising among highly educated people in great cities. What you really start with is ritual, myth, and mystery, the death and return of Balder or Osiris, the dances, the initiations, the sacrifices, the divine Kings. Over against that are the Philosophers, Aristotle and Confucius, hardly religious at all. The only two systems in which the mysteries and the philosophies come together are Hinduism and Xtianity; there you get both Metaphysics and Cult (continuous with the primeval cults). That is why my first step was to be sure that one or other of these had the answer. For the reality can't be one that appeals <u>either</u> only to savages <u>or</u> only to high brows. Real things aren't like that (e.g. matter is the first most obvious thing you meet—milk, chocolates, apples, and also the object of quantum physics).

There is no question of just a crowd of disconnected religions. The choice is between (a) the materialist world picture: wh. I <u>can't</u> believe. (b) The real archaic primitive religions: wh. are not moral enough (c) The (claimed) fulfilment of these in Hinduism. (d) The claimed fulfilment of these in Xtianity. But the weakness of Hinduism is that it <u>doesn't</u> really join the two strands. Unredeemably savage religion goes on in the village: the Hermit philosophies in the forest: and neither really interferes with the other. It is only Xtianity wh. compels a high brow like me to partake in a ritual blood feast, and also compels a central African convert to attempt an enlightened universal code of ethics.

Have you tried Chesterton's <u>The Everlasting Man</u>? The best popular apologetic I know.

Meanwhile, the attempt to practice the <u>Tao</u> is certainly the right line. Have you read the <u>Analects</u> of Confucius? He ends up by saying "This is the Tao. I do not know if any one has ever kept it." That's significant: one can really go direct from there to the <u>Epistle to the Romans</u>.

I don't know if any of this is the least use. Be sure to write again, or call, if you think I can be of any help.

Yours sincerely,

C. S. Lewis[205]

The Man Who Received "A Severe Mercy"

Van thought through very carefully what Lewis wrote over the course of the next week. At the same time, he read *The Pilgrim's Regress* and *Miracles*. Then something startling happened. One day during that week, Davy, while simply crossing from one side of the room to the other at their Woodstock flat, lumped together all that she was, all that she feared, hated, loved, hoped, and she committed her ways to God in Christ.[206]

While their intellectual positions with regard to Christianity had been the same, Davy was in a completely different emotional position. She had a sense of sin, pain, and need for Christ. The sense of sin that began for her during their time in New Haven had not abated.[207] Furthermore, at Yale, she had been thought to have some obscure ailment; a doctor had recommended an extended rest.[208] However, she still wasn't feeling better two years later. In fact, an Oxford doctor thought Davy might have Boeck's sarcoid, a disease that results from inflammation of tissues in the body. (It can appear in almost any body organ, but it starts most often in the lungs or lymph nodes.)[209] As if Davy's own health problems were not enough, before leaving for England, she found out that her mother was dying of cancer. Her sister had practically commanded her to go to England anyway. Now, a few months later, her mother had died. All of these things contributed to Davy's sense of need for Christ and in the end, pushed her over the brink.

Van sensed that Davy had been taken away from him; he felt alone and betrayed.[210] Nonetheless, he wrote again to Lewis on December 21. As a result of reading *Regress*, Van began to see that a relation might exist between the glimpses of the "Island in the West" and God. Furthermore, Lewis convinced Van that Christianity was unique among religions and that he needed to accept it all the way, if he could accept it at all.

However, Van felt like Lewis' character, Virtue, in *Regress*; he simply could not see his way beyond a certain point, or edge. He noted that the most repugnant demand of Christianity was, to him—humility, surrender, the bowed head and knee, saying to God: Not my will, but yours be done. Yet, Van wrote to Lewis, would not he accept the Master with Joy, accept the humility, rather than face the horror of nothingness after death? That, to Van, was the worst, the idea of ceasing to be. Then, he made a most startling, almost prophetic statement to Lewis: "If I were ever driven to Christianity (I hope it will not be so), it would be because my wife were dead and I could not face her extinction or because my own end were at hand and I could not face that."[211]

Van went on to outline for Lewis all the benefits he saw if Christianity were to be found true. Furthermore, he asserted that he would accept any humbling for it to be true. However, his fundamental dilemma was still that he couldn't believe in Christ without faith and he couldn't have faith without believing in Christ. From whence was he to acquire such faith?

He asked Lewis if there was an intellectual proof of Christianity. Would he find such in Lewis' book *Miracles* after re-reading it and thinking it through? Could Reason carry him over the gulf without faith?

Van promised Lewis that he would keep the Tao if he could, but he suspected that he would often fall. He also promised that he would read Chesterton and, especially, the New Testament. It occurred to Van that he might someday look back on this season as a significant Advent and Christmas.

Lewis wrote back two days later, on December 23, 1950....

> The contradiction "we must have faith to believe and must believe to have faith" belongs to the same class as those by which the Eleatic philosophers proved that all motion was impossible. And there are many others. You can't swim unless you can support yourself in water & you can't support yourself in water unless you can swim. Or again, in an act of volition (e.g. getting up in the morning) is the very beginning of the act itself voluntary or involuntary? If voluntary then you must have willed it, you were willing it already, it was not really the beginning. If involuntary, then the continuation of the act (being determined by the first movement) is involuntary too. But in spite of this we <u>do</u> swim, & we <u>do</u> get out of bed.
>
> I do not think there is a demonstrative proof (like Euclid) of Christianity, nor of the existence of matter, nor of the good will & honesty of my best & oldest friends. I think all three (except perhaps the second) far more probable than the alternatives. The case for Xtianity in general is well given by Chesterton; and I tried to say something in my <u>Broadcast Talks</u>. As to <u>why</u> God doesn't make it demonstrably clear: are we sure that He is even interested in the kind of Theism which wd. be a compelled logical assent to a conclusive argument? Are <u>we</u> interested in it in personal matters? I demand from my friend a trust in my good faith which is certain without demonstrative proof. It wouldn't be confidence at all if he waited for rigorous proof. Hang it all, the very fairy tales embody the truth. Othello believed in Desdemona's innocence when it was proved: but that was too late. Lear believed in Cordelia's love when it was proved: but that was too late. "His praise is lost who stays till all commend."[212] The magnanimity, the generosity which will trust in a reasonable probability is required of us. But supposing one believed what was wrong after all? Why, then you wd. have paid the universe a compliment it doesn't deserve. Your error wd. even so be more interesting & important than the reality. And yet how cd. that be? How cd. an idiotic universe have

produced creatures whose <u>mere dreams</u> are so much stronger, better, subtler than itself?

Note that life after death, which still seems to you the essential thing, was itself a <u>late</u> revelation. God trained the Hebrews for centuries to believe in <u>Him</u> without promising them an after-life; and, blessings on Him, he trained me in the same way for about a year. It is like the disguised prince in the fairy tale who wins the heroine's love before she knows he is anything more than a woodcutter. What would be a bribe if it came first had better come last.

It is quite clear from what you say that you have <u>conscious</u> wishes on both sides. And now, another point about wishes. A wish may lead to false beliefs, granted. But what does the existence of the wish suggest? At one time I was much impressed by Arnold's line "Nor does the being hungry prove that we have bread." But surely, tho' it doesn't prove that one particular man will <u>get</u> food, it <u>does</u> prove that there is such a thing as food. i.e. if we were a species that didn't normally eat, weren't designed to eat, wd. we feel hungry?

You say the materialist universe is "ugly." I wonder how you discovered that? If you are really a product of a materialistic universe, how is it you don't feel at home there? Do fish complain of the sea for being wet? Or if they did, would that fact itself not strongly suggest that they had not always, or wd. not always be, purely aquatic creatures? Notice how we are perpetually surprised at Time. ("How time flies! Fancy John being grown-up and married! I can hardly believe it!") In heaven's name, why? Unless, indeed, there is something about us that is not temporal.

Total Humility is not in the Tao because the Tao (as such) says nothing about the Object to which it would be the right response: just as there is no law about railways in the acts of Queen Elizabeth. But from the degree of respect which the Tao demands for ancestors, parents, elders, teachers, it is quite clear what the Tao <u>would</u> prescribe towards an object such as God.

But I think you are already in the meshes of the net! The Holy Spirit is after you. I doubt if you'll get away!

Yours,

C. S. Lewis

This second letter gave Van much to chew on, and the last paragraph frightened him. Alarm bells were going off in his head, but where could he run? He began to resent Davy's conversion, not so much her becoming a Christian, but things like her going to church without him. He even resented her acts of goodness toward him; he suspected she was doing it for God and not primarily for him.

There, on the brink of Christian faith, Van hung for three months. He continued to read and think deeply. He even considered changing the subject of his B.Litt. to something theological, or even studying for the priesthood. He wrote to Lewis twice about this issue, but eventually decided to continue with his studies in history.[213]

Van knew that his Christian friends were praying for him, but he regarded such activity with suspicion. He even regarded his own upsurges of emotion with caution; he was half in love with Jesus, but was afraid to commit.[214]

However, in late March, Van read something that struck him with considerable force. It was the words of Mark 9:24 where a man says to Jesus, "Lord, I believe; help thou mine unbelief." [215] This was exactly Van's problem. Perhaps it would be enough for him to say the same to the Lord.

One day after reading this important statement in Mark 9:24 Van had a second intellectual breakthrough. He suddenly realized that he could not go back to his old, easy-going yet vague belief in God. There was a gap behind him as well as before him. Perhaps the leap of faith *toward* Jesus was a gamble, but the leap *away* from Jesus also contained a risk. If he were to now reject Jesus, he realized that he would forever be haunted by the thought that he had, perhaps, rejected God. Van could not bear this thought. He could not reject Jesus. There was only one thing to do: fling himself over the gap toward Christ.

It was a damp, English morning with a hint of spring in the air, four days after Easter, Thursday, March 29, 1951.[216] Van wrote in his journal and to C. S. Lewis, "I *choose* to believe in the Father, Son, and Holy Ghost—in Christ, my lord and my God."[217] Later, Van wrote a sonnet about this all-important choice:

> Did Jesus live? And did he really say
> The burning words that banish mortal fear?
> And are they true? Just this is central, here
> The Church must stand or fall. It's *Christ* we weigh.
>
> All else is off the point: the Flood, the Day
> Of Eden, or the Virgin Birth—Have done!
> The Question is, did God send us the Son
> Incarnate crying Love! Love is the Way!

The Man Who Received "A Severe Mercy"

Between the probable and proved there yawns
A gap. Afraid to jump, we stand absurd,
Then see *behind* us sink the ground and, worse,
Our very standpoint crumbling. Desperate dawns
Our only hope: to leap into the Word
That opens up the shuttered universe.[218]

C.S. Lewis at his desk at The Kilns

Photo Courtesy of Walter Hooper

St. Ebbe's

Author Photo

XIII

THE OTHER SIDE OF THE GAP

> "Come," said the Guide at last, "if you are ready let us start East again.
> But I should warn you of one thing—
> the country will look very different on the return journey."
>
> C. S. Lewis, *The Pilgrim's Regress*

Lewis responded to the good news from Van in a letter written on April 17, 1951:

> My prayers are answered....
>
> There will be a counter attack on you, you know, so don't be too alarmed when it comes. The enemy will not see you vanish into God's company without an effort to reclaim you. Be busy learning to pray and (if you have made up yr. mind on the denominational question) get confirmed.
>
> Blessings on you and a hundred thousand welcomes. Make use of me in any way you please: and let us pray for each other always.[219]

Davy had already started attending worship services at St. Ebbe's Church in Oxford along with many of their Christian friends, so that is where Van went too.[220] St Ebbe's was and is an evangelical Church of England parish in the center of Oxford. The present church building was constructed in the early 19th century but it stands on the site of a church dedicated to St. Ebbe before AD 1005 when the church was granted to Eynsham Abbey. A 12th century Norman doorway stands at the west end of the building.[221] St Ebbe's rector during Van and Davy's time in Oxford was Maurice Wood, an evangelical Anglican who served as a Royal Navy Commando Chaplain during World War II; Wood participated in the landing on the beaches of Normandy on D-Day, and he conducted the first worship service on liberated French soil. Wood was a keen evangelist and supporter of Billy Graham's crusades in England. He later served as Bishop of Norwich from 1971 to 1985.[222]

Van and Davy visited the other Anglican parishes in Oxford: the University Church of St. Mary the Virgin and St. Mary Magdalen in particular. They found the Anglo-Catholic Mass beautiful and they came to accept the high-church view that the Anglican Communion was and is a part of the one Catholic Church. However, Van was more enraptured with Anglo-Catholic worship, with its emphasis on the altar and sacraments, than Davy ever was;

she was, from start to finish, much more evangelical in her leanings.[223] Despite their different preferences, Van and Davy always returned to St. Ebbe's where they especially enjoyed the singing of the *Te Deum Laudamus* in a manner that made a triumphant proclamation of the line: "Thou art the King of Glory, O-O-O-O-O Christ!"[224]

In addition to *The Gap*, Van wrote a series of Sonnets about his newfound faith that he sent to C. S. Lewis for comment. Lewis responded with a brief note, typed by his brother Warren:

> Thank you for a letter I prize very much. The sonnets, though in a manner which will win few hearers at the moment (drat all fashions) are really very remarkable. The test is that I found myself at once forgetting all the personal biographical interest and reading them as poetry.[225]

Coming from Lewis, a quite experienced poet with very exacting taste, who never spared appropriate literary criticism, this was high praise indeed.

Van and Davy continued to read deeply in Christian theology. They found the works of Austin Farrer and Charles Williams to be especially meaningful and helpful. However, they were disconcerted upon their encounter with certain German theologians, the "demythologisers" like Rudolf Bultmann. For Bultmann, the Resurrection and Ascension of Jesus, along with many of the claimed miracles in the Gospels, were all myths, not historical occurrences at all. However, Van was not swayed by the Bultmannian arguments, for Oxford had certainly taught him to challenge unverified, fundamental assumptions. Bultmann, was clearly, to Van's mind, bringing *unverified* assumptions *to* the text of the New Testament, not reading such conclusions *out of* the text.[226]

In the spring of 1951, at the end of Trinity Term, Van and Davy apparently made a decision to stay on longer at Oxford than they originally planned. No doubt, this choice was influenced by the fact that Van had accomplished very little research toward his B.Litt. degree. When one takes into consideration the massive amount of reading Van did in Christian theology over the previous several months it seems quite clear that he had little time for anything else during his first year at Oxford. Thus, Van negotiated a more extended leave of absence from Lynchburg College.

The Van Aukens spent the Long Vacation[227] during the summer of 1951 traveling around England. They visited Hampshire, the Cotswolds, and Essex. Then there was a fortnight trip to Wales; there Van climbed Cader Idris and Mount Snowdon, an excursion that resulted in back problems for Van for quite some time.[228] Van wrote to Dr. Osborne at Wabash College from the Oxford & Cambridge University Club in London on 29 September 1951 saying, "We're quite in love with England and with London.... I hope very much to be able to come back from time to time—but I'd best not count on it."[229]

The Man Who Received "A Severe Mercy"

Van's main reason for writing to Dr. Osborne was to express his interest in returning to Wabash to teach some day. He'd written to Byron Trippet, also of Wabash, on the same subject in July. Trippet was not too encouraging about the possibility of a position for the 1952-53 school year, but suggested writing to Dr. Osborne with his request. Van made clear that he was on leave from Lynchburg College and felt duty-bound to return there in the fall of 1952. He also said that he liked it in Lynchburg and would be disinclined to move, unless it was to Wabash, a location with a special place in his affections. Van went on to detail his perceived strengths and weaknesses as a teacher of both English and history. No job offer came immediately from Van's query, but the possibility of a change was in the offing.

After the Long Vacation, with their lease on the Woodstock flat at an end, Van and Davy began looking for another place to live in Oxford. A student friend of theirs had been leasing a tiny flat in the very heart of town.[230] This friend had completed his studies and thus the flat was available. It couldn't have come at a better time. Van and Davy snapped it up.[231]

The Van Auken's address at their new location was 3 St. John Street, just behind the Ashmolean Museum. However, the entrance to their flat was actually on cobblestoned, gas-lit, Pusey Place.[232] A red door opened from the street into a garden and then another door announced "The Studio." The flat had a very small kitchen on the ground floor and an extremely narrow staircase leading to the second floor where there was one long room with a fireplace, skylight, and windows overlooking the garden. From The Studio, Van and Davy could listen to all the bells of Oxford, but especially "Great Tom" at Christ Church, which they would hear boom out 101 times every night at 9:05.[233]

The Studio, being so centrally located in the heart of Oxford, became a meeting place for all of the Van Aukens' friends.[234] Because of their return to Christian faith, the Van Aukens' number of Christian friends increased. Geraint Gruffydd, an expert in Welsh and Celtic Studies, was doing a D.Phil. at Oxford and, like Van, was a member of Jesus College.[235] Geraint met Van and Davy before their move to The Studio, on a bus to North Oxford one Sunday after church service.[236] Geraint found Van, from the outset, to be a very able, somewhat aloof, but unfailingly courteous person, whose friendship he came to value highly. Geraint thought Davy was much more outgoing—indeed self-giving—fun to be with, possessing an infectious laugh but with a deep underlying seriousness. In short, Davy was an easy person to like. Furthermore, Van and Davy's marriage impressed Geraint as being rock-solid.[237]

The Van Aukens invited Geraint around to their flat and thus began a lifelong relationship. Van later said that Geraint could read poetry in such a way that it would put chills down the spine of a statue.[238] Van and Davy once paid a visit to Geraint's home in Wales, during the Long Vacation (July-September) where they argued about the merits of burgundy versus claret. This resulted in numerous visits to wine merchants, followed by countless wine-tasting sessions after the manner described in Evelyn Waugh's *Brideshead Revisited*.[239]

Another important Christian friendship that began for the Van Aukens at Oxford was with Julian Stead. Julian was the son of William Force Stead, Anglican priest, poet and one time Chaplain of Worcester College, Oxford, who baptized T. S. Eliot. William and his six-year-old son Julian were received into the Roman Catholic Church by Dominican Father Bede Jarrett at Blackfriars, in St. Giles Street, Oxford, in August of 1933.[240] Julian's mother, Anne Frances Goldsborough, was the sister of Mary Goldsborough who married Dr. John Askins. Dr. Askins was the brother of Mrs. Janie King Moore, C. S. Lewis' adopted mother who lived in Lewis' home, The Kilns, from 1930 until her death in 1951.[241] Julian was born in Oxford, educated at Worth Priory in Sussex, England and Portsmouth Priory in Rhode Island. He later joined Portsmouth Priory as a monk and was sent by the Priory to study, first in Rome and then in Oxford, where he was attached to St. Benet's Hall.

Julian had a friend, Christopher Fullman, who was also a Catholic priest, returning to St. Vincent's Abbey in La Trobe, Pennsylvania after being educated at Oxford. Chris had been the only Catholic member of the Van Auken's circle of Christian friends and he thought it would be good for Julian to take his place in that group.[242] Thus, Chris took Julian to The Studio one day to meet the Van Aukens and their Christian friends. There were four or five others there and while the rest were talking, Van, following some kind of sixth sense, came over to Julian and quietly said, "I'd like to read your poetry." Thus began one of the greatest, if not *the* greatest friendship of Van's life.

Van and Davy attended Julian's ordination as a Catholic priest in April 1952 at Blackfriars. It was one of the first times either of them had been present at a Mass. Afterwards, Davy said very enthusiastically to Julian, "It was so religious!" Years later, Julian said that such intensity was characteristic of Jean, as he called her. He remembered her as small of stature, pleasant looking, though not stunningly beautiful, and enthusiastic. She was not as intellectual as Van, nor did she write much poetry, except for one poem that she wrote for Julian, some years after they first met.

The Van Aukens' marriage struck Julian as being an extremely close one. However, Jean once said to Julian of her marriage, "Sometimes, it's really hard." Julian saw Van as being a bit domineering in the marriage, and possessive.[243] He had a desire for oneness and unity, but unfortunately, it included control. Julian mentioned this to Van years later, but Van denied it vehemently, that

The Man Who Received "A Severe Mercy"

Jean ever found their relationship hard. However, at the time, Julian saw this as a vulnerable spot for their marriage; it could conceivably break up because Van was too controlling.[244]

Despite growing tensions in Van and Davy's marriage, life at The Studio was, generally speaking, quite happy. Julian was the one who later captured the spirit of the place in his poem at the beginning of *A Severe Mercy*:

> Ah Studio! We'll meet again.
> It won't be gaslight in the lane,
> But just as gentle, only brighter.
> And Jack on Aslan's back.
> We'll sing His glory
> Around those two: One Love-truth.
> Old world will give one final 'crack!'
> Our hearts could not be lighter.[245]

Julian was also the one who led Van to accept the Catholic view of Mary. This was expressed especially in Van's poems, *The Heart of Mary*[246] and *Our Lady of the Night*.[247] Julian once explained how this came about:

> I was the only Roman Catholic in the inner group [at the Studio], and I remember as though it were yesterday Van asking me one night to explain Roman Catholics' devotion to the Blessed Virgin, something strange, if not actually repugnant, to most of our friends who, if they were not members of a Welsh Chapel or Baptists, were "low-church" Church of England, worshipping mostly at St. Ebbe's, the most evangelical of the Church of England parishes in Oxford. I was a mere theological student, but I did my best to explain it in terms familiar to Catholics which had been helpful to me, comparing Mary to the moon; her purity and faith, her sanctity, are derived entirely from her Son, as the light of the moon is really sunlight reflected (as Sebastian Moore has summed it up: she is "the perfect recipient"); the moon is closer to us than the sun, and Our Lady is closer to us than the Incarnate Word of God. Such a feeling is admittedly the opposite of the truth; speaking ontologically, it is the Incarnate Word who has identified Himself with each of us. See the Epistle to the Hebrews and the word of the Saints: "He is closer to us than we are to ourselves." But speaking psychologically, the feeling that she is in some sense—being *only human*—closer to us in certain circumstances is understandable and theologically defensible.
>
> Precisely because He is God and, therefore, everything

to the Christian (including Catholics and Orthodox), the supernatural power of Jesus is dazzling to the mind of the believer and not so easy to relate to, in a sense, as the goodness of His humble, merely human mother. A Catholic would not hesitate to subscribe to the assertion that there could be no holiness, goodness, or compassion in Mary, which we turn to in our despair, which is not also in God and derived from God, so that Marian devotion is less justifiable logically than psychologically. In some such inadequate words as these I explained that whereas Christ sometimes or in some ways dazzles us, Mary does not. As the moon shines at night, so the human Mary shines when perhaps the light of our faith in God has seemed to go out, to have set. We have recourse to Mary who can see Him, as the moon can "see" the sun shining not on us but on her.

As we talked, slowly and gently in the dimly lighted Studio, I remember glancing up through the big skylight at the moon herself shining down on us. And as the conversation ended, I could see that Van was visibly more than satisfied with my response, and his mind was held by the analogy which was new to him. And that very night, or the next day, he hatched what is one of the theologically richest poems addressed to Mary in the English language.[248]

PUSEY PLACE, LOCATION OF THE STUDIO

Author Photo

THE EASTGATE HOTEL

Author Photo

XIV

C. S. LEWIS & OTHER FRIENDS

> Two friends delight to be joined by a third, and three by a fourth,
> if only the newcomer is qualified to become a real friend.
> They can then say, as the blessed souls say in Dante,
> "Here comes one who will augment our loves."
>
> C. S. Lewis, *The Four Loves*

While Van and Davy's friendship with Julian certainly became the closest and most important over the years, there were other valued friends as well. These included David Griffiths of Worcester College and Tom Harpur[249] of Oriel, both studying for the Anglican priesthood. David shared with Van a love for Anglo-Catholic worship, whereas Tom was more evangelical. There were also friends from St. Ebbe's, like young Jane and her friend Mia, who were studying for university entrance. Davy brought them to The Studio where Jane, especially, would listen intently as Van read from T. S. Eliot's *Four Quartets*.[250]

Poetry readings were very much a part of the lively life in Christ shared among the Van Aukens' friends at The Studio, not only the reading aloud of the published poetry of famed writers like Eliot, but also the then unpublished poetry of Van, Julian, Geraint and others. At the end of every evening Van and Davy would walk their friends out into misty, cobblestoned Pusey Place and wish them farewell with the words of Charles Williams: "Goodnight; go under the Mercy." And their friends would often respond, "Sleep under the Protection; goodnight."[251]

However, life at The Studio was not simply that of a Christian coterie. Van and Davy continued to develop friendships with non-Christians as well, who were always welcome in their home. One of these non-Christian friends was Richard, from Corpus Christi. One night Van provided Richard with a very illuminating analogy, explaining the Incarnation by comparison to an author writing a novel and putting himself as a character into his story.[252]

Throughout their time in Oxford, Van and Davy also took day-trips and more extended journeys throughout the United Kingdom and Europe. They spent Christmas in Yorkshire with one of Van's college friends, Trevor. There was a two-week journey to Wales, not only with Geraint but also with Peter and Bee Campion.[253] Another of the original "Christian Five", Thad Marsh, borrowed a car, leading Van and Davy on an exploration of the nearby Cotswold countryside. Another frequent caller at The Studio, Peter Crane, invited Van and Davy to his parent's home, Fritham, in the New Forest.

Edmund Dews, the friend who had introduced Van to Binsey, had recently purchased a Morris Minor. Dying to try it out on a long trip, he invited Van and Davy to join him on an excursion to the south of France where they enjoyed cathedrals, Roman ruins and the Caves of Lascaux, as well as a joyous ride into Paris on a glorious spring day. Van's novel, *Gateway to Heaven*, written and published many years later, has a chapter entitled "Journey to Provence." That chapter represents a sort of itinerary of Van and Davy's trip to France with Edmund, though some of the characters in the story are created almost from whole cloth.[254]

As much as they enjoyed all their other friends, very much at the heart of Van and Davy's Oxford experience was C. S. Lewis. In the autumn of 1951, Lewis invited Van to dine at Magdalen College for the first time.[255] Upon meeting Lewis face to face, Van was surprised to find him looking more like a jolly, red-faced butcher than the thin, gaunt, ascetic he anticipated. As Van later put it, Lewis was the picture of John Bull himself, come to life.[256]

Knowing that Van would want to talk about his newfound faith, Lewis suggested it would be best to save such discussion for his rooms after dinner in hall and port in the Senior Common Room. This was not the first hint Van had that Lewis' vocal Christian faith was not very well accepted by other Oxford faculty. The Oxford intelligentsia would have tolerated Lewis' Christianity as a private matter, but not as something to be noised about in popular books on the subject, especially since Lewis was not a trained theologian. Van's first intimation of the dislike of Lewis by his fellow dons came from his friend, Thad Marsh. On February 8, 1951, when all the MAs of the university were to vote for the Professor of Poetry, Thad was walking along the High Street and overheard one don remark to another, "Shall we go and cast our votes *against* C. S. Lewis?"[257] However, Lewis certainly had his friends at Oxford as well. In the end, he lost the Professorship of Poetry to Cecil Day-Lewis by a mere twenty votes.

Van's deep friendship with Lewis began at their first meeting on that November night in 1951. Van later said that no other man did so much to shape his mind, as did Lewis; and Van never loved any man more.[258] That November meeting was the first of many in Lewis' white-paneled, book-lined rooms with their splendid view of cloister and Magdalen Tower on one side, deer park on the other. Lewis "strolled" with Van Auken around Addison's Walk[259] more than once. The first time Van was ready to adjust his stride for an older man, until he discovered that Lewis "walked" like the Legions on the march!

Van also heard Lewis lecture on a number of occasions in the Examination Schools[260] at Oxford University as well as listening to Lewis engage in debate at meetings of The Socratic Club.[261] However, their most usual meeting place was for lunch at the Eastgate Hotel, across the High Street from Magdalen. At that time, the restaurant at the Eastgate, a converted coaching inn, was more like a pub, with its wood paneling and crests of the various Oxford colleges lining the walls. Lewis would enter and immediately boom out: "Any pies today?" Steak and kidney pie along with a pint of bitter was Lewis' usual choice.[262]

On 15 March 1952, Lewis sent Van a postcard inviting him to dine at the Eastgate at noon on Saturday, the 22nd. Van showed up but Lewis forgot. The following Monday, Lewis sent another postcard around to Van:

> Porcus sum, I am a pig, porcissimus, the piggest of pigs. I looked at my diary at about 3 o'clock on Sat. afternoon and found to my horror that I had failed a tryst with you at 12. Please forgive a nit-wit. Will you prove your charity by meeting me at the Eastgate 12 o'clock next Saturday? Even I seldom make exactly the same howler twice! I'm really v. sorry; I had been much looking forward to it.
>
> C.S.L.[263]

At their meetings, whether in Lewis' rooms, along Addison's Walk, or at the Eastgate, Van and Lewis talked of countless subjects, not just Christianity. There were conversations about science fiction, poetry, "the Island in the West" from Lewis' *Regress*, definitions of the novel, the "bent" world in Lewis' science fiction and in Gerard Manley Hopkins' poem "God's Grandeur." There were also talks about human frailty, beer, prayer, literary sources and favorite books. They both agreed that reading certain books over again was the sign of a real book lover.[264]

May 1952 was a beautiful month for the Van Aukens in Oxford. On the first day of the month, at six o'clock in the morning, Van and Davy sat in a punt[265] on the Cherwell River and listened to the choirboys sing in the May with the *Hymnus Eucharisticus* from the top of Magdalen Tower, followed by the change-ringing bells echoing throughout the city. As the bells were still sounding, Van pushed off down the river to the place where he and Davy ate the picnic breakfast they had brought with them.[266]

One Sunday in that same month, the Van Aukens along with Peter and Bee Campion, walked across Port Meadow to Binsey to attend Mattins at St. Margaret's.[267] However, they had got the time of the service wrong and consequently were the only ones in attendance. Undaunted, Davy played the tiny organ, Peter read the first lesson, Van the second, and Bee gave the sermon. The most beautiful part for Van was the sound of their four voices filling the church as they sang their favorite line from the *Te Deum*: "Thou art the King of glory: O Christ."[268]

On May 16, 1952, Lewis wrote to Van accepting an invitation to dine with he and Davy at The Studio on May 29 at 7:30 pm.[269] The appointed evening having arrived: Lewis and the Van Aukens lifted their glasses of sherry in a toast, followed by a dinner of mutton and new potatoes. Brilliant conversation ensued on all manner of topics: word origins, Americanisms and the "cockney" accents of Chesapeake Bay residents, boats and sailing adventures. Eventually talk turned to more spiritual issues: namely prayer. At the end of the evening Van and Davy walked Lewis part way back to Magdalen, saying their goodbyes beneath the Martyrs' Memorial in St. Giles.[270]

At the end of Trinity Term 1952, a number of the Van Aukens' friends were leaving the university, including a very sad Julian who had to return to his monastery in Rhode Island. That autumn Julian wrote of his wishing to be in Oxford again and sent the Van Aukens the following poem:

> Sometimes I light my pipe and the fall evenings are long
> And getting cool, gone the summer song,
> Somehow my mind returns
> My mind and heart and lungs long to return
> To the Studio fireside, to Van and Jean,
> To the maroon armchair, sinking there
> We will talk of prayer.
> And the gaslight and perhaps the evening rain
> Will rise in mist from the lane,
> As our wills to God to mortal eyes unseen.[271]

That autumn, Van and Davy often went to the Lamb & Flag pub, across the street from the Inklings' preferred pub, the Eagle & Child, in St. Giles.[272] With many of their friends gone from Oxford, The Studio all but quiet, Van and Davy felt like they were discovering each other again. They talked over their years at Oxford and all they had learned, including the most momentous event of both their lives, their return to Christian faith. Both Van and Davy felt they needed extended time to talk over the implications of this newly rediscovered faith for their lives and for their marriage. However, soon they had to return to "everyday life", the more ordinary life, of Van teaching at Lynchburg College.[273]

Michaelmas Term concluded in early December 1952. On their last full day in the great university town, Van and Davy wanted to take in all of the "grey magic", listening to the city "whispering from her towers the last enchantments of the Middle Age."[274] From The Studio it would not have taken them very long at all to walk and look longingly one last time at all the great sights of that magnificent town. Thus, they strolled that morning from The Studio up Beaumont Street past the Ashmolean Museum and the Randolph Hotel. Crossing St. Giles they would look again at the Martyrs' Memorial and St Mary Magdalen Church. Up Broad Street, they would pass

The Man Who Received "A Severe Mercy"

every bibliophile's dream: Blackwell's. Then turning right on Catte Street, they would be near the great Sheldonian Theatre as well as the place Van spent countless hours during the previous two and a half years: The Bodleian Library. From there, they made their way under The Bridge of Sighs along to New College. This part of the walk would have taken them into the seemingly oldest parts of Oxford: honey-colored walls of ancient Cotswold stone, black wrought-iron lampposts, then countless bicycles lining Queen's Lane and out on to the busy High Street and modern life again. Up the High they went; then, turning around on Magdalen Bridge, they gazed at that splendid tower, remembering the sound of the choirboys from the previous May Day. As they walked back down the High, and approached St. Mary's Church, as if on cue, the bells rang out, reminding Van it was this church spire that "inspired" him to have that important second look at Christianity.

Van met Lewis for lunch back up the High, at the Eastgate once again. There they talked, over meat pies and beer, about what awakening after death would be like. They agreed that whatever heaven would be, it would feel like "coming home." Out on the High they shook hands and Lewis said, "I shan't say goodbye. We'll meet again." When Lewis had crossed the street on his way back to Magdalen, he turned at the last moment, and bellowed across the traffic to Van standing in front of the Eastgate: "Besides, Christians never say goodbye!"[275]

The next morning Edmund Dews fed Van and Davy a farewell breakfast and took them to Oxford Station. Then the Van Aukens went up to London where they had just enough time for lunch at the Oxford & Cambridge Club. Afterwards, it was on to the train to Liverpool where that night Van and Davy boarded their ship to cross back over the Atlantic again. However, one question must have lingered in their minds: "Are we going home, or leaving home behind?"[27]

Li'l Dreary

Author Photo

XV

LI'L DREARY

> And English air that was my breath
> Remained my mortal life till death.
>
> Theodore Maynard, *Exile*

On February 5, 1953 an article appeared in *The Lynchburg Daily Advance*:

> Sheldon Van Auken, assistant professor of history and English at Lynchburg College, is a tall, powerful man with a scholarly air about him.
>
> Generally speaking, the physique of a professional football lineman and scholarliness don't go together. But on him they rest well.
>
> "The worst part about going away," he said this morning, between pulls on his pipe in his office at Lynchburg College, "is coming back."

It was indeed difficult for the Van Aukens returning to Lynchburg. Their sense of displacement was typified by the name they gave to their new, rented house, one half mile from Lynchburg College—Li'l Dreary. However, the quaint, craftsman-style bungalow at 503 Oakridge Boulevard was really not that dreary; plus Van and Davy had the joy of reunion with Flurry, whom they had entrusted to a friend during their sojourn in Oxford.

What was happening to the Van Aukens has taken place in the lives of countless other people who have lived in "foreign" countries and then returned "home": reverse culture shock. Everything about Lynchburg suddenly seemed strange: *The Daily Advance* instead of *The London Times*, cold American lager in place of warm English bitter, the drab Virginia winter supplanting evergreen England, "semi-illiterate" students in Van's classes versus the intelligent repartee of the Oxford elite.[277]

However, in their parish church the Van Aukens found some solace and reminders of the England they had loved and lost. They discovered Grace Memorial Episcopal Church only a couple of blocks away from Li'l Dreary on New Hampshire Avenue. The building was built of Virginia greenstone, reminding Van and Davy of soft Cotswold limestone. The Rector, L. Stanley Jeffery, and his wife, were from Cornwall, thus giving the Van Aukens a sense of connection back to their spiritual home. In this church, Van and Davy began to make some very good friends. One of these was Miss Preston

Ambler,[278] a retired high school teacher from Cape Charles on the Eastern Shore of Virginia. Miss Ambler was a songwriter, author of *Early Episcopal Churches in Piedmont Virginia* and one of the Van Aukens' neighbors. Another church friend, Mr. Shirley Rosser, was a 1940 graduate of Lynchburg College who returned to teach physics and astronomy in 1942. Years later, Dr. Rosser taught physics and elementary nuclear engineering to the crew of the *Savannah*, the first nuclear-powered merchant ship.[279]

Van and Davy made other friends within the college community. There was Belle Morton Hill, a 1936 graduate of Lynchburg College who had lost her husband recently and was making a new life for herself, first as Head Resident and later teaching English at her alma mater.[280]

The Reverend Joseph Nelson was another teacher at the college who became acquainted with Van and Davy. Rev. Nelson came to Lynchburg in September of 1952 to teach social science and history. Later he taught religious studies and Greek. He was associated with the Disciples of Christ denomination and on one occasion went door to door throughout the neighborhoods around Lynchburg College with a Disciples of Christ pastor. On that occasion, he encountered Van and Davy at their home on Oakridge. The Disciples' pastor accompanying Joe Nelson invited the Van Aukens to a preaching series at his church. However, Van and Davy politely declined since they were already involved at Grace Church.

In fact, the Van Aukens were quite committed to work in their local parish. Davy began teaching a high school Sunday school class and worked diligently at her preparation for it. In addition to attending worship services at Grace on Sunday morning, Van and Davy sometimes went with Father Jeffery to another church where he led an Evensong service. At home, the Van Aukens would say family prayers together from the Book of Common Prayer every morning and evening as they knelt before a wooden cross.[281]

In March of 1953, Davy obtained a job in the bookkeeping department of their local bank. At the same time, Van was teaching a somewhat heavy load of courses at college. In a class on world civilizations Van happened to mention that no author of textbooks could ever be completely objective; his or her bias would always show through. Van went on to give the example of a so-called "enlightened emperor" of China who invited missionaries of other religions to present their teachings in his country. Van noted that such an emperor might properly be called "open minded", but to call him "enlightened" when he didn't have any faith himself revealed a certain bias on the part of the textbook writer. This example raised a number of objections from Van's students. One girl in particular continued to insist that such an emperor was "enlightened" in some fashion. At the end of class, she asked Van if she might come to his house sometime to discuss the issue further.

The Man Who Received "A Severe Mercy"

When the student came over, Van and Davy thoroughly discussed the matter with her. They even ventured to share with her the sort of enlightenment they had experienced at Oxford. As a nominal Christian, she was fascinated to meet two Christians who really believed that Christianity might actually be true. At the end of their time together, the girl asked if she might come again to the Van Aukens' home to talk more about Christianity. She also wanted to know if she could bring a friend.

Thus, without Van or Davy planning it, a Christian student group was born in their house that day. Not only did that first female student bring along her friend, eventually the group grew to include about a dozen students. They started meeting every week. Some dropped off, while other students stayed with the group and brought even more friends. Van would read to the group from the writings of C. S. Lewis, Charles Williams, Dorothy Sayers, and others. Davy would serve refreshments and talk to students individually. Even Flurry was a part of it all, often lying in the center of the room. On one occasion, Van told a true story about Flurry and Gypsy in order to illustrate the Christian teachings about the fall, original sin and free will. At the end of every meeting, the Van Aukens would kneel with all the gathered students, the room lit only by the glow from the fireplace. Van would begin the prayer time with the words: "In the name of the Father, the Son, and the Holy Ghost", then invite each of the students to pray silently. As each would finish their prayer they would say their "Amen", then all would depart with the benediction "Go under the Mercy." Because of those meetings, many of the students who came to the Van Auken home became committed Christians.[282]

Shortly after the Christian student group began, Van wrote to C. S. Lewis, thanking him again for his role in their conversion, and expressing his dismay at some of the "semi-Christians", priests especially, he was encountering in Lynchburg. Lewis wrote back on April 22, 1953, saying rather humbly, "Think of me as a fellow-patient in the same hospital who, having been admitted a little earlier, cd. give some advice." Lewis continued, "The semi-Christians (in dog-collars) that you speak of are a great trial. Our College chaplain is rather of that kind. I'm glad you have something better in your own church." Lewis urged Van not to be too concerned about those moments when he felt about Christianity, "How could I—I of all people—ever have come to believe this cock and bull story." Lewis suggested that such feelings are the flipside of the just recognition that the Christian truth really is amazing.[283]

On April 23, Van and Davy spoke to the Lynchburg College Faculty Women's Club about their time in England. The meeting took place at the home of Mrs. Dorothy Freer, wife of Ruskin S. Freer, professor of biology. One of the other hosts that evening was Belle Hill. Van later remembered all the ladies' smiles disappearing when he started lashing out at all the things he disliked about American culture: car horns blasting, drinking and anti-drinking attitudes, McCarthyism.[284]

As 1953 progressed, Van struggled, not only with the lack of high civility in Lynchburg, which he had known in England, but also with the feeling that God was distant. He deeply missed Oxford, that "holy city" in which he had experienced conversion, in which he could hear from The Studio the ever-present sound of change-ringing bells. He also found the "pagan impulses" of his former life recurring increasingly, and it was worrisome to him. He longed to be alone with Davy again, on the schooner, outward bound to some distant island. However, how did such desires fit in with their new Christian faith? He was unsure of the answer.[285]

As Van began to drag his feet along the Christian pathway, Davy threw herself more relentlessly into her Master's service. She worked hard and long, preparing for her Sunday school class every week. She wanted Van to speak to some of the more difficult boys in the class, but it didn't happen because Van failed to follow through on Davy's suggestion. Van simply wasn't that interested in a high school Sunday school class.

When Davy wasn't reading the Bible to prepare for her class, she was reading it for her own growth. Reading Christian literature consumed her free time. Most of the time, she was reading the Bible, but she supplemented this with Brother Lawrence's *The Practice of the Presence of God*, and other devotional books. Van felt she was going overboard in her commitment, becoming too fanatical. However, how could he say to his wife: "You are loving God too much"? Thus, Van remained silent, and read the Bible less himself, while Davy steeped herself in it.

Davy knew something wasn't right but what could she do about it? Before their conversions if Van or Davy had felt something wrong in their relationship one or the other or both would have called for a "Navigator's Council." Everything would have been discussed. They would have asked, "What is best for our love?" However, now they both knew that the most important question was not this one. Rather the question had to be: What would be best to further our love of God? Davy was quietly pursuing the answer to that question all the time. Van, on the other hand, was not really facing the question at all.[286]

As spring came into full bloom that year, Van was feeling a sense of discontent. Davy continued with her spiritual reading while he read other things: novels and mysteries mostly. No longer were they reading the same books together. Yes, they continued their prayer times and regular attendance at worship, but something was missing.

Because of her deep devotion to God, Davy was changing in relationship to her husband. She was trying to follow, for the first time, the Apostle Paul's command: "Wives, submit yourselves unto your own husbands, as unto the Lord." (Ephesians 5:22 KJV) Davy was becoming more domestic, doing more cooking and baking; Van was afraid that if he issued a command she would obey it. He almost wanted a fight, but what he really wanted was the old, pagan Davy back.[287]

They talked together about when they would fulfill their Grey Goose dream. *Ettarre* still lay at anchor on the Eastern Shore of Maryland.[288] They remembered fondly their days of adventure in the Florida Keys and on the Chesapeake, as they sat on their back porch at Li'l Dreary after dinner each night, enjoying the oncoming spring. However, both Van and Davy were too busy with work, church, and the Christian student group, to take time out for sailing.[289]

Spring semester ended at Lynchburg College and Van agreed to teach summer school to make a little extra, needed money. Davy continued working at the bank. It was a typical hot and humid Lynchburg summer. The Van Aukens longed for the coolness of England.

Davy was struggling physically. She found herself tired all the time. Another worrisome sign was that her ankles had begun to swell slightly. Van urged her to see their doctor who, in turn, encouraged Davy to cut back on work. Van insisted she stop altogether. Davy secretly thought she was going to die. She did not tell Van this, but she prayed for one more year of life for the sake of their student group.[290]

In August, their young friend Jane came from England for a three-week visit and stayed with Van and Davy at Li'l Dreary. Jane was at university now, but her parents were in New York, so she had decided to visit the Van Aukens. Davy was still working at the bank, having just given her notice. Thus, Van had to do most of the entertaining. Jane attended Van's summer school class in English literature. Sometimes after class, they would walk around town. In the evening, they would read poetry aloud together: Van reading T. S. Eliot of course, and Jane reading one of her favorites—Emily Brontë.[291]

Jane had come to faith about the same time as Van at Oxford. In addition to their shared delight in poetry, Van and Jane also had in common a love for Anglo-Catholic worship. Thus, they talked for hours about poetry, Oxford and the High Church Anglicanism of St. Mary Magdalen Church.[292]

Van and Davy had been getting along in Lynchburg without a car, but they had both desired, since returning from Oxford, to have an MG two-seater. At last, just a few days before Jane was to return home, Van saw a black MG TD[293] for sale. He took Davy for a test drive and they fell in love with it. They bought it on the spot and, for the next three nights, they drove all around the Virginia countryside, top down, with Jane in the very small backseat, under a full moon.[294]

On the last night of Jane's visit, all three of them enjoyed the most beautiful drive of all. When they returned home late, Davy, who was still feeling very tired all the time, went to bed. Van and Jane stayed up all night reading poetry, talking, silently holding hands, and feeling grief over Jane's departure.

After Jane left the next day, Van told Davy all that had happened the night before. He told her that he wished Jane were his sister. However, there was more. Reflecting on it years later, Van realized he had been in love with Jane, and she with him. He thought of it as a consequence, a result of "The Shining Barrier" being breached by Christ. Van felt he never could have fallen in love with anyone other than Davy during their pagan days together, precisely because they had worked so hard at protecting their love. However, now a third person, Christ, had invaded their relationship. Perhaps, if Van had been as close to Christ as Davy was, he would not have permitted himself even such a temporary dalliance with Jane. However, he was not pursuing a relationship with Jesus with the intensity that Davy was. All of this Van did not understand fully at the time; all he knew was that something had thrown off the fine watch mechanism of the love he had once shared with his wife.[295]

The unbearably hot and humid Lynchburg summer ended in early September that year and life seemed to go on as usual. Van and Davy invited Joe Nelson and his wife and children over to their home for a picnic. The Nelson children enjoyed playing with Flurry; they were fascinated with the Van Auken's MG and so Joe took a photograph of his children sitting in it.[296]

However, Van and Davy enjoyed their English roadster more than anyone else. Now that the days and nights were cooler, Davy was starting to feel better. Thus, the Van Aukens, with Flurry ensconced in the back seat, went exploring, all over the central Virginia countryside in the car that they named "The Trout." On their drives, they would often stop at St Stephen's Church in Forest to kneel and pray by one of the venerable stone crosses in the cemetery. Van and Davy loved the old country church so much they even came for Sunday services on occasion, though they felt they could not abandon Grace Church. Not far from St Stephen's they found a deserted house they named Ladywood. This was just the sort of place they had envisioned during their talks at the Lamb & Flag in Oxford, a place where they could be alone together to reconcile Grey Goose and Christianity. Van and Davy dreamed of buying the house, but they didn't have enough money at the time.[297]

One night, just before the autumn term of 1953 began at Lynchburg College, Davy had a restless night. She decided to get up and sleep in their guest bedroom. However, she didn't sleep. Rather, she spent the entire night in prayer. That night she offered up her life for her husband that his soul might be fulfilled.[298]

The Man Who Received "A Severe Mercy"

Autumn term began at Lynchburg College and the Christian student group started meeting again at Li'l Dreary. As before, the group talked of Christ and they read Julian's unpublished poems. The fire glowed on the hearth, and the Lord in whose name they gathered, was a palpable presence in the room.[299]

On Christmas Eve, Van gave Davy a special present. With only one lamp illuminating the living room, he ushered her in with eyes closed, the Sanctus from the Mozart Requiem Mass playing on the record player at full blast. When Van told Davy she could open her eyes, there before her was a large, framed photograph of the piers and vaulting of Bourges Cathedral. Davy had tears in her eyes. Later that evening, she told Van about offering up her life for him.[300]

Thus, the variously troubled year of 1953 ended for the Van Aukens. It was a year of transition, from England back to America. It was also the year, when both Van and Davy realized: they were not as close as they once had been. Still, they ended on a note of love, with hopes for a brighter new year in 1954.

MOLE END

Author Photo

XVI

MOLE END

> The Mole had been working very hard all the morning,
> spring-cleaning his little home.
>
> Kenneth Grahame, *The Wind in the Willows*

On the last day of 1953, Van and Davy moved house. Whatever the reason was for their move (perhaps their lease could not be renewed), they were happy to leave Li'l Dreary behind. They were even more thrilled to move into a beautiful ante-bellum mansion set amidst great oak trees and wide lawns.[301] The house was once owned by Henry E. McWane, one of several of Lynchburg's industrial and business leaders who moved from one of the older sections of the city to "the suburbs" in the early twentieth century. The façade of the house was embellished with a handsome, two-story portico. A balustered railing protected the flat deck of the hipped roof. Sometime after 1927, the house was conveyed to Lynchburg College and converted into apartments.[302] The house is located at 110 Langhorne Lane, very close to Lynchburg College. Van and Davy were to move into the basement apartment. However, their moving arrangements were complicated, and so on the last night of 1953 their furniture was in the basement but they had to spend the night in an upstairs room.

Thus, on New Year's Day, they woke up to bright sunshine in a many-windowed sunroom. Van enjoyed watching a dozen squirrels scamper around the branches of a mighty oak tree outside, while Davy wheeled in a magnificent breakfast on a tea trolley they inherited from some departing former residents of the house. That day reminded them of the first New Year's Day they had spent together at Glen Merle, seventeen years before. They toasted each other with their teacups raised saying, "If it's half as good as the half we've known, here's hail to the rest of the road!"

Mole End was the name Van and Davy gave to their basement apartment, after Mole's home in Kenneth Grahame's wonderful children's book: *The Wind in the Willows*.[303] The apartment had and has a "forecourt" under the front steps of the McWane House just like Mole End in the story. One can still see the large, opaque, glass-brick window near the front door to the basement apartment. Van and Davy placed their wooden cross on the inside of this window and would say their prayers together, kneeling before the cross, morning and evening.[304]

The Van Aukens would often go in the evenings to Grace Church, to which they had a key, and Davy would play the organ. The small sanctuary with its stained glass windows and hammer-beam ceiling would be filled with the sounds of Bach's *Toccata and Fugue*, or his "Little" Fugue in G Minor, or the Van Aukens' favorite, the *Te Deum*. Van and Davy would kneel and pray together at the white, marble altar with the words inscribed: "Holy, Holy, Holy."[305]

Back at Mole End, the Christian student group resumed their meetings. One of Van's English students, Betty Wright Smith (Class of 1956), remembers visiting Mole End for evening discussions and poetry readings hosted by Van and Davy. She recalled the room being lit by candles and the glow of the fireplace. Van would read poetry in his deep voice. Davy very much played a behind the scenes role and was quiet though cordial, serving tea and coffee. The love that Van and Davy had for each other was transparently evident. Their deep connection in life, interests and background was clear. All the girls wanted to grow up to be like Davy and have the kind of love she shared with Van.[306]

During the first few months of 1954, Davy renewed her artistic endeavors at painting, which she had not done since Oxford. One of these, which Van called *The Wave of God*, was begun at Oxford. The Van Aukens had been to an exhibit of William Blake's artwork at the Tate Gallery in London. Inspired by Blake, Davy had begun a small painting in earth tones of a nude female lying down with one arm covering her head as a great wave of the sea was poised to crash over her. This painting Davy now completed. Shortly thereafter, Davy painted another scene depicting herself and Van; her figure lay in an attitude of surrender before a low door. Van, on the other hand, was being directed to a high door by a magnificent angel. This work of art revealed, not only much of how Davy saw Van, but her own deep humility as well.[307]

In the month of March, Julian came from his abbey in Rhode Island for a visit. Van and Davy drove him in "The Trout" out to St Stephen's, where they all knelt by the stone cross to pray. Back at Mole End, they had long conversations about England and Oxford and Christianity. At the end of Julian's stay, Van took him to the train station with the top down on the Trout, despite an unusual fog that was hanging in the air that morning. Both Van and Julian remembered for years to come the sight of Davy, standing in her dressing gown in front of the McWane House waving goodbye. To Julian she seemed small and alone; he had a premonition, unspoken to Van and Davy, that this would be the last time he would see Davy in this world.[308]

April and May were beautiful that year. Father Jeffery celebrated Holy Communion for Van, Davy and Shirley Rosser (who had been ill) at Mole End. Springtime meant drives in the MG in the Blue Ridge Mountains with Redbud[309], the dogwood trees, lilacs in bloom, and the song of the whippoorwill.

Earlier in the school year, a female student had come to talk with Davy alone, and a male student wanted to talk with both of them. They wanted to know what Van and Davy thought, from a Christian perspective, about homosexuality. In their pagan days, Van and Davy's attitude had been: if that's what some people want, why not? They had at least one close friend who was a lesbian. However, now that they were Christians, Van and Davy didn't know what to say to the two students who came seeking their advice. They sought the counsel of Father Jeffery who was strongly disapproving of homosexual practice. Thus, Van and Davy wrote to C. S. Lewis for a second opinion.

Lewis wrote back on May 14, saying that he would discuss the matter with those whom he thought wise in Christ and that what he had to say on the matter was only an *interim* report. Lewis said he believed that the *physical* satisfaction of homosexual desires was sinful. However, he stated, that leaves the homosexual no worse off than any other person who is, for whatever reason, prevented from marrying. Furthermore, Lewis suggested that speculation on the cause of homosexuality was irrelevant; we must be content with ignorance. Then Lewis gave a corollary from John 9:1-3. He said that the disciples of Jesus were not told *why*, in terms of efficient cause, the man was born blind. They were only told God's final purpose in the matter: that the works of God should be made manifest in him. Thus, Lewis asserted, the works of God could be made manifest in a homosexual person just as in anyone else. Lewis believed that in the challenges faced by the homosexual there was concealed a vocation to be discovered. Once found, this vocation would turn what might appear to be a disability into "glorious gain." According to Lewis, homosexuality, like every other tribulation, must be offered to God and his guidance must be sought in how to use it.[310]

Lewis, as promised, sent Van another letter dealing further with this issue. This second letter was lent by Van to another person seeking his advice on the issue and was never returned.[311] This was not the last time that Van would have to deal with homosexuals seeking his counsel. He would turn again to Lewis' words for guidance many times. It was, in fact, an issue he would deal with in novelistic form many years hence.[312]

June was a month of excitement and decision for the Van Aukens. George Kendall, the Dean of Wabash College, telephoned Van to take him up on his offer of 1951 to serve on the faculty. The position suggested was one in the English department. Kendall wanted to know if Van was still interested and, if so, would he come to Indiana and discuss it with them?

There were a number of points in favor of the move. Van felt that Wabash was, academically, a better college than Lynchburg. Secondly, Wabash was offering him higher pay. Thirdly, Lew and Mary Ann Salter, whom Van and Davy had known so well at Oxford, were now at Van's alma mater. Fourthly, Van really liked a number of people at Wabash: Kendall, Osborne and Trippet, to name a few. Finally, serving on the faculty at Wabash would put Van and Davy closer to Van's aging mother who was still living in Indianapolis. However, there were points in favor of remaining at Lynchburg as well. These included: the beauty of Virginia itself, the Christian student group, and Van's attachment to Dean John Turner at Lynchburg College. What to do?

After Lynchburg College's commencement, just as it was time for the Van Aukens to travel to Wabash for the big interview, Davy came down with some sort of virus. She wasn't too bad off, but still it seemed best that she stay home while Van went on to check out things in Indiana. Before he left, Van made Davy promise that she would see their family physician, Dr. Craddock.

When Van returned, he and Davy decided to accept the position at Wabash. Van wrote to Dean Kendall on June 21 to discuss the details. He expressed doubt as to whether he was adequate for the post in the English department. His attitude was conditioned, at least in part, by the awe with which he regarded some of his former teachers at Wabash like Kendall and Osborne. He also felt at a bit of a loss due to never having taught a full English load since he had taught history *and* English at Lynchburg. Furthermore, his work at Oxford and Yale had been more in the area of history. Nonetheless, Van promised Dean Kendall he would work all the harder to live up to their expectations of him. He pointed out that he would not be able to move to Indiana until September 1, since he was teaching again that summer at Lynchburg College. Van closed by saying that the decision to accept the position at Wabash was a hard one, but now that it was made, he was glad to be going there.[313]

Back home in Virginia, all of Van's students in the Christian group were very disappointed. The Lynchburg College President, Orville Wake, felt he was losing one of his best teachers. The Van Aukens began to grieve the oncoming loss of Mole End, Grace Church, St. Stephen's, and all their friends in Lynchburg.

Davy got over the virus she'd been suffering, but she still felt tired all the time. Thus, Dr. Craddock suggested she should make a journey north to Charlottesville, to the University of Virginia Medical Center for tests.[314] Davy didn't think it was necessary but she complied with her doctor and Van's request. She had to stay in hospital for a few nights during the testing period. Overall, she was feeling better and she and Van talked on the phone every evening.

It was Monday, July 26, when Van drove up to Charlottesville to meet with Davy's doctor and hear the results of the testing. The doctor did not

The Man Who Received "A Severe Mercy"

sugarcoat his answer: "She's a very sick girl. I'd say no more than a 20% chance of survival, and that's allowing for a miracle. She may live for another six months at best."

Van was overcome. He asked what exactly was wrong. The doctor explained that it was Davy's liver; it had passed the point of no return. The doctors did not know what had caused the liver damage. They thought perhaps it had been a virus picked up in Hawaii, or maybe more recently. They just did not know, nor was there anything they could do to cure the problem.[315]

Van, determined to be strong when he broke the news to Davy, put it off until the following day. Still, Davy knew something was wrong when she saw Van minutes after he'd spoken with the doctor. Tears came to Van as he drove away, alone except for Flurry, in the MG. All he could think to do was keep praying: "Thy will be done."[316]

As soon as Van got home to Mole End, he began to clear the decks for action. He immediately sent telegrams to C. S. Lewis and Maurice Wood in England; he called local friends like Shirley Rosser, Belle Hill, Preston Ambler and Father Jeffery. Van told everyone what the doctor had told him and asked all to pray. Julian, having a strange feeling that Van and Davy needed help, had offered a Mass for the Van Aukens the day before at Portsmouth Abbey. That night, Van went alone to pray, kneeling beside the old stone cross in St. Stephen's churchyard.[317]

Feeling strengthened by all the prayers, Van felt ready the next day to tell Davy. As he drove to Charlottesville he offered up his life to God for whatever Davy's best good might be, death or life. A rainbow appeared over the Blue Ridge Mountains to the west after he prayed.

Van brought yellow roses to give to Davy when he told her. When the nurse went out to find a vase, he broke the news to his wife. They both smiled through tears as they embraced each other and thought of all the people praying for them, perhaps at that very moment. Davy's response was simple, though hard for her to get the words out: "Let all be according to His perfect will."[318]

VIRGINIA BAPTIST HOSPITAL

Author Photo

XVII

LIGHTEN OUR DARKNESS

Lighten our darkness, we beseech thee, O Lord;
and by thy great mercy defend us from all perils and dangers of this night;
for the love of thy only Son, our Saviour Jesus Christ. Amen.

The Book of Common Prayer

On Thursday, July 29, Van wrote to Dean Kendall at Wabash College telling him the situation with Davy. He told the Dean that even if the move itself wasn't impossible, he didn't want to take Davy away from her world, her friends, home and priest. Van was already convinced that his wife would die in Lynchburg. There would be no more opportunity for both of them to explore new worlds or experience brave adventures together. Van explained to Kendall that though Lynchburg College had already hired another man to fill his vacant post, the board had voted to keep him on, breaking their budget. Van told Dean Kendall that he was truly sorry about not going to Wabash but that it was one regret swallowed up in an unbearable sadness that nevertheless, he had to bear. In closing, Van promised to keep the Dean posted on developments through Lew and Mary Ann Salter.[319]

Davy's sister came to visit her in hospital in Charlottesville. Many other friends visited, and departed feeling like they had received more encouragement from Davy than they were able to give to her. A bishop came and, laying hands on her, prayed for Davy's healing, if it was the Lord's will.[320]

Eventually Davy was able to return home. Shirley Rosser drove the Van Aukens from Charlottesville back to Lynchburg in his large, comfortable car. Shirley offered to Van all of his savings if he should need it to pay for medical bills.[321]

Davy was happy to be home. Van moved her bed into the large living room at Mole End where she entertained guests like a queen holding court. Van did all the cooking and tried to make Davy's salt-free diet palatable. He also massaged his wife's back, trying to provide some comfort, and gave her the injections of medicine she needed each day.

Countless friends, and even strangers, offered financial help. Anonymous envelopes filled with cash came in the mail. Students lined up to offer the blood Davy needed, some twenty or thirty pints. Though Van's blood was the wrong type, he too donated blood for others in need.

Van and Davy spent that month of August, sitting outside every afternoon under the oaks that then surrounded the McWane House. As they sat in the shade of the trees, they remembered Glen Merle and read their journals of happy times long past. At night, they would say their prayers together kneeling beside Davy's bed, and Father Jeffery came once to give them the Sacrament.[322]

That August was a happy month for the Van Aukens, despite the build-up of fluid in Davy's abdomen. However, in early September, she had to go into their local hospital, Virginia Baptist, to have it drained. Van drove her to the hospital, expecting she would be able to return home soon, but she was not able to do so. Despite his teaching duties, Van didn't miss visiting Davy every day.

After Davy went into hospital in September, there arrived an encouraging gift from their friend Julian. He sent a medieval crucifix carved out of wood which showed not only Christ on the cross but an image of the Father in a cloud above, the Holy Spirit descending in the form of a dove, and Mary standing below with a sword piercing her heart. The Van Aukens kept the crucifix close by Davy's side throughout the coming ordeal[323] along with a poem that Julian wrote for Davy:

> In the valley where the creeks run dry
> Plant this my cross; hold it before your eye
> The sap that flows from the wounded side
> Of this tree's fruit, our Savior Christ, Who died
> That you might live, will stream to you
> with life that cannot die.
>
> In the valley where this world's lights won't shine
> Look at the mother moon and the sun divine
> On this dark wood. And from their two pierced hearts
> Let light come in that counterparts
> The sorrow and the joy in your two hearts and mine.[324]

During her entire illness, Davy drew strength from Scripture. In August 1954 she marked Psalm 116:6 in her Bible, "The Lord preserveth the simple: I was brought low and he helped me." On September 25, her seventeenth wedding anniversary, she read and marked Isaiah 35. Verse 10 must have been especially meaningful: "And the ransomed of the LORD shall return, and come to Zion with songs and everlasting joy upon their heads: they shall obtain joy and gladness, and sorrow and sighing shall flee away." Then, on October 7 she marked two verses: "But they that wait upon the LORD shall renew their strength; they shall mount up with wings as eagles; they shall run, and not be weary; and they shall walk, and not faint." (Isaiah 40:31) and "Fear thou not; for I am with thee: be not dismayed; for I am thy God: I will strengthen thee; yea, I will help thee; yea, I will uphold thee with the right hand of my righteousness." (Isaiah 41:10)[325]

Throughout the autumn months, Davy felt moderately well. That was partly because of cortisone treatments that had a euphoric effect. However, the weather bothered her; just as in the previous summer, it was terribly hot. The heat wave lasted until October when Hurricane Hazel finally knocked it out.[326]

Davy did everything the doctors and nurses urged her to do. That is, she did everything except remain in her hospital bed. She simply could not stay put when she heard some other patient in need. The hospital staff repeatedly found her at night, sitting at the bedside of another patient—holding their hand, praying with and for them, providing any comfort she could. Despite her disobedience in this regard, the doctors and nurses at Virginia Baptist Hospital couldn't help but love Davy, and she loved them too.[327]

That autumn, in hospital, Davy wrote down her "Christian Maxims":

I. Thou shalt <u>love</u> the Lord thy God ... and <u>if</u> thou canst not yet love Him, thou shalt <u>trust</u> Him with all thy mind, soul, and heart.

II. Him <u>only</u> shalt thou serve with all thy heart, and soul and mind. And Him only shalt thou desire, above all forever.

III. Thou shalt not do anything contrary to love, nor shalt thou forget thy blindness, <u>for</u> in Him only—not thy reason, virtue, or vision—shalt thou find salvation and freedom.

IV. Thou shalt not sully the Light He giveth thee, nor shalt thou dull thyself—His instrument—for thus is the coming of the Kingdom deferred.

V. Yet be thou mindful that His purposes are <u>best</u> served by a willing and teachable spirit, for He may choose to use thy own distress for another child's blessing.

VI. Therefore, thy reason cannot always be thy guide, nor innocent pleasure thy right. In Him are no rights, no questions, no understanding; for His ways are unfathomable and His knowledge past finding out.[328]

Davy's room was on the second floor, left-hand side of the hospital as one faces it from Rivermont Avenue. She was at the end of a corridor where there was, just beyond, an outdoor veranda.[329] Every day that autumn, Van would take Davy in a wheelchair out on to the porch where she could look down and wave to Flurry in the MG parked in front of the hospital. Out on the veranda they would talk and read poetry and share their love with one another. On Halloween, Van brought yellow roses for Davy as he often did. However, this time, he teased her and said that he had made a special trip to Glen Merle to get them. Thus, they talked much of Glen Merle that night and Davy said, "Perhaps we shall be allowed to meet again at Glen Merle." Van agreed saying, "A heavenly Glen Merle. If there is anything I'm certain of, it is that heaven will be like coming home. For us that is Glen Merle." That night, Van went home and wrote a poem that he read to Davy next day entitled *All Hallows Eve*, and on All Souls' Day he wrote another entitled *Dying*. These poems Davy pinned on the wall by her bed along with the poem from Julian.[330]

On November 23, C. S. Lewis wrote to Van, anxious for news of Davy's condition. He told Van that he never woke in the night without remembering both of them in prayer. Lewis remarked further that he never liked "two young people" more. The letter concluded with: "Whatever has happened and in whatever state you are (I have horrid pictures in my mind) all blessings on you."[331]

In December, Davy slipped into a coma. One of the doctors told Van that she would not come out of it. Still, when Van held her hand and kissed her, Davy responded: "Oh, love …" The next day the hospital staff began feeding Davy through an IV. She was unresponsive to doctors and nurses but Van could get a response out of her whenever he spoke of Laddie or Glen Merle. He even was able to feed her. At that point, Van gave up teaching his classes in college and stayed at the hospital as much as he could, regardless of visiting hours.[332]

Fifty-five years later, Van's colleague Joe Nelson recalled: "When Davy became extremely sick, the administration [of Lynchburg College] allowed Van to miss classes so that he could be with her at the hospital. And what the others of us in the History department did was that each one of us took a class. And for a period of time, I taught this class of his, and somebody else taught that class, and so on.... Eventually, of course, Davy's system just broke down, and we all felt for Van, but there was nothing that we could do."[333]

Against all predictions, Davy came completely out of the coma, but then the awareness of her impending death returned. Van reminded her that she had given to him her fear of death, in a "Charles Williams" type of exchange, and that he would bear that fear for her.[334]

On Christmas Day, Van and Davy enjoyed a merry little dinner together in hospital. Van gave Davy a poem, his *Song of Two Lovers*, as a present. She listened to Van read it with tears in her eyes. Then, by special arrangement with the hospital, Van brought Flurry into Davy's room for a visit. It was a joyous evening.[335]

However, after a few good days, Davy's health began to go rapidly down hill. She knew she was dying. She even told Father Jeffery: "It will be one more week—perhaps a little longer." She made Van promise, that after her death,

The Man Who Received "A Severe Mercy"

he would not take his own life, as they had planned, so long ago, to do.[336] Van promised that like the lone Grey Goose flying on without his mate, he would try to live on without her.

On the night of January 16, Van and Davy prayed together at her hospital bedside as they always did, and he read to her one or two things from C. S. Lewis and George MacDonald. Then Davy asked him to read his poem again, *Song of Two Lovers*. Afterwards, looking at Van, Davy smiled and said, "My golden one!" They both remembered that day when she had first called him by that name so long ago, the day of her first flight in the bi-plane. After this, Davy was sleepy and so Van departed for home.[337]

However, at three o'clock the next morning a phone call came to him from the hospital. Davy's pulse was slowing down. Van quickly washed, and shaved and then drove to the hospital, as ready as a husband could be for such a moment. He raced through the wintry night with the top down on the MG and Flurry beside him. The four and a half mile drive never seemed so long before.[338]

Van found Davy awake and not in pain. She was simply slowing down. She was thirsty, so Van gave her a drink of water. Then he prayed as they often did: "Lighten our darkness …"[339] Following this, Davy prayed for the hospital and the doctors and nurses, each by name, including their favorite nurse whom they called St. Joan. Van and Davy whispered their love to one another. Then Davy asked God to take her, and Van released her saying, "Go under the Mercy."[340]

Time passed. The sky outside the hospital window began to lighten. Then suddenly, in a clear voice Davy said to Van, using their old term of endearment: "Oh, dearling, look …" What she saw at that moment in the realm of the Spirit, Van never learned, for those were her last words this side of eternity.

More time passed. Davy reached up to touch Van's face. Then, as the day dawned, Davy was taken up into the light, and breathed her last.[341]

PART THREE
WANDERING
1955-1973

I wandered lonely as a cloud
William Wordsworth

The Old Stone Cross in St. Stephen's Churchyard where the Van Aukens Prayed

Author Photo

XVIII

VAN'S GRIEF OBSERVED

> Is my gloom, after all,
> Shade of His hand, outstretched caressingly?
> Francis Thompson, *The Hound of Heaven*

On January 18, 1955, Van received a small, light box containing Davy's ashes. When he looked at the ashes that night, he thought of the line from Shakespeare, changing "his" to "her":

> Of her bones are coral made.[342]

Late that night, Van made the ten-mile drive out to St. Stephen's Church in Forest, Virginia. While he was driving along he thought of how he and Davy had argued, in days long past, of whether Robert Browning's poem, *The Last Ride Together*, referred to riding horses or riding together in a carriage. Davy had insisted it was a carriage ride, and now she was proven correct, here Van and Davy were riding, side by side in their carriage—the MG. The last stanza of Browning's lovely poem ends on a note of hope:

> What if we still ride on, we two
> With life forever old, yet new,
> Changed not in kind but in degree,
> The instant made eternity, —
> And heaven just prove that I and she
> Ride, ride together, forever ride.[343]

At St Stephen's, Van knelt by the stone cross and prayed. Then, under the bare branches of the mighty oak trees, he scattered some of Davy's ashes and laid one of her yellow roses on the cross. As he did so, it began to snow. Van couldn't help but think of the last line of the first poem he ever wrote for Davy: "Beneath the deathly snows."[344]

Just as there was nothing unique about Van and Davy's love except for what they made of it, so also there was nothing extraordinary about Van's heart-wrenching grief. What *was* unusual was how Van chose to handle the loss of Davy. Unlike many another lover, many another bereaved husband, rather than stuff it down, run away, or otherwise try to avoid the pain, Van faced it all, head-on.

At first, Van had all the normal duties of a grieving widower to attend to. There were services at Grace Church and St. Stephen's. Following Davy's request, he ordered tract racks for both congregations. He went through her things quickly, and gave away certain items to the friends she had designated. Davy had made Van promise that he would transfer the notes she had written in her father's old Bible that was falling apart into their newer one. Now Van did so.[345] He also wrote approximately sixty letters to friends and family, many who had been praying for Davy. He ended each letter with the words of St. Julian of Norwich that had become so dear to his wife: "All shall be well."[346]

One burden Van was relieved of bearing was that of Davy's medical bills: Dr. Craddock and the Virginia Baptist Hospital both refused payment. They said that Davy had done more for them than they were ever able to do for her.[347]

One of the first letters of condolence that Van received came from Dean George Kendall at Wabash College. He wrote:

> Lewis Salter tells me the last news of your Jean's illness, as he has through these last months told me how things were going with you. We want to say, Yvonne and I, that our sympathy has been strongly with you and is now. I do not know what comforting word or thought there may be in the face of a sorrow like yours. I think perhaps there is no comfort, only courage.[348]

Another friend, from Oxford days, Geraint Gruffydd, responded to Davy's death by writing a poem in Welsh. Translated by the author into English it reads:

> Jean has gone from us
> To the place of her heart and her treasure
> Where her King and Brother stands
> In the midst of His bright array.
> Full, full is her joy there,
> The Vision fills her heart,
> And the tears of her gratitude fall
> Along the new beauty of her cheeks
>
> But empty is our life without her, empty
> For Van and for us who loved her.
> How shall we forget for long
> The clear smile on her face
> (And the hidden cross in the heart)?
> She was our company's candle,
> Salt of our savourless earth,
> Her love was a warm hearth

The Man Who Received "A Severe Mercy"

> Her faith food for our journey.
>
> May our place be with her at our ending
> In the bright feast, in the full circle:
> Will not her welcome be gracious
> To the circle, and to the feast?
>
> But fathomless still are the seas of our longing.[349]

Amazingly, on Wednesday, January 19, two days after Davy's death, Van returned to teaching his classes at Lynchburg College. He was determined to face his grief alone and not show it to others. He was even able to calmly read a poem about loss to one of his English classes. Even Van was amazed at how life, simply, went on. Of course, all his students knew the ordeal he was going through. One of his students remembered years later how Van looked like a shell of his former self.[350] On that first day back at teaching, when he went home, the first sight of his empty MG brought a flood of tears.[351]

Van thought, perhaps, he could bear the grief if only he could tell Davy about it. They had always shared everything. So now, he shared the grief with her too, through letters. Other than the evening when the Christian student group came to Mole End, Van spent his nights alone. He stayed home and wrote to Davy about what he was experiencing. He also found himself dreaming about her, but only once per month for the first year after her death. It was as if, like their beloved Peter Ibbetson and Mimsey of long ago, Van and Davy were communicating to each other through dreams. For over a year there was not a day Van did not shed tears, but always alone.[352]

One of the first letters Van wrote, the day after Davy's death, was to C. S. Lewis. He told Lewis of Davy's passing and he asked his mentor if he would be willing to scatter some of Davy's ashes, as she wanted, at St. Margaret's Church in Binsey. Van didn't hear back from Lewis so assumed he was away from home. Therefore, he sent Davy's ashes straightway to their Oxford friend Edmund Dews with a note attached. Edmund was surprised to receive such a package in the mail, but was happy to serve his friend Van in this way. Thus, on a winter's day, with the "grey magic" of Oxford in the air, Edmund walked across Port Meadow, and scattered Davy's ashes in the ancient churchyard, saying as he did so: "Under the Mercy."[353]

Lewis did write to Van on February 10, 1955, saying that he had heard from Edmund Dews and he was sorry that his answer to Van's letter had apparently been lost in the mail. He assured Van that he would have assisted with the "sacred office" of scattering the ashes even though he always felt uncomfortable carrying out ceremonial acts. Lewis went on to tell Van what a privilege it was for him to be "admitted to such a beautiful death, an *act* wh. consummates (not, as so often, an event wh. merely stops) the earthly life."[354]

He went on to note how reassured he felt by Van's use of the word "sad."[355] The use of this simple word suggested to Lewis a "clean wound." It is never, he said, sadness that does harm, but the many other things that are often mixed with grief: resentment, dismay, doubt, and self-pity. Lewis also noted how all earthly loves must be crucified before they are resurrected. He concluded the letter by assuring Van that he was always in his prayers even upon waking in the night.

Van was startled by Lewis' suggestion that death might be the easiest way to lose one's love, and that all earthly loves *must*, in some way, be lost. He wondered: was Davy's death somehow necessary to the crucifixion/resurrection process Lewis spoke of? At that point, Van was, understandably, far from being able to accept what Lewis had to say on this subject.[356]

Despite the pain brought on by this first letter, Lewis proved to be Van's greatest friend as he walked the winding road of grief. Van wrote again to his mentor on Valentine's Day and Lewis responded on February 20. In response to Van's supposed change of "luck", Lewis reminded him of the Lord's words to St. Teresa of Avila when she complained to the Lord during a time of trial, "Teresa, this is the way I treat My friends" and Teresa's response: "Ah, my God, that is why you have so few." At the end of this letter, Lewis invited Van to stop using "Mr." before his name. Lewis always addressed Van as Van Auken, the way fellow students would address each other at school.[357]

As a way of facing his grief completely, Van set about what he called "The Illumination of the Past." In preparation, he wrote to all of Davy's friends and family asking that they lend him her letters. He was already learning much about her and her spiritual growth by transferring the notes from her father's old Bible to their new one. Van also read again some of their favorite books.

Two months after Davy's death, Van was thinking a lot about her offering up her life for him. He also meditated on his offering up *his* life for *her* best good and the rainbow that attended that prayer. He wondered about the meaning of the rainbow and thus, wrote to Lewis about it.[358]

Lewis wrote back to Van on April 6 saying: if we have accepted the omniscience and providence of God, then, in a sense, everything in life becomes significant, not just the rainbow—all things have meaning. Van had also asked for Lewis' thoughts on publishing his Oxford thesis jointly under his and Davy's name, because he thought she would have liked it. Lewis warned Van that the phrase "what Jean would have liked" could come to have its dangers. The better question to ask would be: What does she will now? He cautioned Van about falling in love with the past and remaining stuck there.[359]

Despite this caution, Van felt that reviewing his life with Davy, and thus drinking the cup of grief down to the dregs was essential. Therefore, in the month of April, he began the Illumination of the Past in earnest. He had gathered and put in chronological order hundreds of letters Davy had written to various people through the years. He also had their journals and her paintings all around. He collected recordings of music to which they had listened at specific periods in their joint life. He even bought some of the perfumes Davy had worn. Then, of course, there were the poems, both his own written for Davy, and the beloved poetry of others. Van saved some of their favorite books, like Peter Ibbetson, to read as part of the Illumination. Thus, everyday after class Van would sit in the large, empty living room at Mole End and travel through the past, at the pace of a month or two per day. Every night he would write to Davy about what he was experiencing.[360]

One insight Van had from this Illumination process was that he had, all along, exercised a loving leadership, an unconscious headship, in his marriage with Davy. Furthermore, this headship was accepted, even desired by his wife, despite their mutual, *conscious* espousals of feminism.[361]

Van found that each treasured memory, brought to the forefront, elicited tears but once, like the MG on his first day back at Lynchburg College. So too, in the Illumination of the Past, each "Davy" of yesteryear, each particular memory of her, came alive for Van but once, then followed a sort of death, then tears, and it was over. Perhaps by facing his grief deliberately, at once, Van avoided having grief ambush his psyche throughout the rest of his life.[362]

Another benefit that flowed from the Illumination of the Past was that Van was able to apprehend a bit more of the essence of Davy, her wholeness—her soul. Many have experienced the same following the loss of a loved one; it is, as Van says, like being able to read the whole novel of that person's life. One begins to see the loved one, perhaps, from a heavenly perspective, the eternal Now.[363]

Inspired by this Illumination of the Past, at the end of April, Van wrote to Lewis. He told his mentor all about "The Shining Barrier", why he and Davy had chosen not to have children (because it might lessen their total sharing), and how they had planned to complete the Shining Barrier with the long last dive, the plan to end their lives together.[364]

Lewis responded on May 8, with, perhaps, the most significant of all his letters to Sheldon Van Auken. He began by complimenting Van on his letter, for it contained a wonderfully clear and beautiful expression of inloveness and one-flesh union often desired by many couples but seldom achieved. Lewis returned Van's letter, inviting him to think through it all deeply and begin to see his experience with Davy from the outside, as the entire human family would look at it from various levels.

Lewis began at the bottom and asked Van to consider: What would the grosser Pagans think? They would say there was excess in what Van and Davy made of their love; it was bound to provoke the retaliation of the gods.

What about the finer Pagans? Lewis suggested they would call "unmanly" each withdrawal Van and Davy made from the claims of common humanity. They would say it lacked a full and appropriate sense of citizenship, belonging to a larger whole. It was uxorious. The Stoics would say that to tear part of the Whole (Van and Davy) out into its own self-sufficing whole would be against Nature.

Then, Lewis mused, what would the Christians say? Yes, Van and Davy had admirably achieved the one-flesh goal of marriage. However, that "one flesh" was not designed to live unto itself. Marriage was made for God and neighbor, as much, if not more than it was designed to please husband and wife. Furthermore, such a marriage, lived for God and neighbor should have been open to the gift of children.

One way or another, Lewis concluded, the thing (the Shining Barrier) had to die. "Perpetual springtime is not allowed." Van and Davy, he asserted, were trying to go against the cosmic grain of life. There are various ways it could have died while both partners went on living. However, Lewis told Van, he had been treated with "a severe mercy."[365] He had been brought to see that he, Van, was jealous of God. From the us-sufficiency of the Shining Barrier Van had been led to "Us and God." Now, Lewis tendered, it was up to Van to move on to "God and Us."[366]

Van's response to Lewis' tough love, was to love his mentor more than ever, like a brother and father combined.[367] However, Van was not certain he agreed with all that Lewis had to say. Perpetual springtime not allowed? Was it wrong for he and Davy to refuse children? On these points, Van was not convinced. One thing he was certain of: he had been jealous of Davy's Divine Lover.[368] Van pondered Lewis' words deeply. He even speculated: what would have happened if Davy had lived? He could think of only three possibilities: either (1) he would have become as committed to God as she was, or (2) he would have attempted to lessen Davy's commitment to God, or (3) he would have come to hate God *and* Davy. The Van who experienced Davy's death cried out against options two and three. However, he realized that only God knew how he would have reacted to Davy's deepening divine love if she had lived. Perhaps Davy's death had saved their love from dying in one of those other, horrible ways. If so, then it was precisely "a severe mercy."[369]

That May, as flowering trees and shrubs came into bloom, Van often journeyed into the Virginia countryside by day, as the Illumination of the Past continued at Mole End each night. He often sat in the doorway of Ladywood, and thought of Davy, sensing her presence in the wind. Because of a dream he had one day, asleep in the tall grass beside their favorite abandoned house, he wrote his poem, *Summer*; it was about a summer bus-ride and walk he and Davy had enjoyed together, years before in England.[370]

The Man Who Received "A Severe Mercy"

The Illumination of the Past caused Van to see how much he and his wife had longed for the timeless, for eternity. On May 20, Van wrote to Lewis about this and the latter responded on June 5 recommending the following reading on time and eternity: Von Hugel's *Eternal Life* and Boethius' *Consolation of Philosophy*. Lewis also encouraged Van to read Dante's *Paradiso*, paying special attention to the point at which Beatrice turns away from Dante "to the eternal fountain"[371] and Dante is content.[372] Van's task, Lewis encouraged, was to keep on with what he was already doing, to say to God: "Take me—no conditions."[373]

Lewis also sent along to Van, with the letter, a series of five sonnets he had written ten years previously; Lewis thought these poems might be helpful to Van at that point in his life.[374] The Sonnets spoke to Van very powerfully indeed. So much so, that he later sent copies of the sonnets to other bereaved lovers.

Lewis closed the letter by asking Van's prayers for his alcoholic brother Warren. Van responded to Lewis' letter confiding in him about his own brother Paul's struggle with alcoholism. On one other occasion, Lewis wrote about Warren and his battles, but Van destroyed the letter.[375]

That June, with thoughts of eternity and God's severe mercy in his mind, Van went traveling north. His first stop was to see his Wabash friends—George and Yvonne Kendall—at their summer home in Duxbury, Massachusetts. He wrote to them later that same month to tell them how much he enjoyed his stay. He noted in his letter that a place cannot properly be judged until one has gone away from it and savored it in memory.

From Massachusetts, he ventured on to Toronto, where he picked up his friend from Oxford days, Tom Harpur.[376] Together they journeyed in Van's MG to Deep River, Ontario, singing old sea shanties all the way. There they spent a month with fellow Oxford friends: Peter and Bee Campion. After that long stop, Van returned Tom to Toronto and continued on to Indiana where he visited his brother and mother. It was on this journey that Van went out on a moonlit night to Glen Merle, where he walked through the gateposts and down to the bridge by the lily pond.[377]

Van after Davy

Photo Courtesy of Lynchburg College Archives, Knight-Capron Library

XIX

FLYING ON "ALONE"

> When a goose falls out of formation
> it suddenly feels the drag and resistance of flying alone.
> It quickly moves back to take advantage
> of the lifting power of the birds in front.
>
> Anonymous

During the immediate years following Davy's death, Van tried to fly on alone, like the grey goose after its mate has died. Among other things, he continued teaching at Lynchburg College and he once again served as Faculty Advisor to the *Prism*, a student run journal.

However, Van felt at loose ends without Davy. There didn't seem to be any purpose to his life. He wondered: "Should I continue teaching in Lynchburg? Should I go to Wabash after all, or should I cut ties with academia altogether and return to the sailing life?"

One evening in the country, Van was praying for guidance from God. Suddenly, a great gust of wind came out of nowhere. Was this a sign from God? If so, what did it mean? Could the wind mean that if he set sail in *Ettarre* again, God would provide the breeze to fill his sails? Van was not certain, so he simply took the great gust as a promise of God's guidance.[378]

However, no guidance came. Van felt desolate without Davy. One more link was broken with her when Flurry died.[379] God seemed remote. After one sleepless night, as the day was dawning, Van decided he was going to have done with God. He got out of bed, dressed, and drove out into the countryside. However, he found that he could not, simply, reject God. He had pledged his fealty to Christ as King. This was something he could not forswear without betraying honor, and doing the honorable thing had been important to him for longer than he could remember.[380]

Of course, Van wasn't truly alone, even in his grief. He wrote to Lewis about all of this and his mentor responded on August 27, 1956. He was glad to hear that Van realized the impossibility of rejecting Christ. Lewis went on to note how it must seem, at times, like God is playing "fast and loose" with us, just as a parent may seem to mislead a child, or a master may seem to mislead a dog. The problem is, as in the case of the wind, that we often misread God's signs. Lewis ended the letter by saying how much he looked forward to seeing Van again.[381]

The two men did indeed meet again, for Van took an extended journey to England in 1957. The main purpose of this trip was to complete the B.Litt. degree at Oxford.[382] Van sailed from Boston aboard the RMS Newfoundland, arriving in Liverpool on February 22. His traveling companion was Gertrude Teller, professor of modern languages at Lynchburg College.[383] Teller's destination was also Oxford; both she and Van stayed at the Beech Lawn Hotel on Banbury Road.[384] One night aboard ship, Van went out on deck and dropped overboard Davy's Grey Goose signet ring and her wedding ring.[385] The Illumination of the Past had indeed brought him to a point of letting go.

However, that did not mean that Davy was out of Van's heart or mind. Two weeks before this trip, he had the most vivid dream he had ever had of his wife. He later called it "The Oxford-Vision Dream", for in the dream he was already in Oxford and met Davy there. He was fully aware that she was dead and that her appearance to him was miraculous. They hugged, kissed, talked. It was all so real. When Van woke up from the dream, he was left with the feeling that "All shall be well and all manner of thing shall be well."[386]

When he arrived in England he planned to spend two weeks in London with his friend and colleague, Gertrude Teller, before both of them were to go up to Oxford. However, while Van was on the train from Liverpool to London, he felt compelled that he should go straight on to Oxford. Thus, he told Gertrude that London was off. He rang up the Beech Lawn Hotel and asked if he could arrive there early, in fact, that very night. Late that evening, he stepped out of the train into the misty darkness of Oxford.[387]

That night, Van was so overwhelmed by the feeling of simply being in Oxford again, the mixture of coal smoke and mist in the air, the sound of distant bells, he just had to walk around and see his favorite places, despite the lateness of the hour. Thus, he dropped his luggage at the Beech Lawn Hotel and walked a mile into the center of Oxford, past his old college on Turl Street, out on to the High where he could peer up at the spire of the University Church of St. Mary the Virgin, then back through Radcliffe Square past the Bodleian. From there he walked down Beaumont Street, took a right on St. John's and another right up Pusey Place to have a look at The Studio. Looking up at the dark, empty building that used to be his home brought tears. Now he just had to go on to Binsey and St. Margaret's Church where Davy's ashes were scattered. He sat a long time on a mossy headstone in the churchyard before returning to his hotel for the rest of the night. It was quite a walk, several miles in physical distance, but an untold number of miles in spiritual distance, seeking a connection with his lost Davy in the night.[388]

Over the next several days, Van found lodging in Wellington Square; he needed a more reasonable place to stay for six months than the Beech Lawn Hotel. During his first week in Oxford, he heard the seemingly incredible news that C. S. Lewis had married. He immediately wrote to Lewis, who now held the Chair of Medieval and Renaissance English Literature at Magdalene College, Cambridge. Lewis wrote back on March 7 confirming that he had indeed married a woman whom he knew to be dying, Joy Davidman, author of a commentary on the Ten Commandments entitled *Smoke on the Mountain*.[389] Lewis went on to explain that Joy was in the Wingfield Orthopedic Hospital in Headington[390] and that he was in the habit of spending as much of the weekend as possible at her bedside. Lewis suggested meeting Van for lunch on Saturday, March 10, at the Royal Oxford Hotel, across the street from Oxford Station, since he would be coming in from Cambridge at that time.[391]

The two did meet at the Royal Oxford that Saturday. At that meeting, Lewis told Van of marrying Joy Davidman in a civil ceremony so that she and her two sons could remain in England; the British government had decided not to extend her visa, apparently because of her former communist party ties. However, as Lewis told Van, he had come to love Joy deeply; in fact, he was *in love* with her. Furthermore, Joy longed for the sacrament of marriage; it was her dying wish to be married to C. S. Lewis in the eyes of God *and* the Church. Thus, Lewis was to marry Joy in an ecclesiastical ceremony in less than a fortnight from his meeting with Van. The Reverend Peter Bide, Lewis' former student, now Anglican priest, performed the service at Joy's hospital bedside on March 21. At that time, Bide also laid hands on Joy and prayed for her healing from bone cancer.[392]

Lewis and Van had many meetings together over the course of the next six months. They often met for lunch, and Van went several times to the Kilns, where he met Joy, who was in bed in the Common Room and not expected to live much longer.[393]

In the spring of '57, Van took the train (the one Lewis called the Cantab Crawler) to visit his friend and mentor at Magdalene College. While there, Van most likely stayed in the Fellows' Guest Room, which then contained a number of items of supposed memorabilia (all 19th century fakes) of Samuel Pepys. There was also, on the wall, a large portrait of the famed 17th century diarist. This may have given Van the impression that he was actually staying in Pepys old rooms. Today, Magdalene College is not certain where the original rooms of Samuel Pepys were located.[394]

After dinner at high table, Van talked late with Lewis in his dark-paneled rooms. It was on this occasion that Lewis invited Van to call him by his nickname, Jack. That night they spoke of love and grief. Lewis, having fallen in love with Joy, had begun to see some of the things Van said about his love for Davy in a new light.[395]

Van journeyed to Cambridge a second time, during the latter part of his 1957 stay in England. On this occasion, he and Lewis talked of poetry, especially Lewis' Five Sonnets, and Greek myth. Van had previously expressed to Lewis that he thought the character of Jane Studdock in Lewis' science fiction story, *That Hideous Strength*, to be a bit too stereotypical. Lewis encouraged Van to have a look at his latest female character, Orual in *Till We Have Faces*. (Inspired, in part by Joy Davidman, that book, a reworking of the myth of Cupid and Psyche, was published in 1956.) Van, indeed, thought Orual a great character, and Lewis' novel he thought to be one of the best of the twentieth century.[396]

At the end of the summer of '57, two weeks before he was to sail back to America, Van traveled to Lincoln, England to visit a friend. When he arrived on the train from Oxford, about sunset, he found his way from the station, up the hill to his friend's lodgings near the great Lincoln Cathedral. As he made the mile-long trek amidst the golden light of the late summer sun, he had an extraordinary sense of Davy being there with him, even though they had never visited Lincoln together. Van was filled with a tremendous sense of peace. As Julian of Norwich had said, and Davy so clearly believed, now Van knew: "All *shall* be well and all manner of thing shall be well." He later thought of that walk up the hill to Lincoln Cathedral as the last thing he and Davy did together.[397]

Van returned for the fall semester at Lynchburg College and established himself in new digs at 400 Brevard Street. Lynchburg College had recently inherited the property immediately adjacent to the campus, beside the library, and during Van's time in England, had the place done over for him, to his specifications. Van called the place "The Birdhouse." He didn't know it at the time, but The Birdhouse would be his home for the rest of his life.[398]

On November 23, 1957, Van was awarded, in absentia, the degree he had worked so long and hard for: a B.Litt. from Oxford University.[399] About the same time, he wrote to C. S. Lewis telling him about the passing of the most poignant period of grief, a grief he, in a way, had clung to, for it called forth a sense of Davy's continuing presence.[400] Lewis responded on November 27, noting what Van had said about this "second bereavement" which takes away the grief itself. Lewis surmised that perhaps what Jesus said about himself, "it is expedient that I go away",[401] is also true about the death of his followers; it is necessary that we lose our earthly loves, precisely so that we may regain them in a fuller, more complete sense, in eternity.

Lewis also informed Van that his own wife was experiencing a quite miraculous healing. In fact, Joy was up and walking, albeit with a cane. He also let Van know that his own bone disease, osteoporosis, was improving. Lewis had prayed that he might bear the pain of his wife's cancer, as part of what Charles Williams called "the co-inherence of lovers." Perhaps because of this prayer, Lewis began to lose calcium in his bones, just when Joy needed to gain it, and did, in her own.[402]

The Man Who Received "A Severe Mercy"

While Lewis and Joy were experiencing a reprieve from death, Van was experiencing what he called "the second death." Poignant grief had passed and now all he felt was emptiness. His mother died and he could not feel anything, despite his love for her. All emotion had, at least for the time being, died.[403]

As 1958 began, Van found himself simply continuing with "normal" life as best he could. His "Day in the Life" chapter from the beginning of *Under the Mercy* well captures the essence of his life from this period.[404] He was often seen wearing the same clothes from day to day: tweed jacket, Jesus College scarf and a riding cap. The bronze bell at the back of Hopwood Hall would summon Van and his students to class at eight o'clock and thus his days would begin.

During term at the beginning of 1958, classes took up about two hours each day for Van. That semester, he taught a class on English history, another on Roman history and a third in English literature. His lectures were usually delivered in Hopwood to at most about twenty or twenty-five students in each class. Van was, by all accounts, a spellbinding lecturer, always helping students to see, hear and even smell important scenes from history using his novelistic flair for description. He would speak somewhat quietly, in a way that made students sit forward in their seats and want to listen. In his English classes, he wanted students not only to see the poets' images, but also hear the power and magic of words. In his history classes, when lecturing on the English Civil War for example, he would help students feel the characteristics of the opposing sides by reading poetry from the time-period. Furthermore, Van wasn't afraid to take sides. His sympathy for the Cavaliers versus the Roundheads would have been clear. However, it wasn't all a one-way monologue; Van would pause in the middle of class and put questions to students or welcome their queries of him. He was always courteous, addressing students as Mister or Miss, but never too formal. One of Van's students remembered his lectures in this way:

> In the classroom Vanauken was magisterial. He spoke knowledgeably of "the glory that was Greece, the grandeur that was Rome." While he lectured, he sat, and bivouacked in his chair he was as immobile as a stump. But the world he drew us into three times a week—a world far removed from my freshman fixation on cheerleaders, draft status, and getting hold of a six-pack for the weekend — was a transcendent and heroic place.... Van was besotted by history, art, literature, and the manifold glories of the mind, and he enabled any student with the attention span of a higher mammal to be besotted as well.[405]

Just as much as students enjoyed Van's lectures, they dreaded his exams. Betty Wright Smith remembered Van saying toward the end of his American Novel course, "I propose we have an oral exam, individually." Betty and the other students had never had an oral exam; it sounded interesting, even though they knew Van Auken might ask them about anything and any author presented in class. All of the students studied like mad. The day of the oral exam, Betty volunteered to be the second person in. Van called forth the name of a particular author. The student regurgitated everything she could remember about the writer in question. Then, as she was making her concluding remarks, Betty suddenly realized she had told Van Auken everything she knew about a *different* author, not the one he had asked about. She panicked, but was silent. Van Auken looked at her and said, "I contemplate giving you a B." "Thank you, sir," Betty responded, gathered up her things and quickly exited the classroom. Later on, she learned that one of her fellow students was asked about Hemingway, one of the authors she knew the most about. Why couldn't Van Auken have given her *that* question?[406]

Bucky Reynolds (Class of 1960) also remembered Van Auken's tests for his Western Civilization class. Van would read out the questions for the midterm. Students would have to write out, usually a one-word answer, being sure to spell each word correctly. If the student's answer was misspelled then he or she received no credit. Bucky had difficulty spelling "Thermopylae" correctly. Then for the final exam there were, once again, ten, single-word answers. Bucky passed the first semester with an A on the mid-term and a B on the final exam. However, the second semester of Western Civilization was more difficult. Below average grades on Van Auken's tests during second semester helped Bucky make the decision *not* to major in history.[407]

During short breaks between classes, Van would step out on to the front porch of Hopwood Hall, behind the Ionic columns. He would perch on the side railing and have a smoke while talking or even joking with students. After lecturing for a couple of hours he would hold office hours in Carnegie Hall for about the same length of time, where students could come and talk to him about their class work or other topics.

The Christian student group continued to meet at The Birdhouse week by week just as they had met with Van and Davy at Mole End and, before that, at Li'l Dreary. There would be discussion, as there had always been, of the Incarnate Lord and what a relationship with him might mean in one's life. There was poetry reading by Van, including the still unpublished poems of Julian Stead. The evening would always end with silent prayer followed by Van's benediction: "Go under the Mercy."[408]

In addition to teaching, and the Christian student group, Van had a number of good friends. One was a great lady—a descendant of one of the first families of Virginia. Van found her to be quite charming and thus he attended many a party and afternoon country outing with her.[409]

Another one of Van's friends was, of course, Belle Hill. She was a beloved English teacher, a lively lady whom students thought to be a real "hoot." Furthermore, it was obvious to at least one student that Belle was in love with Van.[410] Many people who knew the two of them often thought they would marry.[411] Van sometimes called Belle "the Blue Butterfly." From his perspective, she was a steadfast friend; Belle had lost her husband in circumstances similar to Davy's death, except that she had a son. At any rate, their experiences of grief made a bond between them. Belle and Van often had conversations that were deep and honest. They even went on vacation together, once to the island of St Pierre and another time to New Orleans. Belle was a cheerful, humorous and valiant companion. Van thought of marrying her, but then he also thought of Davy, Grey Goose and The Shining Barrier. Thus, marriage to Belle never transpired.[412]

Another friend of Belle and Van was Don Evans, professor of art at Lynchburg College. They were often seen together and thus thought of as Lynchburg College's "three musketeers." One student remembered how all three "smoked like chimneys."[413] Another student recalled fondly Don's classes on the top floor of Hopwood Hall. He always had a number of slides of famous artwork accompanying his lectures; talks that were invariably delivered with his eyes closed.

However, despite beloved friends, interesting students, and work to do, Van still sensed a Davy-shaped hollow at the center of his life. He still had no sense of overriding purpose or direction. Once again, he wrote to his mentor about this in April of 1958. He told Lewis he was considering a "drastic act" that he would not name, except to assure Lewis it was not suicide. This "drastic act" Van was still considering was that of resigning his position at Lynchburg College, buying his dreamed of deep-sea schooner, and taking off for the South Seas.[414]

Lewis wrote back on April 26 informing Van of Joy's continued miraculous improvement and assuring him of his prayers. He told Van that whatever he should decide about his direction in life, it would not prevent God from bringing good out of it. "More and more I see how useless it is to try to play Providence to oneself or to another. All we can do is to try to follow the plain rules of charity, justice and commonsense and leave the issue to God."[415]

In the autumn of '58, a new semester began and Van had still not taken off for Tahiti or Tuamotu. The dinghy (*Ilikea Moana*) still hung in Van's garage beside the Birdhouse, the compass of *Ettarre* was at the ready, and the figurehead of "the witch woman" was above the mantelpiece, looking like she couldn't wait to dip her breasts in the ocean waves.[416] However, Van waited, weighing his options, writing to Lewis about a great "irrevocable step" that he still would not name.[417]

Van kept that option of sailing the South Seas for another day. Meanwhile, he came to a bend in the road, the 1960s, and the Davy-shaped hollow was partially filled with other things.[418]

VAN CHECKING HIS CAR OUT OF THE LIBRARY

Photo Courtesy of Lynchburg College Archives, Knight-Capron Library

XX

THE IDEALISTIC YEARS

> The road is long
> With many a winding turn
> That leads us to who knows where
> Who knows where
> But I'm strong
> Strong enough to carry him
> He ain't heavy, he's my brother
>
> Scott & Russell

The year 1960 brought with it the opportunity for Van to be an encouragement to C. S. Lewis, just as his mentor had walked with him through his times of grief. He wrote to Lewis in April of that year to see how Joy was doing. Lewis wrote back asking for Van's prayers because Joy's cancer had returned and the doctors were not offering any hope for recovery.[419]

After receiving this letter, Van wrote several letters to Lewis, all but commanding him *not* to reply unless he had news about Joy. He told Lewis of his love for him and for Joy. He told him more about Davy's illness and how he was able to reach her while she was in a coma. He assured Lewis of his continued prayers. In addition, he sent to his mentor a sculptured reproduction of a twelfth century Norman Christ. The reproduction was about seven or eight inches high, mounted on a walnut plaque.[420]

Lewis wrote back to Van in the summer of 1960, telling him, sadly, of Joy's death on July 13. He commented on the Norman Christ, saying that he didn't like at first, though Joy did, but he was growing to like it more. In fact, Lewis had the sculpture above the head of his bed in the last years of his life.[421]

Lewis wrote again on September 23, 1960. He noted that he and Van were much at one in their reaction to grief. Some of Lewis' comments to Van on the subject of grief later made their way into his book, *A Grief Observed*. He noted that, like Van, he couldn't imagine real Eros coming twice. He still felt married to Joy.[422]

While Van was exchanging a number of letters with Lewis throughout 1960, he was, of course, continuing with his everyday life and work as a teacher in Lynchburg. Part of that life included the ongoing Christian student group, and one member of that group was Clifton Potter, who was destined to become, eventually, one of Van's colleagues.[423]

Belle Hill's son, Morton, was a friend of Clifton Potter, whose family lived in Lynchburg. Thus, Clifton first met Sheldon Van Auken at Morton's house, when the two boys were still in high school together. Clifton began his studies at Lynchburg College in the fall of 1958. Before arriving at the college, he had already decided to major in history; thus, he was bound to have a number of classes with Van Auken.

Clifton had Van Auken as a teacher for Greek, Roman, and English history. He also had Van for a class called senior seminar that Clifton took in his junior year. Clifton wrote his paper on Cardinal Wolsey. He remembers meeting at Van's house every Tuesday and Thursday at 4:30 in the afternoon. One student wrote a paper that quoted certain French poets. Another student complained that the poems were not translated into English. Van's response to the student who complained was simple and straightforward: "Sir, all scholars read French."

Clifton learned a lot from Van about how to write. Van was a stickler for proper grammar, spelling, and variety in writing style. He taught Clifton and his other students simple things like: never use the same key word twice in the same sentence, use a synonym instead. However, Van did not put sufficient emphasis on bibliography. He could create a wonderful mood in class but didn't emphasize the scholarly side of research in history and English literature.

When he entered Lynchburg College, Clifton Potter chose to join the staff of the school newspaper, the Critograph, and the school literary magazine, the Prism, because he had been involved in similar activities in high school. A number of students on the staff of the Critograph and the Prism all went over to Van's place, the Birdhouse, on Tuesday nights. The meeting would begin around seven o'clock and sometimes last until 11 pm when the women had to be back in their dormitory. Van would provide coffee and cookies. This group, that Van called simply "the Christian group", would talk about everything under the sun—ethics, history, and literature—not just religion. As Clifton later recalled, Van was, politically, a liberal at the time and Tuesday night discussions took a turn in the direction of Van's interests.

In the fall of 1960, the group drove to Roanoke Airport to see, hear and meet John F. Kennedy during the presidential campaign. Clifton remembers shaking Kennedy's hand, and his tremendous grip. "I had a new college ring and Kennedy's grip on that ring left a dent on my finger."

Every spring Van's Tuesday group would present a petition to the officials of Lynchburg College asking them to integrate. They never did at that time, but Van's group kept agitating for change. In this regard, Clifton remembered a unique experience. He was waiting at a bus stop in Lynchburg when a black man came up to him and asked: "Why are you so afraid of us?" Clifton shared the story with the Tuesday night group and they talked about it for the rest of the evening.

The Man Who Received "A Severe Mercy"

On December 14, 1960, two young men from Van's Tuesday night group participated in a sit-in at Patterson's Drug Store in downtown Lynchburg. Their names were James Hunter and Terrill Brumback. They joined two black students from Virginia Seminary—Kenneth Greene and Barbara Thomas—as well as a couple of white students from Randolph-Macon Woman's College—Mary-Edith Bentley and Rebecca Owen. They simply walked into the drug store on Main Street and sat down at the segregated lunch counter. When they refused to leave at the request of the owner, they were arrested.[424]

Terrill and Jim had informed Van about the sit-in before it happened. When they were arrested, Van went down to the jail to tell them the Dean's ruling that they would not suffer any academic penalty for their absence from school. Van got into an argument with the jailor who simply could not understand how these young men could each need half a dozen textbooks to do their schoolwork while they were locked up.[425]

In February 1961, the Prism published Van's letter to the editor entitled *A Question of Justice*. In that letter, Van voiced his support for his students' act of civil disobedience. He compared their stand to that of Socrates who was condemned to death for not believing in the gods in which the city believed. Van asserted that a believing Christian must, and a true patriot should, stand ready to put conscience above the law, if necessary.[426]

If participation in Van's Tuesday night group shaped the political outlook of certain Lynchburg College students, it also shaped their religious outlook. Some came to the group who did not have much religious experience at all before college. Some of these students eventually came to Christian faith. Others, who were already Christians, became Episcopalians like Van. Simone Reagor was one of these.[427]

As was the case with many of Van's students, Simone became a friend. In his English history class, and in the Tuesday night group, Van referred often to his time at Oxford. Then one day in his office in Carnegie Hall, when Simone was talking about graduate school, Van asked her if she would like to go to Oxford, and offered to help get her there. Simone was overwhelmed at the thought of it; studying at Oxford seemed like an unattainable dream. However, she and Van became dedicated to making that dream a reality. Being a keen feminist Van relished the thought of getting one of his female students to Oxford.

Thus, Van and Simone spent many hours planning her future together during her final semester at Lynchburg in the first months of 1961. Because they were spending so much time together, they became quite close. Van encouraged her to read C. S. Lewis, and this reading, led Simone to become a committed Christian in March of that year. She was confirmed at Grace Memorial Church, at which time Van gave her, as a gift, a copy of the Book of Common Prayer. He later referred to Simone as his daughter in Christ.[428]

That spring, Van and Simone went for long drives in the country. (Van had traded in his old MG-TD for another British sports car—a Triumph two-seater he called the Jaybird.) This friendship between teacher and student was based upon a shared love of Oxford, England, Virginia and Christianity. However, there was a bit more to it than friendship. As Van later admitted, he was in love with Simone.[429]

One of the funniest incidents, for which Van has been long remembered at Lynchburg College, had to do with his new Triumph. There was, at that time, a group of students on campus known as "The Pranksters." They had been responsible, among other stunts, for surreptitiously rolling a Civil War cannon from Miller Park two and a half miles to Lynchburg College, where they placed it in the middle of the green campus oval one dark night in February 1960. This group was constantly on the lookout for new and ever-more creative pranks. Perhaps their most famous stunt was carried out on Sunday night, May 21, 1961, into the wee hours of Monday morning. Their plan was to put Van's powder blue TR-3 in the middle of the college's Knight Memorial Library reading room. In the end, it required six maintenance men and a host of curious students thirty minutes to remove the car from the library. Van watched the process of extrication with a smile occasionally fleeting across his lips. According to the *Critograph*, he called the prank a "jolly good show." Furthermore, he said, "I fully intend to purchase an anchor." Commenting on the Pranksters, Van noted that they were "silly asses" to have done it but he found the prank funny nonetheless.[430]

The spring of 1961 was a busy time for Van. In April, he was promoted from associate professor of history and English to being a full professor. Then in May, Van and Simone decided to strike a blow against segregation at their parish church. They were friends with a black couple whose black Episcopal Church had welcomed them to a service. Therefore, Van and Simone decided to return the favor by inviting their friends to Grace. The Reverend Jeffery had moved on, but the current Rector was supportive of Van and Simone's plan to bring their black friends to church. He simply asked that they not tell him in advance which Sunday it would be. When Van and Simone did bring their friends, the Rector happened to preach on the evil of segregation. Some members of the congregation left before the end of the service to avoid having to greet Van and Simone's friends. Others later called Van and Simone "nigger-lovers", and claimed that the Rector or some outside agitators had put them up to their stunt. Because of the rumors flying around, Van felt compelled to write a strongly worded letter to the Vestry. In that letter, Van stated very pointedly why he believed segregation at the altar of Christ was completely unacceptable, and he supported his position using various New

The Man Who Received "A Severe Mercy"

Testament scriptures. Van ended the letter by saying that if Grace Church was to be a private club of "the respectable", then the Vestry should let the real Christians know so that they, black and white, could find an old barn or catacomb somewhere to raise an altar and worship Christ.[431]

In response to the letter, one of the churchwardens came to call on Van. He warned that if Van brought blacks to a service at Grace again, it would split the church. In return, Van asked him which he would prefer: that he would bring his black friends whenever they would wish to attend, or that he would leave the church. As a representative of the Vestry, the warden told Van it would be better for him to leave than to cause a church split.[432]

Van and Simone had already visited the Church of the Covenant on a few occasions; it was the only "white" church in Lynchburg at that time that welcomed blacks. Now Van and Simone began to attend there regularly. However, because Van was a believer in the sacraments and apostolic succession he went on occasion to an Anglican Church for early communion.

The Reverends Beverly Cosby and Irving Stubbs had started the Church of the Covenant on the first Sunday of October 1954.[433] Van was attracted to the church, not only by their stand on racial integration,[434] but also by what he sensed in their midst of what he called "the lively life in Christ." The church reminded him of the group of friends that met at The Studio in Oxford; there was a real interest in talking about Christ and the meaning of the Christian life, something Van didn't see in the other churches he was acquainted with in Lynchburg at that time.[435]

After Van had been attending Church of the Covenant for some time, the Rev. Bev, as he was known to all and sundry, invited Van and several others to write an account of how they became Christians. The result was that Van wrote at considerable length about his still recent conversion at Oxford. Van called his paper *Encounter with Light* and the Rev Bev was so impressed with it that he asked Van's permission to publish it as a thirty-page little booklet. Van wrote to C. S. Lewis and obtained his permission to use the first three of his letters to him in the pamphlet. Church of the Covenant gave away thousands of these booklets; people from as far away as India wrote, asking for copies. The booklet was first issued anonymously, but was later published under Van's name by the Marion E. Wade Collection of Wheaton College in Wheaton, Illinois. The booklet was then, and is still, not under copyright. Thousands more have been given away and sold by the Wade Center over the years.[436]

The Church of the Covenant also operated a coffee house called the Lodge of the Fishermen. Van became a member of the church and as such worked in the Lodge waiting on tables. In addition to writing *Encounter with Light*, Van wrote several small leaflets to hand out to visitors explaining what the Lodge and the church were all about.[437]

In early June 1961, Simone graduated from Lynchburg College. After receiving her diploma, she paused as she came off the platform long enough to smile at Van who was seated among the faculty. Van later said that as much as he had given to her as a teacher, Simone had also given something to him; she had partially filled that Davy-shaped hollow. Through Simone and her friends, as well as through Jim Hunter and others, Van began to see life through their eyes; the protest movements of the 1960s gave them something to be friends about.[438]

Simone spent the summer of 1961 working alongside Van and others at the Church of the Covenant. They continued their drives together through the Virginia countryside. At the end of that summer, Van drove Simone to Smith College in Northampton, Massachusetts, where she became a Woodrow Wilson Fellow. (After obtaining her master's degree from Smith, Simone did go on to Oxford as a Marshall Scholar where she earned a D.Phil. in history.)[439] En route to Massachusetts, Van and Simone stopped in New York City where they saw plays (*Camelot* and *A Man for All Seasons*) and dined in Greenwich Village.[440]

In 1962, Van began writing a novel that would eventually be published under the title: *Gateway to Heaven*.[441] He wrote most of the book during a two-year span from '62 to '63, substantially completing the book in the later 1960s with some final touches made before publication. *Gateway* was eventually dedicated to Simone in these words: "To S, nonetheless: for her winged vision."[442]

The writing of *Gateway to Heaven* was interrupted by a grant for travel in Asia that Van received and a sabbatical in England. Van wrote to his mentor, C. S. Lewis, about his travel plans and Lewis answered on June 30, 1962. He was glad to hear that there was some hope of seeing Van and insisted that they must talk of a thousand things during his visit.[443]

Van departed in the autumn of 1963 and spent a month in France, then another month or so in England visiting friends and traveling about. When he arrived in Oxford he contacted Lewis, not knowing his mentor had been in a coma and almost died during the previous summer.

Lewis invited Van to tea and, the day having arrived, Van took the bus from Oxford out to Headington Quarry. It was a good walk from the bus stop on the London Road to The Kilns; Van had to walk it with a typical November English rain descending, and the wind blowing quite a bit. Van couldn't help but think of the lines from Shelley's poem:

> O wild, West Wind, thou breath of Autumn's being,
> Thou, from whose unseen presence the leaves dead
> Are driven, like ghosts from an enchanter fleeing[444]

The Man Who Received "A Severe Mercy"

Lewis met Van at the door of the Kilns. During the six years since they had last seen each other, Lewis had aged tremendously, and looked in very ill health. Nonetheless, Van and Lewis talked about all manner of subjects, first in the Common Room and then in the kitchen over tea and biscuits, while the rain pelted the windows, and the wind whistled around the Kilns. The conversation naturally floated toward talk about Davy and Joy, how much they missed them and still felt married to them. They also discussed their publications: Van's *Encounter with Light*, that Lewis liked very much, and Lewis' essay: "We Have No Right to Happiness", later printed in *The Saturday Evening Post*. Van told his mentor of his involvement in the racial struggle and Lewis approved heartily of his stand.

Finally, when it was time for Van to go, Lewis made him promise to return in a couple of weeks, and they set a date. However, on the day Van was to meet with Lewis again, he read in the Oxford Mail over breakfast: "C. S. Lewis Funeral Today." Coincidentally, Lewis had died the same day as John F. Kennedy and fellow writer Aldous Huxley. Thus Lewis' passing was overshadowed by news of Kennedy's assassination. Van chose not to attend Lewis' funeral that day. Instead, he walked over to the Eastgate Hotel and stood outside for a few minutes thinking of Lewis' words from so many years before: "Christians never say goodbye!"

A month or so later, Van was on a plane to India to spend the spring semester at the University of Bombay. Later in the year, he traveled to Istanbul and the Ionian shore of Turkey. He visited Troy and then he went on to Greece itself. However, these travels were, as Van said years later, only a happy interlude to the real story of the 60s.[445]

VAN IN THE MORGAN

Photo Courtesy of Lynchburg College Archives, Knight-Capron Library

XXI

THE ANGRY YEARS

> Yes, how many deaths will it take till he knows
> That too many people have died?
> The answer my friend is blowin' in the wind
> The answer is blowin' in the wind.
>
> Bob Dylan

In his book, *Under the Mercy*, Van notes that the marches of the 1960s became angrier as they changed from support for civil rights to protest against the escalating "police action" in Vietnam. Van felt the Christian case for civil rights was clear and compelling. He was less certain what the Christian position should be regarding the war.[446] He read a lot on the topic and didn't like the way the United States was conducting its activities in Southeast Asia. In 1966, Van saw a photograph showing American troops dragging the body of a Viet Cong soldier behind their M113 armored personnel carrier. That was a turning point.[447]

Van's actual involvement in the anti-war movement began with a 1966 protest in support of conscientious objectors who were jailed in a Virginia prison. Though Van was not a pacifist he was willing to support those who were. Lynchburg College students invited Van to join them, along with students from some other local colleges, in supporting the religious conscientious objectors. Van, in his TR-3, with cap pulled down low over his forehead, led the small group of thirty or forty protesters down the main street of the town where the prison was located. Though he wanted to show his support for the religious COs, he didn't want to get in any trouble with any authorities. Thus, Van was grateful for the "crazy" blonde girl sitting beside him in the car who suddenly stood up, waving a placard, whooping and hollering for their cause. At least she drew attention away from him.[448]

Despite activities like these, the later 60s weren't, for Van, all about protesting the war. In the summer of 1967, he vacationed, once again, in England, exploring, among other things, Hadrian's Wall. He also purchased a new car—a Morgan 4-seater—direct from the factory in Great Malvern, England, near the location of C. S. Lewis' former boarding school. Van named the car "Morgan le Fay" after the powerful female magician of Arthurian legend. Later, he re-named his beloved car, "Colonel Morgan" after John Hunt Morgan of Kentucky, and painted it an appropriate Confederate grey.[449]

There was no escaping news of the war and the growing student protests. Van was among a third of the faculty at Lynchburg College who signed an anti-war protest in '67. He also helped to form a local chapter of the Southern Students Organizing Committee, the southern counterpart of the Students for a Democratic Society.[450] The SSOC was involved in a number of political and social issues: civil rights, anti-war protests and the feminist movement.

When Van returned from England to Lynchburg in the fall of '67, he was instrumental in aiding a small group of students at Lynchburg College in submitting a petition to the Student Government Association asking to charter their L.C. chapter of SSOC. The SGA Senate denied the students' request, supposedly because their SSOC constitution was not properly formulated in writing. Furthermore, the Senate stated that: "the presence of such a minority viewpoint would not add to campus life and would be detrimental to college relations in the community." Undaunted, the SSOC continued to meet off-campus under Van's direction. In fact, they often met at the Birdhouse to discuss issues and to organize for marches and rallies.[451]

The largest and most important event in which the unofficial LC chapter of the SSOC participated was the March on the Pentagon that took place October 21, 1967. Estimates are that on that day 70,000 demonstrators descended on Washington, D.C. to "confront the war makers." Van and John Molfase, a psychology instructor at Lynchburg College,[452] and a group of thirty LC students were among the thousands.[453] Lynchburg's President, Dr. M. Carey Brewer was personally opposed to these "peaceniks", as he called them, parading in protest against the war. "They are dead wrong," he said, "and if they prevail we will all be dead."[454] The Lynchburg College contingent made the two and a half hour trek to Washington anyway.

The event was initiated and organized by the National Mobilization Committee to End The War in Vietnam (MOBE). This entity was a loose coalition of 150 smaller groups like the SSOC. David Dellinger, MOBE coordinator and radical pacifist, asked Jerry Rubin to be project director for the march. Rubin had run the Vietnam Day teach-in at Berkeley on May 21-22, 1965 and other anti-war actions on the west coast since then. It was his idea to target the Pentagon, but it would not be the only place of protest that weekend. The largest rally was held at the Lincoln Memorial. During the afternoon, people lined the reflecting pool and listened to speeches. Dellinger said the time had come to go from protest to resistance. Dr. Benjamin Spock, world famous for his book on baby and childcare, told the crowd that he felt betrayed by President Johnson. He had campaigned for LBJ in 1964 because he promised not to escalate the conflict in Vietnam. Four months after the election the President sent massive numbers of American troops into battle.[455]

The Man Who Received "A Severe Mercy"

Van later conveyed the spirit of the occasion through the eyes of his fictional characters Richard and Mary in his novel, *Gateway to Heaven*. It was a beautiful Indian-summer day. Van and the others from Lynchburg sat near the Reflecting Pool, listening to the speeches, waiting for the march to begin. There were banners and signs all around expressing the anti-war sentiments of those who had gathered. Van later remembered the mood as lighthearted and friendly. Marijuana was smoked and passed about freely.[456]

After the speeches at the Lincoln Memorial, about 50,000 people set off for the Pentagon. It took them about an hour and a half to walk two miles across the Memorial Bridge and down a service road to the north parking lot where a second rally was scheduled. While a few dozen chanted, a few thousand marchers bypassed the parking lot for the Pentagon entrance where 2,500 federal troops and 200 U.S. marshals formed a human barricade protecting the Pentagon steps.[457]

A couple thousand demonstrators chose to spend the night. No one forced them to leave, though many did depart as the temperature turned cold. The rest lit bonfires made from picket signs and stayed up all night singing, talking, and confronting the soldiers. Some protestors tried to talk to the troops facing them with sheathed bayonets; some taunted them; some put flowers in their gun barrels (as Van's character Mary did[458]); some just stood and stared.

When the sun rose, a few hundred people marched to the White House to wake up President Johnson with chants. Some were arrested for picking flowers in Lafayette Park. Most of those who spent the night at the Pentagon left on Sunday after a small afternoon demonstration. Very early on Monday morning, police arrested the couple hundred protesters who remained at the Pentagon; the total number of arrests for the weekend came to 681. One hundred people were treated for injuries.[459]

There were many other protest marches in which Van participated from 1967 to 1971. One of these was a march down Fifth Avenue in New York City at the same time as the Columbia University Sit-In.[460] SDS at New York University organized the march. It was part of the "International Student-Faculty Strike to Bring Our Troops Home, End the Draft and Racial Oppression." This was a weeklong event consisting of anti-war protests and discussions, culminating on Friday, April 26, in a boycott of classes and a Saturday march down Fifth Avenue. At the same time, Columbia University was shut down by a student strike in which officials of the university were taken hostage. These student demonstrations followed on the heels of the assassination of Martin Luther King, Jr. earlier in the month.[461]

In addition to protest marches, Van participated in draft counseling on numerous occasions, often going with one of his students to confront the Draft Board. One such student, Tim, became a close friend. Tim had decided after viewing the film, *The War Game*, that he could not and would not carry a draft card. Thus, he returned his to the Draft Board, who responded by attempting to draft him, despite the fact that he was 4-F. When Van and Tim were unsuccessful in arguing their case before the local draft board they went to Richmond. When that effort also failed, Tim decided to head for Canada where he would renounce his American citizenship. Van drove him up to Toronto, and even visited Tim there a couple of times, the second occasion happened during the demonstrations at the Democratic Convention in Chicago in the summer of '68. During that second visit to Toronto, Van and Tim decided to try LSD. They got hold of two six-hit caps and had a "terrific trip", all the while listening to Tim's recording of the film soundtrack to *2001: A Space Odyssey*.[462] Van later described the experience in some detail, albeit under the guise of fiction, in *Gateway to Heaven*.[463]

When he returned to Virginia, Van made yet another house move, but on this occasion he was like a turtle taking his shell with him. Lynchburg College had decided to build a library extension that required the land on which the Birdhouse was situated. Being rather attached to the old place, Van purchased it and the accompanying garage from the college for the huge sum of $200 and had both moved down the hill to 100 Breckenbridge Street, where he would live for the rest of his life.[464]

In the fall of 1968, in addition to changing his home address, Van took an active role in the United States presidential election. He served as one of twelve presidential electors in Virginia for African-American candidate Dick Gregory and his running mate, Dr. Benjamin Spock, representing the Peace and Freedom Party.[465] While Van's political party was not successful in the presidential election that year, he did see positive movement on another front.

Van continued to battle for official recognition of the SSOC at Lynchburg College. In October of '68, the group was denied advertising space in the college newspaper, the *Critograph*. The reason given was: because the SSOC engaged in draft counseling, forms of which were unconstitutional. Van fired back, charging that the editor had given up on the facts and was relying on "indiscriminate innuendo." He went on to assert the legality of the group's draft counseling.[466]

In the end, Van and his group of "rabble-rousers" were victorious. At the beginning of November, the student senate voted to approve the charter of the SSOC. By this time Van was no longer an official faculty advisor to the group, however he must have been happy to see his students achieve their goal.[467]

Now, no longer officially involved with SSOC, Van continued his crusade for social change in other ways. Among other activities, he was a member of the executive board of the Lynchburg chapter of the American Civil Liberties Union. In February of 1969, they were responsible for bringing to the area a showing of the film, *Change of Seasons*, about the Chicago riots that had taken place the previous summer. Once again, the Lynchburg newspaper tried to insinuate, as they had in the past, that Van was a communist. In reporting about the film, the editor of the paper stated: "The American Civil Liberties Union is a leftwing organization with many Communist members and Communist connections."[468] As Van stated years later, the charge that *he* was a communist was rather silly. In actuality, he didn't like communist totalitarianism in the 60s any better than Nazi totalitarianism in the 40s. The editor of the Lynchburg paper had only to obtain a free copy of *Encounter with Light* from the Church of the Covenant in order to find out that Van was under the influence of Jesus Christ, not Leonid Brezhnev.[469]

If any further proof was needed that Van was still, at least somewhat, under the influence of Christ in the late 60s, one only need read the sermon he was invited to give in Snidow Chapel of Lynchburg College in the spring of 1969. The sermon was entitled *The Image of Jesus*.[470] In the message, Van attempted to correct and humanize the image of Jesus that he thought might be in the minds of both students and faculty in his audience. He invited his listeners to picture Jesus in blue jeans, looking like the typical 60s radical. Van even managed to work in a reference to LBJ and "Tricky Dick." By the time of preaching this sermon, Van was also sure where Jesus would have stood in regard to the war in Vietnam; to Van's mind Jesus was clearly a peacenik. He concluded the sermon by echoing the words of Dorothy Sayers about Jesus, "He was emphatically not a dull man in His human lifetime, and if He was God, there can be nothing dull about God either."[471]

Van's continuing commitment to Christ also came across in at least one meeting of the SSOC that took place in his home around this time. David Hartman remembered the event in this way....

> The students sprawled on his floor that night went into the usual 60s cant about the evils of the Establishment and the imperatives of dialectical materialism. It was only when one young radical launched into a soliloquy on how God had betrayed him that Van quietly interrupted and gave a most persuasive defense of orthodox Christianity. The room fell silent. If I had been taken aback by his [Van's] politics, they were taken aback by his faith. His hair length and antiwar convictions allowed him passage through their barricades, but his profoundly unfashionable faith seemed to put him back beyond the pale. I loitered after the others had left, and mentioned that I was intrigued by what he had said about Christianity. He gave me a booklet he had written entitled "Encounter with Light" (in which I recall seeing for the first time the name C.S. Lewis).
>
> It is a fact about Vietnam-era idealism that many male collegians

were considerably more exercised about the draft than about the war. Because Van was a former naval officer, decades past draft age, and had no draftable son, his own opposition to the war was free of self-interest…. It wasn't until years later that I fully appreciated the depth of Van's courage and the purity of his convictions.[472]

Van's involvement in the anti-war movement at this time was often conducted in small ways, such as picketing the Lynchburg Post Office, the only federal building in town.[473] Nonetheless, these seemingly harmless activities caught the ire of then president of Lynchburg College, Carey Brewer. By the summer of 1969, Brewer was threatening Van with firing, despite tenure, if he did not cease and desist all his so-called radical activities. Brewer never did fire Van, but by the end of 1969, there was a faculty rebellion in the works. It all started with the actual firing of two teachers at the school: one who was an alleged homosexual and the other was a professor of political science who had criticized the administration. Soon, a third, beloved faculty member was leaving—the college chaplain. An emergency faculty meeting was called. The only way Brewer was able to keep control was by threatening even more of the faculty with firing.[474]

On the national scene, Van didn't like the escalating violence of the anti-war movement. He addressed this concern in one of his last anti-war essays entitled *The Peacemaker*. He warned those gaining power in the Movement using the words of Lord Acton: "All power tends to corrupt and absolute power corrupts absolutely."[475]

In 1969, the SSOC published a pamphlet Van wrote entitled *Freedom for Movement Girls—Now*.[476] He penned his tract for the times in late 1968 using only his last name as author, thus not revealing whether he was a man or a woman. In the booklet, he argued that man defines himself primarily in terms of brain, or at least hand and brain, whereas man defines woman in terms of vagina and womb. The only real superiority of man over woman is that of sheer physical power, but such animal strength is of virtually no importance in a world dominated by machines. In such a world brains are what count. Therefore, Van concluded, we should stop wasting half the brainpower of the world on household duties and secondary jobs.

Van later claimed that in this pamphlet he had invented the terms "sexist" and "sexism."[477] Others also attributed the coinage to him. However, the term "sexist" was actually coined in 1965 by Pauline M. Leet, director of special programs at Franklin & Marshall College, Lancaster, Pennsylvania, in a speech that was circulated in mimeographed copies among feminists. The term "sexist" was popularized by use in print in Caroline Bird's *On Being Born Female* published in November 1968.[478] Van may have picked up the term from one of these earlier sources without realizing it.

THE MAN WHO RECEIVED "A SEVERE MERCY"

At any rate, Van talked about the "sexist myth" that woman is primarily a biological being driven by overwhelming maternal instincts. The truth, Van insisted, is that a woman or girl (his preferred term) is a human being with a brain first and only, incidentally, capable of bearing children. Her unique female function requires only eighteen months (to produce the two children per couple society can afford), so what is she going to do with the other sixty-eight years or more of her life? Van's answer was that women might take over, and run the world and make it a more peaceful place.

Two little asides in the tract are of some interest. He notes that a girl is not being unfeminine or lesbian when she demands her human rights. After all, Van suggests, what does it matter if she is a lesbian, we are freedom lovers, and so a girl's sexual orientation is no one else's business. Similarly, men should not be allowed to tell women what they may and may not do with their own bodies, particularly in the matter of abortion. *Freedom for Movement Girls—Now* reveals just how far Van had swung to the left in his social perspective and is rather fascinating when compared to his later swing back to the right.

The last of the great anti-war demonstrations in which Van took part began on May 1, 1971. It was the brainchild of Rennie Davis along with Jerry Coffin of the War Resisters League and Mike Lerner, a defendant in the "Seattle Seven" trial. The goal of the protest was simple: if the government won't shut down the war in Vietnam, we'll shut down the government. The tactic for doing this was to block the bridges of Washington D. C. with thousands of protesters. Davis gathered his recruits from college campuses across the country.[479]

Years later, Van recalled traveling to SSOC headquarters in Nashville for planning of the Mayday demonstration. A couple of others rode with him in the Morgan and a van followed them with many more. On the return trip, Van had car trouble; consequently, the group didn't arrive back in Lynchburg until 2:30 in the morning, too late for the girls to return to their dorm. Thus, the whole crew spent the rest of the night "sleeping" on the floor of the Birdhouse. Van lit a candle and placed it on the mantelpiece while playing Joan Baez at low volume on his record player.[480]

Saturday, May 1, 1971, saw 35 to 45,000 protesters camped out in West Potomac Park, listening to a rock concert and planning for the shutdown of DC. Van and the Lynchburg College SSOC group were among them. Van told the group that if any of them were arrested during the weekend that once they were released he would meet them at a certain corner of the Justice Department building at a specific hour.[481]

On Sunday morning, police descended on the park to evict the protesters from their encampment. About half of the gathering decided to go home at that point. However, Van and his group hung in there. Van later recalled several hundred protesters sitting outside the Department of Justice, shouting "Jump!" whenever Attorney General Mitchell and others came out on to the balcony above them. When Van and one of the Lynchburg College girls went to meet one of their contingent, Jake, who had just gotten out of jail, they happened to run into a large group of police officers with tear-gas. There was no way Van and his two compatriots could break through the police line to get back to the rest of their group. They had no choice but to get into Van's Morgan and drive around the scene, cheering on the protesters with peace signs.

Early on Monday morning, the remaining protesters moved into position to block their targets. The government was ready with a combined force of 10,000 police, National Guard and federal troops, with 4,000 more, ready in reserve. Skirmishes took place all over the city, but the government prevailed in the end, making thousands of arrests.[482] Van, by sheer luck, wasn't among those arrested; nonetheless, he decided on the trip home to Lynchburg that he wasn't going to participate in any more protests. Many others were deciding the same thing, for as it turned out, that was one of the last major demonstrations of the anti-war movement.[483]

What began after the Mayday Protests Van later called that curious tail of the '60s: the flight to the country. Suddenly, countless "Movement people" were discovering the joys of rural living. Van and a friend were among them; they bought a log cabin in Amherst County, not far from Lynchburg, on 150 acres, between Bear and Cedar Mountains. Van and his friend named the place "The Rock" and Van used the location as the setting for what he called the "Gateway to Heaven" in his novel of the same name.[484] Van's novel in many ways summed up the life he had lived in the 60s. By the end of the decade, Van had adopted the whole hippie look: blue jeans, long hair and the ever-present peace symbol slung around his neck. However, all that was about to change.

One more link with the past was broken when Van's brother Paul died. He had been an alcoholic for many years and had a much more difficult military experience than Van had in World War II. At the end of his life, Paul was a patient at the Veteran's Hospital in Salem, Virginia and Van would visit him there.[485] Now Paul was gone, the sixties were over, and a new life stretched in front of Van. He never could have imagined what that life was going to entail.

PART FOUR
RETURN TO THE OBEDIENCE
1973-1996

… obedience to which, if joyful, if free,
proves to be not only no slavery,
but to anyone whose intuition is perspicacious,
is itself obviously the highest liberty.

Charles Williams, *The Figure of Beatrice*

Van wearing peace pendant

Photo Courtesy of Lynchburg College Archives, Knight-Capron Library

XXII

TWITCHES UPON THE THREAD

> I caught him with an unseen hook and an invisible line
> which is long enough to let him wander to the ends of the world
> and still to bring him back with a twitch upon the thread.
>
> G. K. Chesterton, *Father Brown*

It was a new decade, and Van felt a sense of starting over. Some friends got together in September 1973 and marked the new era by giving Van the gift of a puppy, a black and white border collie that he named in a way reflective both of the times and of his love of English literature. The dog's first name was Nelly (after the old nurse in *Wuthering Heights*). Her middle name was Dean after John Dean of the Nixon White House, and her last name was Watergate.[486]

Around the same time Van set about restoring his house in its new location: a fresh coat of paint inside and out, refinished furniture from Glen Merle, and new Persian rugs. It was now, no longer, "the 60s pad" but "a gentleman's residence" once more. To symbolize the change he also gave the house a new name; students from the 60s who had known it as the Birdhouse were mostly gone, new friends referred to it as "Van's house", but Van preferred to call it a cottage, which indeed it was. Thus, the house at 100 Breckenbridge became known thereafter as "Vancot."[487]

However, it wasn't simply Van's cottage that underwent renovation, the man who lived there did too. He cut his hair short once again, put on a tie, and as he put it years later—"rejoined the faculty." During the 60s, Van had identified more with his students than his colleagues, and certainly not with the administration of Lynchburg College. He even tried to dress a bit like his students and appear younger than he really was.[488] Now all of that changed. Van was even inviting colleagues and their spouses over to Vancot for sherry parties.[489]

In a way, Van was returning to the man he had been before the detour of the 60s. However, it wasn't a simple return to his life as it was in the 50s. For one thing, he wasn't going to church at all by this time.[490] In the early 60s, Van had been attending and actively involved in The Church of the Covenant. He was often there with two of his close friends and colleagues, Belle Hill and Don Evans. However, about the time that the Surgeon General of the United States began issuing warnings about the dangers of cigarette smoking, in the late 60s and early 70s, The Church of the Covenant reconsidered its position on the matter. The Church decided to tell its members and attendees they could no longer smoke inside the church house or the Lodge of the Fishermen. Smoking was still allowed on church property *outside* the buildings, but that wasn't good enough for Van or Belle or Don. All three left the church and never returned.[491]

However, the year 1975 proved to be for Van what might be called "The Year of the Twitches on the Thread" pulling him back to God and the Church. The first twitch came with Van's belated realization that the Episcopal Church planned to revise the 1928 Book of Common Prayer.[492] Van and Davy had used this edition to say their morning and evening family prayers. How could the Church think of changing this sacred language?

Van had been very protective of prayer book language even while attending The Church of the Covenant. That congregation used a hymnal that contained a version of the General Confession from the Book of Common Prayer. However, like the revision of the prayer book that was in the works, the Covenant church hymnal left *out* of the General Confession the key word "miserable."[493] The original confession was stated as follows:

> Almighty and most merciful Father, We have erred and strayed from thy ways like lost sheep, We have followed too much the devices and desires of our own hearts, We have offended against thy holy laws, We have left undone those things which we ought to have done, And we have done those things which we ought not to have done, And there is no health in us: But thou, O Lord, have mercy upon us **miserable** offenders; Spare thou them, O God, which confess their faults, Restore thou them that are penitent, According to thy promises declared unto mankind in Christ Jesu our Lord: And grant, O most merciful Father, for his sake, That we may hereafter live a godly, righteous, and sober life, To the glory of thy holy Name. Amen.[494]

Van, noting the sacrilege of leaving out the key word "miserable", wrote *in* the missing word in every hymnbook his hands touched at Church of the Covenant.[495]

Van's concern for retaining the original language of the old and dear prayer book had not changed by the early 70s. Even though he was not going to church at the time, he was still horrified by the thought of this revision. Thus, he shot off letters to the Episcopal hierarchy, Episcopal journals and to the rectors of local parishes.[496] That was the first twitch on the thread.

The second twitch followed on from the first. One of those local rectors, to whom Van had written, came calling on him. It was the Reverend Louis Fischer from St. Stephen's Church in Forest, where Van had scattered Davy's ashes twenty years before. Fischer suggested to Van that if he was going to fight for the old prayer book then he needed to be a church-going Episcopalian with a church home. That made sense to Van and so he showed up at St. Stephen's one Sunday morning in the Morgan with his dog Nelly in tow. Van felt like he was returning home, not only because of St. Stephen's as a place, with its connection back to Davy, but because of the people there. Shirley Rosser from Lynchburg College, now married with children, was attending. In addition, Van made new friends with others like the woman he called "Lady Frances"; she was the wife of James Barnett "Barney" Hodges. The Hodges lived at Elk Hill, an eighteenth century red brick house set on four hundred acres, just down the road from St. Stephen's. Their home reminded Van of Glen Merle, and so, in a different way, gave him a sense of coming home, just as St. Stephen's itself did.[497]

Elk Hill, which Van visited often, is an old plantation house of great interest, added to the Virginia Landmarks Register in 1972 and the National Register of Historic Places in 1973. The house was built in 1797 for Waddy Cobbs, uncle of Nicholas Hamner Cobbs, the first rector of St. Stephen's Church. Waddy Cobbs later gave the house and plantation to his daughter and her husband along with several slaves. The farm was later owned by three generations of the Nelson family. Dr. Thomas Hugh Nelson was the great-grandson of Brigadier General Thomas Nelson, Jr., Governor of Virginia during the siege of Yorktown and a signer of the Declaration of Independence. Famed chronicler of the Old South and relative of the owners, Thomas Nelson Page, often visited Elk Hill and did some writing there. Sometime in the 1930s, the poet Robert Frost spent a week at Elk Hill with the Hodges family, who had acquired the property in 1928.[498]

Returning to May of 1975, on Rogation Sunday Van brought Nelly to St. Stephen's as usual. Only this time Nelly was allowed to participate in the traditional blessing of the animals, and a march around the boundaries of the churchyard. After the service, there was a picnic under the great old oak trees. Some of the women of the church begged Van to allow Nelly, now safely ensconced in the Morgan once again, to return for some meat scraps. Van shouted: "Abandon ship!" and Nelly came running. This gave Nelly the idea that she could be a regular and faithful member of St. Stephen's. Thus, on the following Sunday, she marched down the center aisle of the church, with the Rector and choir. Van gave her a scolding, but at the same time, he shared her joy at being part of such a loving church family.[499]

A third "twitch upon the thread" that drew Van closer to God was the death of his cousin Ann, killed in an automobile accident. Because of her death, Van started thinking more of eternal things and the Christian hope of everlasting life.[500]

A fourth pull upon the thread came in the mail one day. The Reverend Newton B. Fowler, Jr. (Lynchburg College Class of 1954 and Chaplain of the College 1968-1970) sent Van a gift from his new post at Lexington Theological Seminary in Kentucky. It was Clyde Kilby's book, *C. S. Lewis: Images of His World*.[501] The book is filled with beautiful pictures by famed photographer, Douglas Gilbert, of the places of Lewis' life in the British Isles, and an excellent text by Clyde Kilby, English professor at Wheaton College in Illinois, who started the world-renowned Marion E. Wade Collection of materials related to Lewis and six other authors. As Van perused and read, the experience brought tears to his eyes, as he thought of his beloved mentor and all the good times he and Davy had enjoyed together during their few years in England. One particular Lewis quote from the book, taken from *The Pilgrim's Regress*, hit Van with considerable force:

> ... If a man diligently followed his desire [for Joy], pursuing the false objects until their falsity appeared and then resolutely abandoned them, he must come out at last into the clear knowledge that the human soul was made to enjoy some object that is never fully given...in our present mode of subjective and spatio-temporal existence.[502]

Van typed the quote on a card and set it on the shelf beside his bed where he often read it again throughout the spring and summer of 1975. He realized that Lewis' statement was a perfect summary of his own life. He had pursued joy, first through a great love—Davy—then down so many dead-end roads in the 60s. Now he was beginning to realize in a deeper way than he ever had before that God was the ultimate source of joy, the One he really needed to pursue.[503]

The next twitch came during a visit to see an old friend in Cincinnati. The friend was George Palmer, with whom Van had been in the Navy and, before that, a radio announcer at WIBC in Indianapolis. George had been in radio for years, then a Channel 12 news anchor in Cincinnati, and finally a feature writer for the *Cincinnati Enquirer*. George wanted Van's help with a story he was doing on a psychic. Van volunteered to have a "reading" with the psychic for possible use by George in his feature article. Expecting nothing but "claptrap", Van was rather surprised when the psychic, "Greener" by name, was able to come within one day of predicting Van's birthday. Greener also correctly surmised that Van had lived in Hawaii and that it had meant a lot to him. Finally, the psychic said: "Oh! I see a great bird flying over the sea. This bird is your highest symbol." Could it be mere coincidence, that Greener identified one of the most important symbols of Van's life—the grey goose?[504]

Greener wasn't finished. With his "sixth sense", he was able to see a woman, and he knew that her name was Jean, that she was Van's soul mate, and that she died of some rare disease. Even more, Greener was able to identify what he thought was Jean's birth date or, possibly, her death date—July 27—actually three days off her birth date and close to the date on which Van learned from the doctors that Davy was going to die. The clincher was when Greener said, "I don't understand this: somehow she *chose* to die...she didn't take her own life and she didn't want to die...but in some way she chose her death. I don't understand how this can be."[505]

Van understood. Though he had gone into this psychic reading not expecting anything, he couldn't help but conclude that somehow Greener was seeing the truth. The importance of this event for Van was that it served as another twitch on the thread, drawing his thoughts closer to Davy, eternity and God.

When he returned from Cincinnati to Virginia, Van had a visit from another friend who, when he left, happened to leave behind his copy of C. S. Lewis' children's book, *The Lion, the Witch and the Wardrobe*. Van had never read Lewis' Narnia stories. Now he read not only *The Lion* but the other six Chronicles as well. It was another twitch.

Next, Van received a letter from Clyde Kilby about the reprinting of *Encounter with Light*. Van wrote back telling Kilby how much he enjoyed his book, *C. S. Lewis: Images of his World*. A correspondence ensued that eventually resulted in Van writing a brief account of the Studio group and what Lewis had meant to them all.

When Van returned to teaching at Lynchburg College in the autumn of 1975, he met a new colleague, Jim, and his wife, Margery. The latter had recently become a Christian, partly through reading C. S. Lewis. The enthusiasm bubbling forth from Margery's soul about her newfound faith, reminded Van a great deal of the joy he and the others in the Studio group had shared so many years before.[506]

As Van was contemplating all these twitches on the thread, he went to bed one evening in October and was happily reading a murder mystery. Suddenly, he felt a compulsion to pull off the shelf and begin reading the first Lewis book he had ever read, *Out of the Silent Planet*. There was nothing particularly significant on the first page, just a pedestrian walking down an English country road at sunset after a thunderstorm, with the church spire of Much Nadderby behind him.[507] However, there was something about re-reading *Out of the Silent Planet* that proved to be the final, ever so slight twitch on the thread, drawing Van back to God. At the beginning of the page, Van was not on speaking terms with the Almighty, but by the time he reached the last words—"The place had changed"—Van had changed. He was back under the Obedience. He prayed, and God was first in his life again.[508]

Van did not return to reading that murder mystery until he had read again, and in some cases read for the first time, everything C. S. Lewis had written. He also read again much of another favorite author, C. S. Lewis' friend Charles Williams. Van was, in the words of Williams, "under the Mercy" once more.

The day after his return to the Obedience, Van wrote to the Bodleian Library in Oxford asking them to send him copies of the C. S. Lewis letters he had given to them in 1969.[509] He returned home late one night after teaching to find the package had arrived earlier that day. Without even taking off his coat or scarf, Van opened the package, sat down and devoured the whole correspondence, with a tear or two dropping on the pages as he read.

One more important step Van took at this time was to confess his sins to a priest. Despite being an Episcopalian, Van chose to confess his sins to his friend and Catholic priest, Father Julian Stead at Portsmouth Abbey in Rhode Island.[510] Father Julian not only heard Van's confession but he acted as an informal spiritual director for many years to come.[511]

In December 1975, Van had his membership transferred from Grace Memorial Episcopal Church to St. Stephen's, thus making his connection to that beloved church official, for the first time in his life.[512] On Christmas Eve, he went to St. Stephen's for the carol service that concluded in the churchyard with "God Rest Ye Merry Gentlemen", candles burning bright in the misty night. Then Van and Nelly went on to Elk Hill for supper, and more carols around the Hodges' family Christmas tree. Thus, the year of the "twitches on the thread" ended.[513]

January 1976 began with Van reading again Lewis' letters to him. In the midst of reading, he paused and wished that Lewis might appear to him, sitting in the chair by the fire and grinning, as he had appeared to J. B. Phillips.[514] No such vision was vouchsafed to him, but less than a minute later, the idea entered Van's mind to write a book he would call *A Severe Mercy*. The thought came to him, he said afterwards, as a vocation from God.[515]

BODLEIAN LIBRARY, OXFORD

AUTHOR PHOTO

Elk Hill
THE HOME OF VAN'S FRIENDS, BARNEY & LADY FRANCES HODGES

Author Photo

XXIII

THE VOCATION

> But all men praise some beauty, tell some tale,
> Vent a high mood which makes the rest seem pale,
> Pour their heart's blood to flourish one green leaf,
> Follow some Helen for her gift of grief.
>
> John Masefield, *Ships*

Van didn't have time to actually begin writing *A Severe Mercy* until the summer vacation of 1976. He wanted to be able to completely immerse himself in the project and that could not happen until he was finished with teaching for that school year. He also realized that writing *A Severe Mercy* would require setting aside work on his novel, *Gateway to Heaven*, for a time. However, it would be worth it; the sense of vocation he had from God was not to be ignored.[516]

In the mean time, Van wrote some other shorter pieces. The first came as a reply to something William H. Marmion, Bishop of the Diocese of Southwestern Virginia, wrote in the diocesan newspaper entitled: "A Letter to a Fundamentalist." Van took exception to the Bishop's statement that "No creed can be final, because inevitably it will be affected by the world view and the psychology and the philosophy of the age."[517] On the contrary, Van insisted, a member of the Episcopal Church who confesses the faith each Sunday in worship may believe *more* than what is in the creeds but not *less*. When we say that Jesus is "very God of very God", either that is a true statement or not.[518] To Van's mind, there was no room to speak of creedal literalism or creedal "illiteralism" on such a monumental point.[519]

Around the same time, and following the same theme of concern regarding growing liberalism in the Church, Van wrote a limerick, later published in the *New Oxford Review*[520] and published in *Mercies: Collected Poems*, under the title "Theology."[521] In the spring of '76, he also wrote *A General Rule for New Testament Criticism*[522] and *The Playwright Incarnate*,[523] the latter explaining the Incarnation and the Trinity by means of the illustration of God being like a playwright who places himself as a character in his play. This miniature play was similar to the illustration Van had shared with a non-Christian friend in conversation in Oxford in the 1950s. All of these small pieces were things Van dashed off in his spare time, on weekends during that spring. However, the real focus of his thought at that time was on the planning of *A Severe Mercy*.[524]

There was one question regarding the writing of the book that stumped Van for a long while: where to begin? He didn't want the opening words to be:

"I was born..." After all, this was to be the story of a great love as told by one of the lovers, not strictly an autobiography. Yet, there were some things that needed to be said, in order to "set the stage" before he and Davy would meet "angrily in the dead of winter." Van wanted to touch on his boyhood code of ethics, his youthful desire to experience a great love, along with the heights and the depths; he also wanted to introduce Glen Merle, so important as the setting for his early romance with Davy. Van went to bed one night that spring, still not knowing how to begin the book. However, the next morning he had his answer before he even opened his eyes. He would begin with his late night walk into Glen Merle, six months after Davy's death. This "overture" would introduce the many important themes in the story to follow.[525]

June 1, 1976, Van began typing with his two fingers by the hunt and peck method on his 1934 Royal Quiet Deluxe Portable typewriter, the one his father bought for him when he went off to Wabash College. The first sentence read: "The country road stretched ahead white in the moonlight and deserted."[526] Years later, Van told me he wrote that first chapter, "Prologue: Glenmerle Revisited", at least twenty times, sometimes the chapter came out longer, sometimes shorter; he wanted to get it just right.[527] The rest of the chapters he wrote three times each before going on to the next. As soon as he was finished with a chapter, he would mail a copy off to Julian Stead for his comments.[528]

In response, Julian wrote a poem entitled "On Reading 'A Severe Mercy'"—

> O triumph! I've waited long
> Through grey wastepaper days
> Through cigarettes and emptied glasses
> Hearing only a single sparrow's song
> —Poor piper, for Davy's death—
> Turning now to my student lasses
> Praying someone will love them too
> Now I dare to believe God's ways
> Contain such unforeseen mercies
> As Davy's resurrection, through
> A book that breathes her breath,
> The faith and love in our undying verses.[529]

Van also shared copies of each chapter in manuscript with Frances Hodges who offered some helpful suggestions. The few times Van went for supper at Elk Hill that summer, with starlight on the vast lawns, reminded him more and more of the vanished Glen Merle he was writing about back at Vancot. However, Van didn't stay long with Barney and Lady Frances on those summer nights, for the next day he would start early at his writing vocation.[530]

The Man Who Received "A Severe Mercy"

Every morning in that summer of 1976, Van was "up" and writing in his bed with his typing desk before him at three o'clock, without pause for even eating until three in the afternoon. Naturally, he drank a lot of coffee to keep going. Every evening he would spend time correcting what he had written. At night, he also read over the diaries for the next period he was to write about. Moment by moment, day by day, he was reliving all his years with Davy. By mid-August, seventy-eight days after he had begun, Van finished his third draft of the entire book.[531]

Edmund Dews, Van's friend from Oxford days, arrived in Lynchburg for a visit. He read the manuscript in one night. He was, in a way, not happy with the book. He thought it contained an element of "wishful thinking" or romanticism on Van's part; it seemed to Edmund that his old friend had portrayed his relationship with his wife as he wanted it to be. The Davy whom Edmund remembered was not one who stood exactly on an equal footing with her husband. Rather, she was a quiet, behind-the-scenes sort of person at The Studio, not the grand hostess.[532] Edmund felt that Van had also idealized him; he didn't think himself to be the great gentleman Van made him out to be. However, Edmund felt he could not share these criticisms with Van, that they would not be taken well, and that his critique would make no difference to Van's writing of the book anyway. Thus, Edmund praised *A Severe Mercy* as "a great work of literature." He felt the way in which Van weaved the poetry, prose and Lewis' letters all together was superb. Though Van was not content with Edmund's response, he did not probe more deeply.[533]

In addition to sharing the story with Edmund, Van gave the manuscript to others to read, others who had not known Davy. The readers included: James Patrick Kelley (a Bonhoeffer scholar then on the faculty at Lynchburg College) and his wife Connie, Simone Reagor, and fellow authors: Clyde Kilby, Thomas Howard, and Paul Holmer, among others.[534]

Van sent off queries, followed by the manuscript, to numerous publishers. Before the year was out, he received a letter from Mr. Edward England of Hodder & Stoughton in London. Mr. England said that H&S would publish Van's book for the former British Empire (less Canada) if they received the final draft by January 10, 1977. Van gladly accepted their offer, even though that left him only one month to finish the final draft. During the Christmas vacation, he did a repeat of his writing habits from the previous summer, up at three o'clock each morning, writing and editing for fourteen hours, drawing little, celebratory pictures at the end of each chapter as he finished the final draft. His only breaks were for Christmas Eve services at St. Stephen's followed by supper at Elk Hill, with another respite on Christmas Day for supper with other friends. By December 30, the final draft was complete, and Van sent two copies off separately to London by airmail. Later, he had the very unusual pleasure for a first-time author, of choosing the publisher for English North America out of three firms making him an offer. His choice was Harper & Row.[535]

If 1976 was the year of writing, then 1977 was the year of editing and publication. As Van later said, he made his editor's life difficult by thinking up many little changes and additions.[536] Indeed, he went over the Hodder & Stoughton typescript of *A Severe Mercy* and the galley proofs with a fine-tooth comb, making detailed annotations on numerous pages.[537] He even sent in three new paragraphs at the last minute; one of these, the paragraph on male headship in marriage in chapter VIII, was too late for inclusion in the first edition.[538]

However, the publishing process did not take up all of Van's time. He was still teaching and writing other little pieces during the year of "exaltation" as he called it. He wrote a very perceptive essay on human free will and the problem of pain entitled "God's Will"; it was later published in *The Living Church*.[539] He also wrote an essay on the issue of the ordination of female priests in the Episcopal Church. This essay marked the beginning of the almost total reversal of Van's earlier feminism.[540] A third piece written was Van's poem about apostates in the Church entitled "The Shepherd's Reformation."[541]

In November 1977, Van received in the mail from London, Hodder & Stoughton's edition of *A Severe Mercy* in its very attractive forest-green dust jacket. The moment when an author holds his first published book in his hands is very special indeed. In Van's case, he felt the sense of a commission discharged.

A few days later, he decided to burn the diaries on which he had based so much of the book. Van did this for a few reasons. First, he and Davy could no longer read them together in old age as they had planned to do, so he thought: why keep them? Secondly, he surmised that perhaps the purpose for the diaries' existence was now fulfilled: *A Severe Mercy* was in print. Thirdly, Van did not want any later biographers rooting around in the thousands of pages he and Davy had written about their life together. Some things he wanted to keep private.[542] Finally, and perhaps most importantly for Van from a personal standpoint, he didn't want to live in the past; he knew himself well enough to realize that if he kept the diaries that is exactly what he would be tempted to do: live his life backward, rather than face forward.[543] Thus, he put the journals on the fire at Vancot, one by one, along with his old photo albums except for about a dozen saved snapshots, and he watched his beloved record of the past burn away.

In a matter of days, the future looked very bright for Sheldon Vanauken; *A Severe Mercy* was mentioned in *Time* magazine in an article about C. S. Lewis.[544] ASM was, perhaps, helped in its sales by the appearance of a number of "new" Lewis volumes that year such as: *The Dark Tower & Other Stories* and *The Joyful Christian*.⁵⁴⁵ In addition, it certainly did not hurt that the name "C. S. Lewis" appeared in larger type even than the name "Sheldon Vanauken" on the cover of the first American edition of ASM. Here is what *Time* had to say about the book:

> In yet another new book, *A Severe Mercy* (Harper & Row), a memoir by Sheldon Vanauken, professor of history and English at Virginia's Lynchburg College, Lewis appears as a ministering angel in tweed jacket. Like so many other unbelievers, Vanauken and his wife Jean dipped into Lewis upon urgings of Christian friends, began devouring all the Lewis books they could find, and wound up, to their surprise, as converts. Then Jean died of a liver ailment, and Vanauken plunged into despair. It was an astringent letter from Lewis that enabled Vanauken to make some sense out of her death—and his life.

Van collected at least eighty pages of reviews of ASM that he later passed on to the archives at Lynchburg College and the Wade Center at Wheaton College. Most of the reviews were glowing—even stating that ASM was "a Christian classic in the making."⁵⁴⁶ However, Van kept the not so positive reviews as well. The one in *Christianity Today* while being mostly encouraging also complained of some "poeticized prose" and "awkward juxtapositions of slang and stilted language", "too many 'whilsts,' 'amongsts,' and 'wonts' scattered throughout the book. The structure, too, is a little awkward at times, causing Vanauken to repeat himself."⁵⁴⁷

John S. Kennedy, writing for *The Catholic Transcript*, began his review with a quote from the jacket of the book: "'Belongs in the same genre as St. Augustine's 'Confessions' and is in some ways greater.' ... It is partly true, partly nonsense, and the book itself evokes an ambivalent response: one part admiration to one part irritation." Kennedy then quoted a passage about Van and Davy's first date and said, "if you find it affected and repulsive, be warned that there is much, much more of the same, which is a great pity, since the book has valuable and even rare substance." Kennedy then concluded by saying, "The author's prose is so mannered that at times it seems almost to be parodistic. An inflated romanticism often threatens to render the book ridiculous. But the theme of a Christian faith found and maturing through adversity is so clearly and vigorously presented that the work's defects can be tolerated if not overlooked."⁵⁴⁸

Van reacted strongly against the repeated criticism of ASM in which some reviewers found romanticism and realism to be opposed. It is perhaps a sign however of Van's maturity that he was able to take himself and his work lightly enough to write a parody of the Prologue of ASM for *The Wittenburg Door* entitled "Jake's Place Revisited."⁵⁴⁹

There were only two reviews Van thought were so wrong-headed they deserved a reply. One by a Mr. Anker appeared in *The Reformed Journal* (November 1978). Apparently, the reviewer suggested that Van (or C. S. Lewis) believed that God killed Davy or allowed her to die, to bring about certain results in Van's life. Van wrote to the *Reformed Journal* to make clear that he was *not* suggesting God intended Davy's death. As far as Van was concerned, his God, and the God of C. S. Lewis, was one of incredible love and mercy.[550]

The other review to which Van replied was by a Mr. Foley writing in *Sojourners*. That reviewer seemed concerned that Van and Davy could go off blithely to Oxford to study or go sailing the Keys or the Chesapeake when there were so many starving people in the world to feed. Van's reply in the December 1978 issue of *Sojourners* was to agree with Mr. Foley, up to a point. However, he also pointed out that if no one sought knowledge or beauty ours would be a dreary world indeed.[551]

As bothersome as a few of the reviews of ASM were, it wasn't so much criticism that Van had to learn how to deal with; rather, he had to determine how he would respond to praise. In addition to the rave reviews, ASM won no less than seven awards, including The National Religious Book Award in 1978 and The American Book Award in 1980.[552] One thing that kept Van humble was the conviction that ASM was really God's doing. Another thing that kept him grounded amidst all this buoyant adulation was the realization that, more important than the awards and the rave reviews and even the royalties, was what the book was doing in people's hearts. Though it is hard to quantify the work of God's Kingdom, Van was beginning to get glimpses through the letters he was receiving from readers of ASM.

One man wrote to say: "I find my marriage to some extent renewed, for creeping separateness is a danger.... Yet more than this happened as your book ripped me apart: you led me into beauty and then into death, and in death and grief I found renewed devotion to living life as a channel for light, to allow God to work his holy mystery in me." A woman who was in the midst of reading the book called it "essential to my personal survival."[553] A man who was a professed non-Christian said of ASM that he was "entrapped by it, finally brought such tears I had to stop for a time. I've now finished it & can only offer mumbled thanks for an extraordinary experience."[554] A pastor of a large Presbyterian congregation preached one whole sermon on ASM and later used it as an illustration in another message.[555] Another woman wrote to say, "You have shown us the possibility of a faith with intellectual integrity, & it is toward that end (or beginning?) we are searching."[556] A grieving widow wrote: "Tears rolled down my cheeks last night as Davy died. Our love was like that: now lost. We are struggling to understand it. Maybe ... through

The Man Who Received "A Severe Mercy"

Religion ... but I want to believe because I cannot do otherwise..."557

Letters poured into Vancot from around the country and the globe, from Christians of all different denominations as well as non-Christians, from people in high school to people in old age, both men and women, from all walks of life. Responses were divided fairly equally between those who were touched by the love story, the conversion tale, and the grief observed. By May 1978, the book had already gone into five printings.558

In addition to being the year of the reviews, and the year of many letters flooding in, 1978 was also a year of travel for Van. That summer he journeyed again to England where he granted interviews to various newspapers and the BBC. David Griffiths, whom Van had known at Oxford, was now a Royal Chaplain at Windsor Castle. He treated Van to lunch one Sunday in the officers' mess of the Life Guards. Van also visited with Peter Crane, who lived on Boar's Hill in Oxford and they lunched together at Jesus College. When Van went round to have a look at the Studio, he discovered it was to be demolished. He decided therefore, to keep one memento: he retrieved the doorknocker and took it home to Vancot. Belle Hill, who was also in England that summer for a conference, traveled with Van to Dorset before they both flew home together.

In the fall of '78, Van traveled to Indiana for the inauguration of Lew Salter at Wabash College. Then he went on to Wheaton College, near Chicago, where he received an award for *A Severe Mercy* and spent time with Clyde Kilby.559

Eternity Magazine gave Van their Book of the Year Award and invited him to write an article for their December issue. His essay was entitled: "Christmas Eve: That Difficult Birth." Once again, in order to explain the Incarnation to those struggling intellectually with the idea, Van offered the illustration of God as the author of a novel putting himself as a character into his own story.560

The Christmas vacation of 1978 was very much like the one two years before. Only this time Van was working all hours on the final draft of his novel, *Gateway to Heaven*. Once again, he paused in his writing sprint to attend the carol service on Christmas Eve at St. Stephen's, followed by supper at Elk Hill. The next day Van enjoyed his Christmas dinner tradition with Jim and Margery Cocking of Lynchburg College and their young son, Van's godson, John.561

The previous four years were very important for Van: the year of "the twitches on the thread" (1975), the vocation (1976), the exaltation (1977) and the reviews (1978).562 However, these years were more about his writing, than anything else. What lay ahead in Van's future were some deep changes in his personal life, and one important step in a new direction he never imagined he would take.

Hopwood Hall, Lynchburg College, where Van often lectured

Author Photo

XXV

LETTERS, A NOVEL & "RETIREMENT"

I get mail, therefore I am.
Scott Adams

When Van began receiving letters from readers of *A Severe Mercy*, he made it his mission, as his mentor C. S. Lewis had done before him, to reply to each letter by return of post. On average, by 1979, he was receiving at least thirty letters per month. That meant writing about one response per day. Usually, Van would respond with a postcard. However, to the more serious inquirers with spiritual questions and problems, he would write a more in-depth letter, sometimes by hand, but usually typed on the same antique Royal Portable on which he had written ASM. Van also kept a record, what he at first entitled "Letters from Strangers," of each response he received to the book. He would quote, sometimes a phrase, perhaps a sentence, or even an entire paragraph, summarizing what each reader said. He also used this device to remember those who wrote to him a second time, often asking them to put the date of their first correspondence in the upper corner of their letter, so he could refer back to what had been said before.

In addition to the letters, there were *visits* from readers; all were welcomed. On one occasion, two women, friends to one another but strangers to Van, came to call because their husbands had left them. Both women were deeply touched by ASM and wanted Van's counsel in their situations. On another occasion, there was a woman who called Van on the telephone in the middle of the night to say that she was thinking of killing herself. She was reading ASM and said she half-believed in Christ but that she believed in reincarnation as well. The conversation, mostly one-sided, went on and on, and was quite strange. Van listened and gently suggested reasons why this woman should not take her own life.[563]

In May, Mike Yaconelli and Wayne Rice visited Lynchburg expressly to interview Van for the *Wittenburg Door*. The two young men were surprised by the simplicity in which the man was living whom they had travelled across the country to meet. Van noted that he never worried about money even when he had little; he always figured something in life would turn up. He also pointed out that he hadn't written ASM to become a successful author, but to tell a story. As was typical of Van, he asked that the two young men not take a photograph of him, though he allowed them to take photographs of the outside of Vancot, of a model of *Ettarre*, one of Davy's paintings—*The Wave of God*, and he gave them a photo of Davy for inclusion in their magazine.

Part way through the interview, Rice and Yaconelli complained, "But all of us can't take a year or two off to cruise the Bahamas." Van's response was to point out, to these young preachers, that if they did take time off from their careers it wouldn't make any difference. Then Van quoted his father, "It doesn't make a damn bit of difference what a man does until he's 45. It's what he does after that." However, Van noted, that if these young men *did* take a year off they would have the time of their lives, something they would never forget. Van concluded by asking them why they didn't do it. Yaconelli and Rice's response was to say they had better change the subject or they would end up quitting their jobs. Yaconelli later said that reading ASM and interviewing Van brought him "face to face with a lifetime of unfinished dreams and unfulfilled longings."[564]

At the end of the month of May, Lynchburg College named Van as the first recipient of their Distinguished Faculty Scholar Award. The honor was created to recognize college faculty "who by scholarly and related activities have brought the highest distinction to Lynchburg College."[565] As one member of the faculty noted years later: through writing ASM Van had done more than anyone else "to put Lynchburg College on the map."[566]

By this time, ASM had sold over 100,000 hardback copies. In the summer of 1979, Hodder & Stoughton in England and Bantam in North America published the book in paperback. In addition, Van had recorded the book on tape for the Martha Arney Library for the Blind.[567] However, all of this success was eclipsed for Van by another loss. Lady Frances, who had helped and encouraged him so much through the writing of ASM, died on August 20 after a long battle with lung cancer.[568]

Van didn't know it at the time, but in a way, God had already planned to provide him with some compensation for the loss of his dear friend, Lady Frances. In September, a fine Southern Lady, a Christian and a widow, who had grown up on a plantation owned by her father, wrote to Van from Hampton, South Carolina. Her name was Loring Ellis; she and Van were destined to exchange countless letters. After a number of years, they gave up writing letters to one another in preference for talking on the phone every evening. Loring's first missive to Van said simply: "I shall always be grateful to you for *A Severe Mercy* which brought me closer to God. Your mastery of the fine art of narrative and the perfect use of the English language is easily on a par with C. S. Lewis."[569]

The Man Who Received "A Severe Mercy"

In addition to responding to the many letters from correspondents, and teaching at Lynchburg College, the other bit of work Van did in 1979 was to revise and do the final edits on his 60s novel, *Gateway to Heaven*. However, Van's only publication during the year was *Jake's Place*, a parody of the opening chapter of *A Severe Mercy* that appeared in the June/July issue of the *Wittenburg Door*, and one other small piece for the *New Oxford Review*, a journal with which he would have a long association. The latter piece was a review of Chad Walsh's book, *The Literary Legacy of C. S. Lewis*. Van's review was entitled: *C. S. Lewis as Literature*.[570]

The highlight of 1980 for Van had to be the publication in May of *Gateway to Heaven* by Harper & Row. The initial print run was 15,000 copies. The flyleaf of the first edition describes the book as:

> ...The story of Richard Vallance, thoughtful and calm, a student at Oxford; Mary, the girl he marries, witty and imaginative, filled with joie de vivre; and their exploration of the complexities of marital love against the turbulent background of the 1960s.
>
> *Gateway to Heaven* tells of a memorable journey to France; the Vallances' stormy sea voyage from London to the Greek Isles, where Mary falls into frightful danger; an idyllic vacation in Hawaii; their response to the antiwar movement, the drug culture, and sexual freedom in the confusion of the sixties.
>
> Richard and Mary are propelled through these scenes of great beauty, adventure, and crises that test and temper their values, Christian faith, and mutual love. Underlying everything is the question of whether their marriage can survive an extraordinary challenge—one that forces them to confront the authentic nature of love.

The response of reviewers to *Gateway* was much more mixed than the reception they gave to ASM. D. Bruce Lockerbie, writing for *Eternity Magazine* found Van's novel to be "a strange and troubling book. Strange because it claims at the outset to be a *romance*, with 'ladies fair and knights on quest and roast dragon for dinner'; hence its improbabilities—miracles, ghosts, voices, and all—contrast too starkly with the March on the Pentagon or the garishness of Waikiki Beach. Romance and realism are a difficult blend to achieve, and Vanauken seems more comfortable with the former." Lockerbie found *Gateway* troubling for a few reasons: (1) Van's use of hesitation in his characters' dialogue, (2) "Mary's infidelity strikes too suddenly and capriciously" (3) "Vanauken's Anglicans have a diluted understanding of biblical authority. For them, apparently homosexuality is merely 'unnatural' like 'eating grapes with your ears.' and (4) Lockerbie maintained that, "commitment to God and his way must govern absolutely, not as some process of reasoning achieved by the dialectics of Oxford's intelligentsia."⁵⁷¹

Van found this particular review "strange and troubling" enough that he felt called to respond. *Eternity* printed his rebuttal to each of these points in their June issue. Responding to the first point, Van reiterated what he had said in response to critics of ASM, that the opposite of romanticism is *not* realism but classicism. All romantic novelists make use of realism in order to secure the suspension of disbelief. Secondly, Van noted that many writers use speech hesitation in fiction and that much of the humor in his book depended on this very quality. He felt it was too bad that Lockerbie was too grave and earnest to take this in. Thirdly, Van admitted that he and other Anglicans might have a diluted understanding of biblical authority, but the unnatural character of homosexual practice is precisely the point made by Paul in Romans 1:26-27. Finally, Van agreed with Mr. Lockerbie that commitment cannot be "in a vacuum" but must be "to someone or something." Mary's commitment in *Gateway* is to her husband; marriage is based upon commitment, not "Oxford dialectics."

However, Mr. Lockerbie was not the only reviewer to be disappointed with *Gateway to Heaven*. David G. Lalka, writing for *Christianity Today*, found GTH to exemplify "fine writing…. Yet the novel is tedious, unrealistic, and at points nearly boring. If one endures, however, he may experience great reward when the novel's symbolism opens to him. That moment may be worth all the others."⁵⁷²

Despite these somewhat negative reviews, GTH also had its admirers. Gregory Wolfe, writing for the Hillsdale Review, found *Gateway* to be "a novel of great beauty and depth, and swift action. The one fault in the book is that it packs so much into its 300 pages that it needs to be re-read. Ah, but this is a *felix culpa*."⁵⁷³ And Edgar F. Shannon, writing for *The American Oxonian* said, "Those who found Sheldon Vanauken's autobiographical work, *A Severe Mercy*, moving and well-crafted … will be gratified to have another volume from the same pen."⁵⁷⁴

One wonders whether Van's novel ever would have been published had he not been the bestselling author of ASM. On the other hand, perhaps the novel suffers from too much comparison to Van's first, autobiographical work. Van's good friend at Lynchburg College, Don Evans, is reported to have said when GTH came out: "Well ASM is really fiction. *Gateway to Heaven* is biography." He felt there was more fiction in the first and more fact in the second than Van would ever admit. Though Van denied the autobiographical element in GTH, it seemed obvious to those who knew him that the book was based, at least in part, on his own life experience. Regarding the reputed fictional nature of some elements in ASM, Clifton Potter once said that: "Van began to see Davy and the past the way an impressionist painter sees a landscape. The lines and memories are softened."⁵⁷⁵

The Man Who Received "A Severe Mercy"

If Potter's assessment of ASM is true, then one may conclude there are many people who love impressionism. By the time *Gateway* came out, sales of *A Severe Mercy* had grown to 175,000.[576] ASM was proving so popular that Harper & Row issued 10,000 copies of a special hardback "Davy's Edition." This included an "Afterword on the Genesis of *A Severe Mercy*", a full color frontispiece of Davy's "Sin Picture", as well as eight full pages of photos, and sketches drawn by Van.

In addition to these publications, there were others in 1980. Van's poem, "Cardinal", was printed in the May edition of *Eternity*. Furthermore, his essay on inclusive language, entitled "The Queen's English", was published in the April edition of *Christian Challenge* and in the May edition of *The Wittenburg Door*.

However, Van's publishing success that year was soured by an unfortunate event that left a bad taste in his mouth for years to come. The administration of Lynchburg College decided upon a policy of compulsory retirement for all faculty members at age sixty-five. Van had reached that high watermark in 1979 but was allowed to continue teaching for one more year, perhaps because of his high profile on campus, in the Lynchburg community, and in the world. Nonetheless, in 1980, he was forced to retire and he was "fit to be tied" about the whole matter. Rather than "retire" as the administration wanted, Van "resigned" in disgust. He retreated to Vancot and refused to even set foot on the campus of Lynchburg College for quite some time.[577]

Some of Van's friends and former students, including Dorothy Potter and Simone Reagor, tried to soften the blow of retirement for Van. To do so, they established The Vanauken Fellowship Fund at Lynchburg College in order to honor "a man who has profoundly altered our view of ourselves and of the world in which we live."[578] Upon Van's request, the fund was named not for him but for Davy. The goal of the organizers of this fund was to raise enough money to be able to send an outstanding rising senior at Lynchburg College to study for a summer at Oxford University. Letters were sent to over 1500 of Van's former students, including many who had known Davy. In fact, enough money was raised to achieve the original purpose of the organizers and the Davy Vanauken Fellowship Fund continues in existence to this day.

While Van certainly did not like being forced to retire from teaching, the event did have at least one positive effect: it freed up time for Van to do even more writing, and some deep thinking about a very important, personal decision....

PORTSMOUTH ABBEY, RHODE ISLAND

Author Photo

XXVI

HOME TO ROME

Everything worth thinking about has more than one cause.
M. Scott Peck, *In Search of Stones*

In the summer of 1980 Van wrote an essay entitled "The English Channel" that was published in the March 1981 edition of the *New Oxford Review*.[579] This essay dealt with the nudges Van was feeling to leave the Anglican for the Catholic fold. There were many factors leading Van to join the Catholic Church. In fact, I have counted about twenty nudges that, all put together, eventually pushed Van over the edge of the white cliffs of Dover and led him to swim the English Channel from Anglicanism to Catholicism.

It all began in Oxford, with Van's return to Christian faith after wandering in the maze of agnosticism, and then a vague theism, for many years. As he looked up at the spire of St. Mary's Church on the High Street, not only was he led to reconsider Christianity, he was led to think about the Catholic Church in particular. After all, he thought, the Catholic Church originally built the spire of St. Mary's, as well as so many other great churches and cathedrals in England. Perhaps her claim to be the one true Church needs careful consideration, just as the claims of Christ do. That was the first nudge.

The second followed on logically from the first. If the claims of Christ to be the Son of God were true, then what of his promise to Peter in Matthew 16:18-19?

> And I say also unto thee, that thou art Peter, and upon this rock I will build my church; and the gates of hell shall not prevail against it.
>
> And I will give unto thee the keys of the kingdom of heaven: and whatsoever thou shalt bind on earth shall be bound in heaven: and whatsoever thou shalt loose on earth shall be loosed in heaven.

What did Christ mean when he said: I will build my Church? Did he mean the Church in the singular, the visible Catholic Church, or did he, as Protestants argue, mean the invisible Church with its countless visible sects? Van concluded that the whole idea of the invisible Church was a sort of rationalization concocted by Protestants after the fact to support their break from Rome.

Next, Van wondered: why is it that the Catholic Church, the one claiming to be founded upon Peter the Rock, with Rome as its geographical center, why is it that this Church is twice as large as all the Eastern Orthodox churches put together, and also double the size of all Protestant denominations combined?

It seemed logical to Van that the claims of Rome should be examined first because it was the ancient center of Christendom. Furthermore, Van believed the Eastern Churches had accepted the authority and primacy of the successor of Peter for a thousand years, until the Great Schism of 1054, and the Church in England had accepted the Pope until Henry VIII came along. If any daughter of the Mother Church was a valid Church then Van was determined to remain Anglican, but the claims of the Mother were logically and chronologically prior, therefore they must be considered first.

There was also, Van realized early on, a strike against the Anglican Church. Her beginnings were not too auspicious. Henry VIII rejected the Pope's authority only so that he could divorce his wife and marry another. To Van's mind, other strikes against the Episcopal Church in the USA included: the decision to revise the Book of Common Prayer, the ordination of women priests, a laissez-faire attitude toward divorce, and seeming approval of homosexual practice. All of these changes in the Episcopal Church during the 70s certainly moved Van closer to Dover.

Some of the nudges pushing Van ever closer to swimming the channel were logical, intellectual, but some were almost mystical. One of these experiences occurred during Van and Davy's years in Oxford. They had gone on holiday to France with Edmund Dews. Attending Mass at a church near Avignon, Van decided he would go forward and take Communion. The thought hit him like a bolt of lightning: here is God in the hands of this wrinkled French priest. As Van received the host, he thought: now at last I have truly received Christ's body.[580]

In subsequent years when Van asked his friend, Dom Julian, if he would serve him Holy Communion, Julian told him he could not, that it was not allowed for him to serve the consecrated elements to one who had not professed the Catholic faith and joined the Church. Van must have felt some frustration at this, but at least the lines were clear: he had to swim that channel if he was going to partake of the Eucharist in a Catholic Church again.[581]

Another nudge toward the white cliffs came in the form of Van's reading. As has been mentioned, Evelyn Waugh's *Brideshead Revisited* was a favorite book ever since Oxford days. Van was quite impressed by the Catholic faith of the Marchmain family and how the Church kept drawing them each back— even Sebastian, battling alcoholism but ending up cared for in a monastery. Then there was Lord Marchmain, resistant to the faith almost to the very end of his life, but then on his deathbed, making the sign of the cross. In some ways, that poignant scene haunted Van for years.

The Man Who Received "A Severe Mercy"

John Henry Newman's *Apologia Pro Vita Sua* was another important influence. Newman's ideas regarding the development of doctrine helped Van tremendously. He especially appreciated what Newman had to say about the "fitness" of God, through the Magisterium of the Catholic Church, "retaining in the world a knowledge of Himself, so definite and distinct as to be proof against the energy of human skepticism."[582]

Van was intrigued by Ronald Knox's statement in his *Spiritual Aeneid* that Anglicanism "is not a system of religion nor a body of truth, but a feeling, a tradition, its roots intertwined with associations of national history and of family life; you do not learn it, you grow into it; you do not forget it, you grow out of it."[583] Perhaps Van was growing out of Anglicanism, just as Knox had, and growing into the Catholic Church. However, he was not there yet.

C. S. Lewis was, of course, the greatest influence upon Van's thinking and life, above any other author. Lewis was a mentor to Van not only through his books, but through his letters and through their personal conversations as well. Van recognized in Lewis a Catholic imagination. One of the chief characters in Lewis' earliest Christian work was Mother Kirk in *The Pilgrim's Regress*. Narnia had a High King—*Peter*. The Grey City in *The Great Divorce* was Purgatory, at least for those who chose to leave it for the solidity of Heaven. Lewis believed in praying for the dead and practiced confession to a priest, albeit an *Anglican* monk. In his theological works, Lewis never talked about Sola Fidei or Sola Scriptura, two of the rally cries of the Reformation. So why, Van wondered, did Lewis never become Catholic? Van had tried to draw Lewis out on the subject, all to no avail. Then, in 1979, Van took a trip to Ireland with Dom Julian Stead. Seeing the sectarian strife there led Van to think that it would have been hard, if not impossible for Lewis to have become Catholic, given his Ulster Protestant upbringing. Suddenly, Lewis' teaching on the subject, and the fact that Lewis never became Catholic, were less important in deciding Van's course of action. All the same, Lewis' Catholic imagination continued to guide Van and prepare his mind for the Catholic Church.[584]

The dangers of modernism and neo-modernism (naturalism) invading the Church, also concerned Van. How was the Church to stand against it? Van began to see an answer in the teaching authority of the Church, the Catholic Magisterium. In fact, he thought, how can the Church survive without the Magisterium? If a relatively simple, almost modern document like the United States Constitution needs the authoritative interpretation of the Supreme Court, then how much more does the Bible (written so long ago and over hundreds if not thousands of years) need the authoritative interpretation of the Catholic Magisterium? Van was convinced that the Holy Spirit had not ceased to infallibly guide the Catholic Church. One of the most persuasive arguments for this, to Van's mind, was the fact that not a single sinful pope down through history had ever altered the Church's doctrine in a wrong direction.

Furthermore, if the Evangelical and Eastern Orthodox wings were again to join with the Church at Rome, what a considerable force for good it would be. Van wished that the Anglican Church as a whole would go with him to reunite with the Chair of Peter. However, the winds of change were not blowing in that direction at the time. What was Van to do?

In 1978, an extraordinary event took place: the selection of Karol Wojtyla as the next Pope, John Paul II. Here was a Pope, Van felt, truly acting as a Father to all the faithful, a Pope who with charisma and *joie de vivre* was showing the world how attractive Christianity could be. In 1980, Van wrote a review of the Pope's play, *The Jeweler's Shop*. It was published under the title "John Paul—Another Dimension" in the October edition of the *New Oxford Review*. Van loved the play and what it had to say about the sacrament of Christian marriage; in future years, Van gave it to many young couples as an engagement or wedding gift.

At this point, as Van stood atop the white cliffs, he could see no doctrinal obstacle to becoming Catholic. The Magisterium and infallibility of the Pope, in his rare *ex cathedra* pronouncements, were selling points to Van, not roadblocks. He had long ago in Oxford, through conversations with Julian Stead, come to accept the Catholic view of Mary. Van had countless reasons *for* joining the Catholic Church, but still he held back. His mind said: "go" but his heart said: "stay." After all, hadn't he been "born again" and nurtured in the Anglican Church? Weren't Davy's ashes scattered in two Anglican churchyards, one in Virginia and one in England? He could hear the gentle, pleading voices of all his friends at St. Stephen's saying: "Don't leave us." Thus, in 1980, while Van published his "English Channel" essay, laying out all the reasons for reunion with Rome, he nevertheless lingered on the white cliffs of Dover.

When Van's essay was published in March 1981, it triggered a variety of responses, some caustic, some praiseworthy, some pleading with Van to remain Anglican, others urging him to join them in the Catholic Church. Van had been camping out on the English side of the channel, every so often dipping his toe in the water and checking the temperature, ever since that visit to Ireland with Dom Julian in 1979. He took some comfort from the fact that it took a while for Newman, Chesterton and Knox to make up their minds; and then there was Lewis who never swam the channel. Perhaps Van could remain in Dover for as long as he wished. Nonetheless, he prayed, hoping something would happen to push him one way or the other.

In May of 1981, Van went to Portsmouth Abbey in Rhode Island to visit with Julian and help prepare for publication his book of Christian poetry, *There*

The Man Who Received "A Severe Mercy"

Shines Forth Christ, for which Van had written the Introduction. However, Van was also waiting for some special act of providence, some sign from God that *now* was the time for him to join the Catholic Church.

Nothing happened. However, Van asked Julian to examine him in the faith just in case. While Van was at the Abbey, Peter Kreeft and Tom Howard stopped by for a visit. Peter and Tom were both authors and college professors; they had come to know Van after writing to express their appreciation of *A Severe Mercy*. Peter was and is a Catholic and, at the time, Tom was an Anglican, but like Van, he too was considering the claims of the Catholic Church. In the course of conversation, Peter asked both Tom and Van a question: if you knew you were going to die tomorrow, what would you do about the Church? Tom wasn't certain, but Van said that he would ask Julian to receive him immediately. After all, Van figured, if he was going to die the next day he couldn't go back to his beloved St. Stephen's, so why not take the plunge into the Channel?

After spending a week in Portsmouth, Van went on to Quebec where he spent some time with Georges Allaire, a Christian philosopher who, like Peter and Tom, had gotten to know Van through *A Severe Mercy*. Georges had helped Van to better understand both G. K. Chesterton and the case for the Catholic Church. However, Georges told Van he couldn't help him make the final determination about what only he, Van, must choose.

Back home in Lynchburg, sometime later, Van thought over all that had taken place on his trip. On the refrigerator door in his tiny kitchen Van had a poster that proclaimed: "Not to decide is to decide." (In fact, the yellowed poster was still there many years later when I visited Vancot.) Looking at that poster, Van realized it was time to stop drifting. Just as he had concluded at Oxford in the 50s that he could not reject Christ, so he now came to the decision that he could not reject the Catholic Church. Van prayed over the decision, then he called Julian. Father Stead, one of the most gracious men anyone could ever hope to meet, had been very patient in answering all of Van's questions about the Church through the years. Furthermore, Julian had never pressed Van to make a decision. Now, the date was set; Van's reception into the Church by Julian at Portsmouth Abbey would be on August 15, the day the Catholic Church celebrates the Assumption of Mary into Heaven. After their telephone call, Julian wrote to Van and told him that he had prayed, every day for thirty years, for Van to become Catholic.

When August 15 rolled around, Julian received Van as planned. Peter Kreeft stood as Van's sponsor. Van chose not to waive the conditional baptism. Bishop Ansgar Nelson of the Order of Saint Benedict anointed Van in confirmation. Cardinal Hume, OSB, from England, was visiting Portsmouth Abbey and he was the first person to whom Van was introduced as a Catholic.

It all seemed so appropriate, as if a hidden hand had arranged it.

Back home in Virginia, Van went to Mass for the first time at Holy Cross in Lynchburg. He had already been introduced to Father Anthony Warner. As the Mass began that Saturday night, Van was astonished to learn that the text for the day was Matthew 16, the Scripture that led Van to consider the claims of Rome in the first place. Again, was there a hidden hand moving the chess pieces of Van's life, was someone smiling on him from above?

Van had already decided he would go to service one last time at St. Stephen's to tell all his friends about his joining the Catholic Church. Then, between Saturday night and Sunday morning, it suddenly hit him: why could he not go on attending St. Stephen's for Sunday morning services so long as he did not take Communion? It seemed there was no reason why not. Yet, it was almost like he had to be willing to sacrifice what was dearest to him before this option was revealed, like Abraham being provided a ram in the thicket *after* his willingness to sacrifice Isaac was quite clear.[585] Van continued to attend services, both at St. Stephen's and at Holy Cross, for many years to come.

St. Stephen's Episcopal Church, Forest, Virginia

Author Photo

Holy Cross Catholic Church, Lynchburg, Virginia

Author Photo

XXVIII

WRITING AWAY

> Of making many books, there is no end.
> Ecclesiastes 12:12

After joining the Catholic Church, Van focused much of his time on writing, both for publication and continuing what he sometimes called his "postcard ministry", responding to readers who wrote to him about his books. On the publication side of things, Van wrote "An Afterword on the Genesis of *Gateway to Heaven*", printed in the September 1980 edition of the *New Oxford Review*.[586] The following year, Bantam published their edition of *Gateway to Heaven*, printing 46,000 copies, thus bringing the total number of copies in print to 61,000.[587]

Now that Van had retired/resigned from teaching, he had more time to devote to writing—especially the writing of essays for publication in various journals and magazines. His piece entitled "God's Will" was published in the June 21, 1981 edition of *The Living Church* and his article entitled "Unisexism: Second Thoughts on Women's Liberation" and his poem, "Pussycat", appeared in the December 81 issue of the *New Oxford Review*.

A number of Van's friends had difficulty accepting his change in viewpoint from his more radical 1960s activist days. Belle Hill, for one, thought Van had gotten too conservative. She grew tired of his "anti-feminist rhetoric" and attributed it to his becoming Roman Catholic. Clifton Potter thought Van was moving in the direction of the Catholic Church as early as the 1960s. He even told Van, "Eventually you will go home to Rome." Van pooh-poohed it at the time. However, when he did join the Catholic Church, Clifton was a bit surprised at just how conservative Van became. Potter later said of his former teacher and colleague, "Van reverted to a very 19th century view of the relationship between the sexes. In the 60s, he thought it was right that he and Davy had chosen not to have children. At that time, he said that having children was a form of enslavement for women. Later on, he regretted that he and Davy had not had children. Van reinvented himself all the time."[588]

Van's story of his latest "reinvention", his turn to the Catholic Church entitled "Crossing the Channel", appeared in the spring 1982 edition of *Communio*. As was mentioned in the previous chapter, Van was fascinated by C. S. Lewis' perspective on the Catholic Church. Thus, a book written by one of Van's correspondents who had also known Lewis, Christopher Derrick, greatly intrigued him. Van wrote a review of Derrick's *C. S. Lewis & the Church of Rome*, entitled "Mere Christian or Divided Man?" It was published in the May 1982 edition of the *New Oxford Review*.

Van's essay, "The Bachelor", written a couple of years before, appeared in the summer edition of the *Hillsdale Review*. In this article, Van argued that it was high time to recognize the role of the bachelor in society as one of dignity with its own rewards. If a bachelor wants to share an apartment with another bachelor, he should do so without a care for what other people think, for the idea that "because a man is not married therefore he must be a homosexual" is ridiculous. If the bachelor finds himself lonely, he should try to find other bachelors with whom he can develop friendships, for true friendship is one of the great gifts of life. Above all, Van asserted, the bachelor should walk through life with his head held high.[589]

As important as Van's publications were, there was another bit of writing he valued even more, and viewed as a sacred trust: his "postcard ministry." In January 1982, that ministry included one Tracy Lee Simmons, a senior at the University of Cincinnati, majoring in English and History. He wrote to Van:

> I've read *A Severe Mercy* and am compelled to express profound thanks that you wrote it at all. I stagger for words. What a gift you've given to all other Christians! I got into C. S. Lewis as a freshman and my life hasn't been the same since. His name on the cover led me to buy *A Severe Mercy*—but what grace that I did! My mother is reading it now and I bought one for my fiancée.[590]

Tracy and Van exchanged a number of letters and postcards in the ensuing months. Tracy wrote again in May to tell of the affect of ASM on his fiancée Sandy:

> She told me yesterday that she has <u>never</u> read a book that touched her so, and <u>meant</u> so much to her as *A Severe Mercy*. Back in January, she said she sat down one Sunday afternoon at 3:30 and read until 10:30, slowly, letting each bit, each phrase sink in. And we both had felt the same on one thing: when Davy's death came, we didn't really feel like crying—at least, not the way we thought we would—we were sobered yet numbed. I for one thought I'd be free from great emotion from then on. But, oh, the Illumination of the Past! The Remembering! I felt pierced as by a sword. It had the same effect on her. And in another way she and I felt alike—and perhaps this is the most important thing—at the end you had the effect upon us that all great literature written to His glory should have: you turned our heads and our hearts upward. There is no doubt that the Spirit worked through you in a more than special way. Sure, He <u>could</u> have said the same things to us through someone else, but the fact is that he used <u>you</u>, and I can't help believing that that says some things about you that I cannot utter.[591]

The Man Who Received "A Severe Mercy"

In June, Tracy asked Van to be his sponsor upon entrance into the Catholic Church. He was the first among a number of people Van led to Catholicism. Tracy offered to come to Lynchburg for the ceremony, but Van's old friend George Palmer who lived in Cincinnati was dying of cancer and longing for a visit. Thus, Van decided to fly to Cincinnati and minister to the needs of two friends, one beginning a new turn in his walk with God, the other still searching for a God he could believe in.

Tracy's reception at St. George's Church was certainly a special time, with Van giving to Tracy the ancient Russian cross that Peter Kreeft had given to him at his reception into the Catholic Church. More meaningful still were Van's talks with his old friend George. Years before, Van had written to George from Oxford, telling his agnostic friend of his return to Christian faith. At that time, Van put the case for Christ to George as powerfully as he could. Now, George admitted that perhaps his thought had remained immature. Was God pulling on the thread attached to George's soul? Van hoped so.

Van and George talked late into the evening, night after night during Van's five-day visit. They spoke of their days as radio announcers, and their time together in the Pacific War. Van even mentioned the television version of *Brideshead Revisited* that he had seen a few months before. He had urged George to see the television miniseries and George had been impressed with the death of Lord Marchmain, making the sign of the cross. George mentioned how so many of his friends who knew he was dying did not come to visit him anymore. Obviously, Van was different. Van was able to speak to George about Davy's death and his strong belief that he would see her again. Then, George made a chance comment about the Shroud of Turin. Van had recently read a good deal about this supposed burial shroud of Jesus and was able to intelligently talk about it with his friend. Was George's interest in the subject a sign of interest in Jesus who, possibly, had been buried in that shroud? Again, Van hoped so.

A few days after Van returned to Lynchburg he telephoned George to see how he was doing. His friend could not stop expressing his deep gratitude for Van's visit. Days later, George died. Had he thought of Lord Marchmain in his final moments? There was no way to know. Nonetheless, Van prayed for George when he heard of his death, and hoped that he would be one like Emeth, received by Aslan in the "new Narnia."[592]

Van wrote up the story of Tracy and George under the title "The Knight's Move." *Fidelity Magazine* published that essay in June 1983. Van wrote another essay for *Fidelity* entitled "The False Sanction of Eros." It appeared in their December issue. That essay in particular had an interesting publishing history. *Christianity Today* accepted the article for approximate simultaneous publication along with *Fidelity*. However, according to Van, Jerry Falwell's

Fundamentalist Journal somehow planned to publish the same article without permission, so *Christianity Today* bowed out. Falwell eventually repaid *Christianity Today* what they had paid Van, paid Van again, and ran the essay in the supplement of the Moral Majority Report, September 1984. The whole experience soured Van's attitude just a bit toward his fellow Lynchburg resident, Jerry Falwell.[593]

Van had four other articles also published in 1984. There was a mini-essay entitled "Genres" that appeared in the January edition of *Motif*. Van's venture in what he called "whatifery" entitled "After the South Won" appeared in the spring edition of *The Southern Partisan*. His essay "Freedom vs. Equality" appeared in the summer *Southern Partisan* and his article "All God and All Man" appeared in the September edition of the *National Catholic Register*.

However, Van's major bit of writing for 1984 was a sequel to *A Severe Mercy* entitled *Under the Mercy*. He began writing the book in January and finished it about six months later.[594] The book chronicled his life after Davy's death up to the time of writing.

Meanwhile, Van's postcard ministry was galloping along at a rapid pace. Every once in a while, old friends were also part of that ministry. In February 1985, Van received a letter from Allene Stidham Lindsey, his friend and Davy's from Indianapolis, the one who shared a pleasant evening with them in Honolulu on December 6, 1941. She wrote to say...

> A strange little story. My granddaughter Kimmy (about 18) was going with a young man named Russ, and she visited his parents and sister—and came down from there to spend a day with us. We were standing in the kitchen talking, she with beach towel, sandwich, sunglasses, and book. She dropped the book, a battered paperback, and I stopped to pick it up: *A Severe Mercy* by an author named Sheldon Vanauken. My reaction was quick. I said, "Kim, where did you get this book?" "It's Russ' sister's," she said. "She's read it at least four times and loves it above everything she's ever read before. I love it too; I've never read anything like it." I said, "Kimmy, I am the Allene in the book!" Can you imagine her reaction?—the whys, hows, whens, and the what-happened-thens? I told her a little of our times together and how we were still infrequently in touch. Then, after she'd gone back to Russ' home, she came back to our house again a couple of days later with a request that quite took me aback: Russ' sister wanted me, of all things, to autograph her book. I demurred—quite strongly—until Kimmy pleaded that I, her Grams, could not deny her anything (quite true, by the way). So I reluctantly wrote on the tattered frontispiece: "This is the story of two remarkable friends of mine. I'm happy that you've met them too. Allene Lindsey."[595]

The Man Who Received "A Severe Mercy"

In addition to the friendships Van cultivated through the mail, there were many other good friends close to home. One of those, who had first written to Van about *A Severe Mercy*, was syndicated columnist Cal Thomas who was then working for Jerry Falwell's Moral Majority. Despite Van's bad experience with the Falwell group over the publication of his essay, "The False Sanction of Eros", Van got on well with Cal Thomas.

In May 1985, Van drove with Cal and his son from Lynchburg to Washington, D. C., to see *C. S. Lewis on Stage* performed by Tom Key at The Kennedy Center. The Washington Arts Group and the C. S. Lewis Institute hosted the event. Jim Houston, one of the founders of the Institute, had known Van and Davy at Oxford. At the event, Van met Senator Mark Hatfield and Representative Don Bonkers who introduced him to the sold-out audience. Van spoke for three minutes about his last meeting with C. S. Lewis, the day of his death, and Lewis' "Christians never say good-bye" comment outside The Eastgate Hotel. A sort of hush of approval followed Van's talk and then applause that lasted almost as long as the speech itself. Van thought Tom Key did a very good job as C. S. Lewis. At intermission and at a reception following the performance, dozens of people came up to Van to tell him how much *A Severe Mercy* had meant to them; one couple said it had saved their marriage. Van had a good talk with Cal, driving home in the rain that night, arriving back at Vancot at 3 am.[596]

Dom Julian Stead

Author Photo

XXIX

UNDER THE MERCY

> Once in a very rare while an absolutely perfect, eternally necessary title emerges. It was with a leap of joy that I read your plan to call your proposed book, not "Beyond 'The Severe Mercy'" but instead UNDER THE MERCY.
>
> Peter Kreeft, in a letter to Sheldon Vanauken

The big event for Van in 1985 was the publication of *Under the Mercy*, printed by American publisher Thomas Nelson in June and British publisher Hodder & Stoughton in the fall.[597] In fact, Van visited England that year to coincide with the release of the book.[598]

The reviews of *Under the Mercy* by Van's friends and correspondents were enthusiastic to say the least. Dom Julian wrote, "Most readers of *A Severe Mercy* will be excited at the prospect of reading its sequel.... *A Severe Mercy* was in the genre of Augustine's *Confessions*; *Under the Mercy* might be comparable to Newman's *Apologia*."

Clyde Kilby called it "a great book ... on plain Christianity!"

Barbara Hoffman, professor of English at Marywood College in Scranton, Pennsylvania, whom Van called "blithe lady Barbara, a guide in the ways of the Church", also loved the book. She wrote, "*A Severe Mercy* is the 'autobiography of a love'—the great love of a lifetime. *Under the Mercy* is the 'autobiography of the man himself—the ideas that shaped his life."

Tracy Simmons, in sharing his opinion of UTM, gave Van this analogy:

> There is a beautiful photo on Father Paul's office wall of a huge seascape and vast sky—all you see except for a tiny sail on the horizon. The caption reads: 'Ships are safe and secure in harbor. But that is not what ships are made for.' I think that not only sums up the message of UTM but is the spirit of all your work: the seeking and striving in order to find and attain, because that is what we're 'made for.'[599]

Of the title, Peter Kreeft said,

> Do you know that there are 'Under the Mercy' buttons? Do you know that a number of people are signing their letters "Under the Mercy" now? A fire is spreading. It [Under the Mercy] is metaphysically exact. It is our cosmic locus, and telos and logos and mythos and ethos. It is how we are born and how we shall die. I think it will be a three-word road map for many souls. Just think: if you and Davy hadn't made it

live, and then made it known through *A Severe Mercy*, few would have ventured into the brambles of Charles Williams to get it (even if they are gold brambles).[600]

Frank Fickes, Van's old friend from Wabash days, editor of *The Bachelor* in their senior year, said this about *Under the Mercy* in a letter to Van: "You write with an ability that would have had Osborne [one of their teachers] nodding approvingly."[601]

Finally, Thomas Howard said of this book, "It is vintage—<u>vintage</u> Van."[602]

However, some readers did not react as positively to this second autobiographical offering from Van's pen. Bruce Nygren, Executive Editor of Trade Books with Thomas Nelson, Van's publisher, wrote to Van in November 1984. He spoke in superlative terms of *A Severe Mercy*, but then of *Under the Mercy* he said, "Parts of the book are brilliant, abundant in wit and insight especially where you take the reader by the hand and walk the trails of your pilgrimage. But…some essays seemed to interrupt the story—<u>your story</u>… particularly 'the South Won'…I wanted to say, 'Interesting stuff…but get on with what happened to <u>you</u>! What happened to that man and his dreams?'"[603]

In Van's defense, it should be noted that Thomas Nelson Publishers suggested that he write a little narrative to "thread" together the essays in *Under the Mercy*. The important things to Van were the essays, not his own life story. In fact, as he says at the beginning of the book, he was hesitant to write a second autobiographical tome. In many ways, he did the best job he could, threading together the essays with narrative, and many who read the book appreciated this.

After *Under the Mercy*, Van continued to write an impressive number of essays, reviews, short satirical pieces, poems and editorials for various publications throughout the eighties and nineties; over sixty of these were published between 1983 and 1996. At the beginning of 1986, the *New Oxford Review* published yet another of Van's essays entitled "Seams in the Seamless Garment." It was a response to an article written by his friend, Peter Kreeft. "The Seamless Garment" was a phrase introduced by Cardinal Bernardin to indicate the weaving together of human-life issues into one, thus affirming the sanctity of life in regard not only to the issues of abortion and euthanasia, but also including capital punishment. Van questioned the implications of this concept, whether it meant that *no* human life could be shortened under any circumstances by deliberate human action. In his essay, Van affirmed his belief in the Just War theory, the right to bear arms and capital punishment.[604]

In April 1986, *Catholicism in Crisis* published Van's article "Listening to the Homosexual." In the essay, Van argued for the importance of, yes, listening to the homosexual in love, but that does not mean that we must, as Christians, condone homosexual practice, which the Bible declares to be sin.[605]

The Man Who Received "A Severe Mercy"

Van's thoughts on this subject certainly had changed over the years. Lynchburg College students asked his opinion on the subject back in the 1950s. Having sought the advice of his mentor C. S. Lewis, Van passed on to those students a conservative stance on the issue. However, in the 1960s, as Van wandered from the church, he also came to the point of approving homosexual practice. It was important enough to him to address the issue in his novel, *Gateway to Heaven*. Then, with his return to the Obedience in the 70s, and his entrance into the Catholic Church in 1981, Van reverted to a conservative position.

Nonetheless, Van was able to show compassion to those seeking his advice about homosexuality. In October 1983, he received a letter from yet another admirer of *A Severe Mercy*, a young man in graduate school. This correspondent wrote,

> I just finished *A Severe Mercy*. A wonderful book, this. I shed many tears and shared much laughter, celebrating your joy in love, life, and God. I found deep comfort in your approach to death, your understanding of time and timelessness, and your jealousy of God. I, too, have felt these things ... and have known, intimately, the bittersweet pain of love and the dark and lonely searchings of a journey towards Christ. Your book was, to an astonishing extent, a version of my life—up to a point. I too have been blessed (all four years at university and still) with a wondrous, loving relationship ... inloveness. And I have, in the past, felt our love to be competing with our faith; but it seems when push comes to shove, God wins. I am a homosexual. My lover is a man. We are both Christians, yet troubled by our sexuality in the face of some religious condemnation ... yet monogamous, committed. In all-out soul searching, we simply cannot understand why our love is damnably sinful. Abstinence seems such an unfair and unjust burden ... it doesn't seem a just or Christian answer. I have read everything, talked to many Christians, and had two years of counseling. I want to share my love for God and for my fellowman and to celebrate the joys of inloveness with my partner in our awe-full, spiritually exciting love. Is it a blessing or am I sinning, and if so, damnably? ... Tell me. Pull no punches.[606]

Van's response to this correspondent was to show sympathy and understanding. He told the young man about his novel, *Gateway to Heaven*, and encouraged him to read it and further share his thoughts. Then Van posed this question, "If you became convinced that homosexual practice was wrong, would you accept celibacy?" Van further suggested that the first and most important question is whether Christ is FIRST. As to whether homosexual practice is sin, Van's response was that of Mary's father to her in *Gateway to Heaven*: "If God has a word for you, He won't speak it to me."[607]

Another essay that displayed how conservative Van had become on certain social issues was "The Iron Law of Home" published in the August 1986 issue of *Fidelity*. In this article, Van pointed out what was obvious to many in the 1980s: the home is endangered. By "the home" he clearly meant the nuclear family of father, mother (who stays at home at least part-time) and one or more children. Van pointed out, rightly, that the creation and maintenance of a home requires a homemaker; that is the "iron law of home." However, Van also maintained that this homemaker should be the woman, a position that certainly not all of his readers would have agreed with. He stated, categorically, that humanity is specialized into protective breadwinners (males) and mothering homemakers (females). Van rightly pointed out that with all the modern conveniences invented in the twentieth century the job of homemaking and the time required to fulfill it had shrunk by half. However, there was still half a job to do. Thus, if the woman were to take a full-time job outside the home, the job of homemaking would be sorely neglected. I imagine that to a number of readers this article begged the question: why could not the man be a homemaker?[608]

In June 1986, Van's fourth book addressed yet another controversial subject: Van's love for the Old South. Southron Press in North America and Churchman's in the United Kingdom published Van's Oxford Thesis—*The Glittering Illusion: English Sympathy for the Southern Confederacy*.[609] As Van stated in the "Author's Note" at the beginning of the book, this thesis was first written in 1952, revised in 1957 and further revised for publication in 1986. The two special essays in the Epilogue, "What the South Fought For" and "After the South Won", were originally published in the Southern Partisan magazine in the spring and summer of 1984. The book raised the question: given the close ties between England and the Southern States in America, why did the British never enter the Civil War on the side of the Confederacy? Van's answer was: because of "The Glittering Illusion", the idea present in the minds of so many in power in Britain at that time that the South simply could not lose the War, not with such great generals and fine men as Robert E. Lee and Stonewall Jackson at the helm.

Van had considered publishing his thesis back in the 1950s, but then he was caught up in the turmoil and grief related to Davy's death.[610] One wonders whether such a thesis as Van's would have found a publisher had Van not already become a bestselling author with the publication of *A Severe Mercy*. His most controversial contention, at least for his Yankee readers, was that the South might have been a better place if the Confederates had won the war.[611]

Years after publishing *The Glittering Illusion*, Van delivered a lecture entitled "C. S. Lewis and The Old South." In that lecture, Van set forth his reasons for believing that the Old South fit precisely into Lewis' definition of "Old Western Man" as articulated in Lewis' inaugural lecture at Cambridge,

The Man Who Received "A Severe Mercy"

in which Lewis referred to himself as a "dinosaur." At the end of the lecture Van stated:

> I close with a question. As Richard Weaver says so powerfully, the Southern tradition is at bay. Does it still survive? Are we who hold to that tradition Old Western man? If we are dismayed by multiculturalism, by deconstructionism, by moral relativism, have we any hope of holding onto and of passing on that tradition? I do not know, I cannot precisely define, what New Western Man is, though there have been many hints along the way—and C. S. Lewis's *Abolition of Man* offers a grim prophecy. Each of us must decide, and decide what he himself is.
>
> "I cannot close without saying, as the Cambridge undergraduates did, that I—to no one's surprise—take my stand as a 'dino.' And hope that I and fellow 'dinos' can make a difference. (*Crisis*, December 1993, p. 30.)

In the late 80s, Van continued to write essays, reviews, forewords and editorials for various publications. The topics touched by Van's pen ranged from Catholicism to evolution, abortion to the death penalty, and various other issues sprinkled in between. Van also continued to faithfully respond to the many strangers who wrote to him, telephoned, or came by for a visit, mostly in response to *A Severe Mercy*. At the beginning of 1987, I was one of those strangers, writing to Sheldon Vanauken, asking him to come and speak at Princeton Seminary. He politely declined, mentioning in passing that he would be in Australia and New Zealand[612] for the month of March, inviting me to stop by Vancot if I were ever to come down to the South. By 1987, I'm sure Van was accustomed to many unusual letters and invitations from fans. However, nothing could have quite prepared him for a phone call he received one day in 1988 from a woman who was touched by ASM in a unique way.

MARION

Photo Courtesy of Elizabeth Rose

XXVIII

THE LITTLE LOST MARION AND OTHER MERCIES

> I once was lost but now am found.
>
> John Newton, *Amazing Grace*

The voice on the other end of the telephone line was not quite like Davy's, more like her sister. Van had waited for this call for a long time, but now that it was really happening, it was truly amazing. It was spring 1988, and Van was talking to Davy's long lost daughter who had been given up for adoption at birth, sixty years before.[613]

The phone call had come about like this. After Davy's death, Van longed to make connection with Davy's daughter, whom she had named Marion. He contacted the agency that had handled the adoption and had discussions with the powers-that-be. He told the officials that he didn't necessarily want to meet Marion or interfere in her life; he simply wanted to tell her about her birth mother and pass on a few precious things that had belonged to Davy. The adoption agency seemed to be close to putting Van in contact with Marion but then, finally, refused. Thus, Van gave up ... for a time.

Meanwhile, Marion was living out her own life on the west coast. She had trained as a nurse and married a doctor. Together she and her husband raised three children. Coincidentally, her husband loved sailing, and their son inherited the same interest. At different points in her life, Marion was on the verge of searching for her birth parents, but she always pulled back. Maybe it would be better not to know.

Over the years, attitudes about adoption changed. A movement began to put children in touch with their biological parents. Being aware of the movement, Van wrote to Betty Jean Lifton—author, adoption counselor and lecturer on the subject. He sent her a copy of *A Severe Mercy*, thus enlisting her help. Lifton, in turn, contacted the adoption agency that handled Marion's case. At first, she was rebuffed, but then she talked a woman at the agency into reading ASM. That woman then telephoned Marion and said, "I'm looking at a photo of your birth mother. She's no longer living, but she was beautiful, and an artist, and her husband is looking for you."

Marion immediately scoured the bookstores for a copy of *A Severe Mercy*. When she found one, she stared for a long time at the photo on the back cover of Van and her mother. Her immediate response was: "Found at last! Incredible, choking joy! Thanksgiving. Yet sadness also—sadness that I could not touch [my mother] hold her, and be held. Smiling with tears on my cheeks."

Next, Marion telephoned Van. That joyful conversation led to many others. Later, when Marion sat down to read ASM, she found it "At once thrilling and scary! My heart pounding. Almost breathless with discovery, unable to sleep till I'd read every word. Excited beyond belief, sobbing, my pillow wet with tears. Seeing my *mother* as a young woman loving the things I loved—beauty, dogs, sails in the wind, music. I had been starving for this—and now the book."

In the fall of 1988, Marion went to visit Van in Lynchburg. They spent a week together before Marion journeyed north to meet Davy's sister and niece. Marion must have seemed to Van like an older version of Davy, small of stature, warm and eager in her personality. Any awkwardness between the two quickly vanished. They had long talks together, went for drives in the country with the brilliant autumn leaves falling down all around; they prayed at the old stone cross in St. Stephen's churchyard. Marion met Van's friends who had known her mother and felt their warm welcome. Van gave to Marion a Caucasian rug on which Davy had played as a child. That night Marion clung to that rug as she went to sleep. Eventually, Marion felt so close to Van she asked if she might call him "Father." Marion later said that reading ASM and meeting Van was "God's answer to my prayer, the completion of a lifetime of longing for my *mother*, and growing closer to her God and mine."[614]

Marion and Van stayed in close touch after she returned home. Van even sent her one of Davy's paintings. In addition, Marion continued to correspond with her newfound aunt, cousin, and friends of Van who had known her mother. An entirely new world had opened up.[615]

Meanwhile, Van's world went on much as it was before. He continued to spend good times with friends. Some were passing, like Shirley Rosser who was laid to rest in St. Stephen's churchyard in the fall of '87.[616] However, others were still around like Belle Hill and Dick Seymann, "a sturdy agnostic with a sense of humor, and a fellow sailor."[617] In addition, Van stayed in touch with many "friends" through the mail. By this time, his postcard ministry had touched thousands of lives, and many of those, fifty or more, became regular correspondents.

In the summer of 1988, Van became aware of one, rather unusual reaction to *A Severe Mercy*. In March of that year, a young couple from Wheaton College, 23-year-old Scott Swanson and 22-year-old Carolyn MacLean, inspired by ASM, had eloped to Lake Geneva, Wisconsin.[618] After a brief, post-wedding visit to see Carolyn's grandmother in Flint, Michigan, the couple planned to drive 350 miles to visit Scott's parents in Elgin, Illinois. Instead, they

The Man Who Received "A Severe Mercy"

abandoned Carolyn's red BMW, putting the keys under the floor mat along with their identification and credit cards, near a Chicago police station, and boarded a flight for San Diego using assumed names. Upon arrival on the west coast, they settled into a $400-per-month apartment in Mission Beach and obtained jobs in a local sandwich shop. There they planned to construct their own "Shining Barrier" of exclusive love.

Meanwhile, back in Illinois, Carolyn's BMW was stolen and later abandoned. The police began an all-out, multi-state search for the missing couple. Scott and Carolyn's families, not to mention their many friends and teachers at Wheaton were frantic with worry. The story made the headlines of *USA Today*, *The New York Times*, *The Chicago Tribune*, *People Magazine* and countless other publications. Scott and Carolyn read those headlines at a local library in San Diego; as they did so, the consequences of their actions began to sink in. Finally, at the end of July, struggling financially and longing for the fellowship of their families, they wrote an eight-page letter to their parents explaining their actions and their whereabouts. The two families were subsequently reunited with their son and daughter.

When Van was interviewed about his reaction to the story he was quick to point out that his message in ASM had been misinterpreted by this young couple. He and Davy, Van insisted, while enjoying time alone together, never would have run off. Van further countered, that even if he and Davy had run away together, they would have dropped a postcard in the mail to their parents. Despite Scott and Carolyn's escapade, Van defended the ideas about marriage he had expressed in his book, written twelve years before.[619]

While Van wrote many different things over the course of his life: history, short stories, autobiographies and a novel, he thought of himself primarily as a poet. Therefore, it was most appropriate that his poetry should be collected and published in a single volume, under the title *Mercies*. Christendom Press released this slim paperback in October 1988. The back cover described the contents as follows:

> In *Mercies*, all of Vanauken's poems are now available, including several that have never been published before: the poems of faith and doubt derived from the years described in *A Severe Mercy*; poems of hope and wonder "written" by the heroine of his novel, *Gateway to Heaven*; satirical and humorous poems which take aim at "progressive" clerics, feminists, and other idealogues. All of the poems collected here reflect the faith, wit, laughter, and tears that mark Vanauken's peculiar imaginative abilities.

One admirer of Van's poetry was a friend of C. S. Lewis, George Sayer. He said of Van's poetry that it "combines technical ability of an order quite unusual today with real lyricism and something of his own to say…. The poems are unusually varied—there are even some very funny limericks—but perhaps Vanauken is at his best in his religious sonnets. In them the lyrical beauty is combined with a sharp intelligence and the sort of intellectual surprises that we enjoy in the seventeenth-century poetry of George Herbert and Andrew Marvell.... My only criticism of this book is that it is too short. I hope that Vanauken will be encouraged by its reception to write a great deal more and that others will be inspired to work with him in reviving the great tradition of English poetry."[620]

Van returned the favor of Sayer's nice comments about his poetry with a glowing review of Sayer's book, *Jack: A Life of C. S. Lewis*.[621] Van's review appeared in the December 1988 issue of the *New Oxford Review*.

Despite Van's accustomed antipathy for biographies and biographers, he found much to like about Sayer's book on Lewis. He noted a few things that contributed to the excellence of it: the fact that Sayer had been one of Lewis' pupils and a close friend, plus the fact that this was a thoughtful, long-considered biography, gracefully written.

Van did not seem to mind that Sayer was willing to point out Lewis' mistakes. In fact, he said, this enabled Lewis to emerge as an even greater man, one who was the more lovable for being human.[622] He admitted, along with Sayer, that Lewis was a difficult person to "get to the bottom of."[623] Despite this, Van especially liked the amount of space devoted to Lewis' ancestry, childhood in Belfast and family background, particularly the focus on Lewis' father Albert.[624] However, Van felt there was one glaring omission in Sayer's biography of Lewis: the fact that Sayer nowhere discussed the question of Lewis and Catholicism, other than to point out the roots of Lewis' anti-Catholicism.

The last several years of Van's life saw him spending his days as he had grown accustomed to do: writing letters to the many people who wrote to him about his books, sharing a drink and a meal with a friend here or there, and continuing to write letters to the editor, essays, reviews and short stories.

This somewhat quiet life was punctuated every now and then by increasing signs of age. In 1989, Van lost another good friend; Lew Salter passed away after a long battle with cancer. Van called Mary Ann a number of times to comfort her in her loss and wrote to his Oxford friend, Geraint Gruffydd, to commiserate. Van told Geraint he thought of Lew and Davy-Jean being together, along with Thad Marsh who had died some time before.

That same year, Van himself suffered a heart attack. Some vague aches in the chest led him, with thoughts of pneumonia, to call his doctor on an August morning. Van saw the doctor that afternoon and received the surprising announcement that he was experiencing a heart attack and would be taken immediately by ambulance to the hospital. While waiting for the

The Man Who Received "A Severe Mercy"

ambulance, Van decided he was going to die and commended his soul to Jesus. He also concluded this was not a bad time or way to go, though he wished for a cigarette!

In hospital, after the heart attack was over, the doctors performed a heart catheterization. Van had a blocked branch artery in the lower part of his heart, but all the main arteries and valves were clear. The doctors told Van he had a strong heart and surprisingly low blood pressure, all this despite what Van himself called a "life of wickedness": smoking, eating bacon and eggs, etc. The doctors recommended a course of exercise that resulted in Van feeling better than he had before.[625]

The heart attack and Lew Salter's passing both served as "a memento mori" for Van—a reminder of the impermanence of life in this world. Nonetheless, Van continued with life as before, writing on an ever-widening variety of topics during his last years. The following list is but a sampling:

- Environmentalism
- Faith
- Evolution
- Awe and mystery in the Mass
- The secession of the Baltic States from the Soviet Union
- The death penalty
- Saddam Hussein's invasion of Kuwait
- The right of individual Americans to bear arms
- C. S. Lewis and his works
- The bombing of Pearl Harbor
- Catholicism
- Homosexuality
- Black fighters for the Confederacy
- Abortion
- Caning
- And the admission of female cadets to the Citadel.

In addition to the shorter pieces he was writing, Van also saw the publication of second editions of two of his books that had gone out of print; *The Glittering Illusion* was re-published by Regnery Gateway and *Gateway to Heaven* by Richelieu Court. In response to the paperback release of *Gateway*, Van was especially surprised and elated. He told the *Lynchburg News & Daily Advance* that *Gateway* was close to his heart; he also admitted that the love Richard and Mary had for each other was like his love for Davy. Furthermore, he noted that when he began writing the book he only had the characters in mind, not a plot. Finally, *The News & Advance* elicited from Van his three "writing rules":

1. Only write until noon,
2. Read many books, and
3. Don't use an electric typewriter or a computer.

On one occasion, Van borrowed an electric typewriter from a friend, but was driven mad by the humming.[626] Of course, Van didn't even follow his own rules when writing *A Severe Mercy* or *Gateway*; when writing those books he often worked from early in the morning until late at night. However, now that he was in his seventies, he liked to take a more leisurely approach.

In some ways, Van's writing in these later years was reaching its peak: at least in terms of volume. Perhaps Van sensed that his earthly journey was nearing its end and he wanted to make the most of every opportunity to express his thoughts. With that terminus in mind, on March 26, 1994, Van sent his own self-composed obituary to the editor of the *News & Advance*. He began his letter to the editor rather humorously by noting that he was not dead yet, nor planning to be, but that it occurred to him the newspaper might like to have an obituary on file for the time when he would die. After all, Van noted, along with Jerry Falwell, he hoped he had done something toward putting Lynchburg on the map.

In 1995, Van lost another dear friend. In August, Tom Harpur in Canada rang up to tell Van the sad news of Beryl Campion in Wales. She had two inoperable tumors in the brain. Van wrote a comforting letter to Beryl's husband Peter, called Mary Ann Salter to tell her the news, as well as writing to Geraint Gruffydd about the matter. By the end of the year, Beryl was gone.[627]

As 1996 began, Van was looking forward to the gathering of his many essays, mostly written over the previous decade, into one volume. That book was to be titled appropriately: *The Little Lost Marion and Other Mercies*. It was to be published by the Franciscan University Press of Steubenville, Ohio. However, the year 1996 also had some things in store for Van that he did not anticipate....

100 BRECKENRIDGE, LYNCHBURG, VIRGINIA 24503   10 OC 96

Dear Will,

Cancer. "It seems, regrettably, that the doctor spoke too hastily in saying "not What comes next I do not know. Chemotherapy, I expect. Seeing a specialist tomorrow. I do not wish this news to be spread abroad. Loving Knows.

I'm enclosing two articles from This Rock. You need not return or comment. Do you have Christian Reflections by C S Lewis, a collection? In it is "Modern Theology and Biblical Criticism" (published elsewhere as "Fern seed and Elephants"). It damns N.T. Biblical Criticism; I think you'd like it.

Bookstores here have had LLM for two or three weeks; they simply rang up the publishers: Franciscan Univ. Press, Steubenville, OH, and ordered. So have individuals. Credit card.

You say, with respect to the mass that "An unbloody sacrifice is no longer a sacrifice." Surely you are wrong? The dictionary says of the word: "An offering to deity of animal or vegetable life; or of food, drink, incense... giving up anything valued for something higher. Synonym: oblation; privation.

You approve of confession as long as the priest also confesses to the people also. Priests do confess (so too bishops amongst the Pope.) — but only a priest (or higher) has the power to grant absolution to the contrite. (If the confessed merely faked contrition or repentance, the absolution does not absolve.) As you know, I don't believe that everything important must be in Scripture, if it is in The Tradition (i.e. in the early Church, coming from an Apostle).

In a novel by C S Lewis's friend, Charles Williams, a little girl is adopted by a practitioner of black magic who has no love for her and will later destroy her, body and soul, by his arts. But the little girl's nanny is disturbed by the fact that she has not been baptized, so the nanny baptizes the child in a London park. (Perfectly valid.) Later in the black magic virus, the girl in desperate straits, she feels herself supported by rough wood — the cross. She survives and the black magic turns against the magician...

I do not accept Mary as co-redemptrix...

If the 12 knew that Peter was to pass on his headship, it still might not have found its way into the Bible.—

Do you mean to say that I cannot ask my beloved Dorg to pray for me ... now? If I ask her to, are you saying she will not hear me? If she can & does hear, she will pray. But how is asking her different to asking St Thomas More or the Lady Mary?

I don't know the words of a priest's vows. I heard of a priest who argued that homosex did not violate his vows — just friendship. — Of course that was nonsense.

I think, and always have thought, that Pilgrim's Regress is a profound and valuable book. Some have said that Mother Church helping him through the crevasses is a very Catholic touch.

I read the W. Confession on justification and baptism. I also read James 2: 18-26 on faith and deeds (works). In 24: "a man is justified by deeds (works) and not by faith in itself (alone)." And 26: "faith divorced from deeds is lifeless as a corpse." It's a wonder that the early Calvinists and (?) Lutherans didn't try to throw this out of the Bible. Anyway, I should think that any real faith would shape one's actions (works), and if not would suggest no real faith. When I think of my own salvation, I hope my faith and works (ASM) are enough. Catholics are not as certain as some Prots that they are certainly saved; but we hope.

No: 1 TIM 3:15 does not say Sola Church: it is the pillar & bulwark of the truth — a truth (it does not suggest) which is in the Church including the Bible, but not limited to the Bible. If Peter passed his headship on, that act is truth because an apostle did it and 'passing on' became part of the truth.

Under the Mercy,
Van

ONE OF VAN'S LETTERS TO THE AUTHOR

XXIX

A GOOD CORRESPONDENT

> And none will hear the postman's knock
> Without a quickening of the heart
> For who can bear to feel himself forgotten?
>
> W.H. Auden

Van wrote his second postcard to me almost a decade after the first, on 12 March 1996. He began by telling me about his new book, due to be published in April. This book was to feature the story of Marion, but also to be a collection of essays, including tales of the years he and Davy spent in Hawaii, as well as the times they spent sailing *Gull* and *Ettarre*.

One week before I was scheduled to meet Van, in April 1996, I had an interesting telephone call. The voice on the other end of the line was clearly that of a very gentile, elderly, Southern lady. Her name was Loring Ellis. She was calling in response to an article in the State newspaper about the C.S. Lewis Society I was starting in South Carolina. In the course of conversation, she happened to mention Sheldon Vanauken and *A Severe Mercy*. I told her that I was going to see Vanauken that very week and she told me that she was a good friend of Van's.

Later that week, Van and I met in Lynchburg. During our visit, Van told me of some of his books with which I was not familiar at that time. I still have the torn piece of an envelope on which Van wrote for me: "GTH Richelieu Court publisher." Later, Van wrote two simple words in his Letter Log about our time together: "good talk." After our visit, I told Van that our afternoon together, for me, had been like "an eternal moment of time." He thought it a "high honour" that I should feel that way.

As soon as I returned home to South Carolina, I immediately wrote to Van. He responded with a neatly typed letter on May 4. That was the first of fourteen letters I received from him in 1996, in addition to three more postcards. Even now, as I reopen those treasured letters, I can smell the faint scent of Van's tobacco.

Along with his May 4 letter, Van sent to me a letter to the editor he had written entitled: "There's no conflict."[628] In the editorial, Van offered a way out of the battle between creationists and evolutionists. It was a piece I really enjoyed because it reinforced my own belief in theistic evolution.

Sheldon Vanauken

I had written to Van about some of C. S. Lewis' advice to writers that I felt Van admirably carried out—enabling his readers to see, hear and feel what he was writing about. In response, Van mentioned how, for most of his life, he had been concerned with the art of writing. In fact, as early as fourth or fifth grade he won a state prize for some story of his that his teacher sent in to a competition.

Our visit and discussion had led Van to read again *Gateway to Heaven*. Reading his own work, he gave it a grade almost as a schoolteacher would; he thought it deserved high marks for its artistry. He enclosed with his letter a review for me to read of GTH, thus urging me to read the book for myself.

In my letter to Van, I had apparently made the mistake of referring to the "dreamy spires" of Oxford. He corrected me, noting that the spires were doing the dream*ing* perhaps of the Catholic Church that built them.

Much of our correspondence discussed the differences between Catholics and Protestants. However, in closing his letter of May 4, Van said: there is more that unites Catholic and Protestant than what divides. Furthermore, he urged that we must stand together against secularism and the anti-Christ. He then invited me to write again about his "English Channel" essay,[629] or GTH or *The Little Lost Marion* when that was published.

Judging by the dates, throughout the rest of our correspondence Van and I must have each replied to the other by return of post. Van's next communication to me was a 3x5 postcard typed on Monday, May 13. He began by asking my forgiveness for the concise reply. I must have had trouble finding some of Van's lesser-known works in my local bookstore, so he told me how I could order them. He also mentioned Christopher Derrick's book, *C. S. Lewis and the Church of Rome*, which I later read at his suggestion. Van felt very strongly that had Lewis lived until the 1990s, in full possession of his faculties, he would have become Catholic, as Malcolm Muggeridge did.

When writing brief postcard replies, Van sometimes ended up with more to say than what could be fit on one side of the card. Such was the case on this occasion. Thus, he continued on the front side of the card with a question: if Jesus built his Church on Peter and gave him the Keys of Heaven, can it be held that the Keys vanished when Peter died—or became twenty-eight thousand keys to pass on to the 28,000 Protestant sects of today?

Our letters to one another did not always deal with heavy theological subjects. Van began his note of June 3 by asking about the pronunciation of my last name. Humorously enough, he had misspelled my family name in various ways, quite accidentally. He began by spelling it: Vaws. Then he got it right: Vaus. Then spelled it: Vaux. He returned to the correct spelling; then he turned to Vaux again! Now he asked if it was pronounced in such a way as to rhyme with boss or loss, moose or loose, pose or rose, or close or dose or gross.

The Man Who Received "A Severe Mercy"

I informed him that my name could be pronounced to rhyme with mouse, house or louse, but that my immediate family pronounced it in such a way as to rhyme with boss. Van enjoyed little word games like this.

The rest of that letter dealt with various topics: Protestant defensiveness, Scripture, the presence of Christ in the Eucharist. Van made it clear that he did not want to argue many points I brought up in my letter. Rather, he wrote to me what he considered to be his own: "confession of faith"—not to shake what he felt was my anti-Catholicism at that time, but to explain where he was coming from. He suggested that if I wanted to read more about the claims of the Catholic Church there were plenty of books to which he could guide me.

Van closed this rather large, typewritten letter (8 ½ x 11 piece of paper, double-sided) with a handwritten note. He asked me if I had ever read or seen the TV film of *Brideshead Revisited*. He said he had read the book again then saw the film with a friend. He was much moved by it and thought the film was a very faithful adaptation of the book, very beautiful, magnificent even.

On June 10, Van wrote to me again, this time a handwritten letter responding to mine, addressing me as "Mr. Vaus." He said he was returning to "Mister" because I had used it for him. Actually, I addressed Van as "Mr. Vanauken" out of respect, not feeling I should be as familiar with him as one of his close friends. However, he signed this letter simply: "Yours, Van." I got the hint and called him "Van" from that point on, and he called me by my first name as well, though he always addressed the envelopes of his letters to me: "The Revd Will Vaus."

I had written to Van about the whole concept of "parish" which I felt was still present in England—the Church at the center of the village with her steeple taller than all other buildings. Van told me he liked the idea of parish as well, but he thought it didn't work anymore in the city, though it used to when whole towns were either Church of England or Catholic. He asked me whether I had ever read Dorothy Sayers book *The Nine Tailors*. Van felt it conveyed what he loved about what he called "the fading C of E"—a strong sense of parish.

In the rest of the letter, Van continued to faithfully, and patiently, address the many questions and concerns I raised about apostolic succession, the canon of Scripture, and the presence of Christ in the Eucharist. Regarding the latter, Van reminded me of the time when he slipped into the line of French folk going up to the altar to receive the Host. It was years later that he officially became Catholic, but he felt he was *really* one from that moment on.

I told Van I had gotten a copy of *Gateway to Heaven* and was reading it. He closed his letter of June 10 by telling me he was looking forward to my comments and those of my wife. He was determined, he said, because of all Davy had told him of what it was to be a girl or woman in the world, to truly create a believable female character—something few men have done effectively in literature.[630]

In my next letter to Van, I wrote about his book *The Glittering Illusion*. I suggested that he displayed a bit of a bias toward Anglo-Catholics in the book. Van clarified, in his letter to me of June 20, that Anglo-Catholics were never his heroes. If anything, he said, he had distaste for them, for not having the courage of their convictions to go all the way and become truly Catholic. He admitted that he might have unconsciously felt a bias *against* the Puritans as extremists. However, he noted that the first chapter of *The Glittering Illusion* on the history of the times was actually written before he became a Christian.

My letter, and Van's response, continued to discuss various issues of Catholic/Protestant difference. In this letter, Van suggested that if I wanted to know more about Catholic doctrine he could send me some tracts from "Catholic Answers." I was interested and he did send the tracts in his future letters.

However, I was afraid I had offended Van in some way by my "attacks" on Catholicism. I told him I was sorry if I had done so. He replied that he was not offended, but that we each needed to recognize that some issues were settled for both of us. I suggested another visit in August, when I would be in Virginia again. Van said he would be glad to see me.

Once again, Van reiterated that he would be interested in my thoughts on *Gateway to Heaven*, which I had not yet given to him. He warned against my viewing GTH as in any way autobiographical. He especially wanted to hear my wife Becky's response to Mary as a character.

Clearly, I was being given homework to finish and I would not be allowed to shirk. I think Van enjoyed playing the role of teacher. It came naturally to him, and I certainly didn't mind being taught. I only wished that I had Van as a professor when I was in college. Short of that, I was happy for the education I was getting from him.

I wrote to Van again on July 3 and he responded on the ninth. He enclosed with his letter four Catholic Answer tracts, the first of more than fifty such tracts with rather detailed explanation of Catholic teaching on numerous topics. Van also enclosed with this letter an op-ed piece he had done for the Lynchburg paper on "Democracy and the nation's Supreme Court."[631] This piece was published the day after the U.S. Supreme Court "discovered" that Virginia Military Institute, with its policy of admitting men only, had been unconstitutional for 150 years.

At the end of his letter of July 9, Van, once again, invited my commentary on *Gateway to Heaven* once I was finished reading it. In commenting on the nickname "Val" for Richard Vallance in GTH, he said that he did not like his own nickname, "Van", but he liked "Val" and that was why he chose it, not because he meant Val to be a portrait of himself. Van closed the letter by asking me, when I would come to Virginia, to call him about a day to come down. He suggested that July 31, August 1 or 2 would be okay.

Van wrote again on July 17, just a postcard this time. He asked me to let him know which Catholic Answer Tracts he had sent me so that he would be sure to send me new ones with his next letter. He also said he hoped I had a nice visit with Loring. I had just visited Loring in her hometown of Hampton, South Carolina. We had lunch together and she had me drive her by Old Field, the plantation on which she had grown up.

The envelope containing Van's next letter to me indicates that he gave it to me by hand during our visit that summer. It was written on July 20. At the beginning of this typewritten letter, Van placed a handwritten note asking me to put "May 96", what he thought was the date of my first letter to him, in the upper left hand corner of my letters. As mentioned earlier, this was his way of keeping track of correspondence, so that he would know *when* his communication with specific correspondents began.

In addition to discussing the history of the Reformation in this letter, Van returned to a discussion of the history behind *Gateway to Heaven*. He talked about how the novel in the eighteenth century (for example: *Don Quixote* & *Tom Jones*) was often picaresque, that is to say they were rogue tales, joined together by the character of the rogue. In the same way, he intended for his characters, Richard and Mary, to tie together everything in GTH, even though his characters weren't rogues.

I had said something to Van about not wholly liking the father's response to Mary's lesbian relationship with Deirdre in GTH. Van told me that he had a letter from another reader that arrived the same day as mine. In it, the correspondent couldn't say enough about the wisdom of Mary's father. It occurred to Van that the reaction of readers to the father in GTH might say a good bit about the readers as mothers and fathers themselves.

I also complained about lack of plot in *Gateway to Heaven*. Van's response to this was that he meant his novel to be more like life—where we don't see the plot in advance. That's why the story is told in the present tense.

Along with this letter, Van sent to me two articles written by Jack Taylor.[632] Jack was a friend of Van's whom he described as a fallen-away Catholic that he helped to bring back to Christian faith, and the Catholic Church, along with his wife Karen. Van thought of Jack, whom I was later to meet, as a mighty warrior for the faith.

On the cover of Van's next letter to me, dated August 17, he said that he wished he lived in a 4-letter town (I lived in Irmo, South Carolina at the time) and had a 4-letter first name and 4-letter last name like mine. He thought if this were the case, it would ease the signing of his name in countless books, not to mention writing an untold number of letters with his return address.

In between Van's letter of July 20 and August 17, we had enjoyed another visit together. On that occasion, we went to one of Van's favorite restaurants in Lynchburg for lunch, Café France. I drove us in my Volkswagen Jetta. I wish Van had driven us in "Colonel Morgan"; that would have been much more fun. However, I thoroughly enjoyed our time together nonetheless. I remember the pants Van wore that day having pockets stained with ink from the fountain pens he inevitably carried around with him. I also remember one snatch of conversation from lunch. I asked him about the Catholic Church's view of contraception and his own view. I remember him saying that he still wasn't certain it was wrong for he and Davy to have chosen *not* to have children.

When I returned from that visit with Van, to my parents' home in Highland County, Virginia, I sent to Van a present for his birthday on August 4. It was a packet of bread mix called "Rebel Bread" with the Confederate flag proudly displayed on the packaging. I also sent along some proper English marmalade. In his letter of August 17, Van began by thanking me for the gift. He especially enjoyed the fact that the marmalade was the "proper" kind: bitter, made from Seville oranges, as opposed to sweet marmalade made from Valencia oranges.

However, Van asked, now that Loring had "improperly" told me the date of his birth, to please "forget it forever." He explained that he had a lifelong allergy to birthdays and that Davy did too. In fact, they had always celebrated a joint non-birthday together elsewhere in the year.

I had told Van that I felt, at times, that *A Severe Mercy* read more like a novel, and *Gateway to Heaven* read more like autobiography. When I asked "why" this was the case, Van said he didn't exactly agree, though he could see how GTH could be perceived as more like real life because the future is not foretold in it, whereas the future *is* foretold in the opening to ASM, making *it* more like a novel. Van felt that ASM *sounding* like a modern novel, because of the opening chapter foretelling Davy's death, was accidental. He preferred to think of ASM being like a symphony rather than a novel, with the opening chapter, "Glenmerle Revisited", being like an overture. Of course, even here, in the title of his first chapter, there is the obvious link between ASM and one of Van's favorite novels—*Brideshead Revisited*.

In my most recent letter to Van, I had asked him if he would consider speaking to our South Carolina C. S. Lewis Society if we were to have a retreat somewhere in Virginia. He was open to the idea but said it would depend upon where and when. Van's letter of August 17, was one of his longest to me, completely taking up two sides of an 8 ½ x 11 piece of paper, typed single-space, covering many aspects of Catholic doctrine. When he came to the end of the second side, having completed the writing of the letter on Sunday afternoon, August 18, Van wrote "out of space" and signed off.

In between this letter and Van's next (smaller) handwritten letter to me on August 27, I heard from Loring that Van was not feeling well. I mentioned this in my next letter to him and he answered that it was true. However, he said, he wouldn't know the cause until his doctor ran some tests the following week.

Around this same time, Van wrote to Geraint Gruffydd in Wales, telling him of Tracy Simmons' plans to study at Oxford that fall.[633] Van hoped to get over to England to see his godson but, as he told Geraint, he wasn't sure he would be physically up to it. Then he quoted from Tennyson:

> We are not now that strength which in old days
> Moved earth and heaven…[634]

VAN

Photo Courtesy of Elizabeth Rose

XXX

THE SETTING OF THE SOUL

> Though my soul may set in darkness, it will rise in perfect light
> I have loved the stars too fondly to be fearful of the night.
>
> Sarah Williams

Van's next letter to me was written on September 9. On the outside of the envelope, he said that he never wrote "Gidding Court" (the street I then lived on) without thinking of T. S. Eliot's "Little Gidding" from *The Four Quartets*. Then, from memory, Van wrote these lines from the poem:

> The dove descending breaks the air
> With flame of incandescent terror
> Of which the tongues declare
> The one discharge from sin and error.
> The only hope, or else despair
> Lies in the choice of pyre or pyre—
> To be redeemed from fire by fire.[635]

Van could have quoted other favorite lines from the same poem:

> You are here to kneel
> Where prayer has been valid.[636]
> Or...
> We shall not cease from exploration
> And the end of all our exploring
> Will be to arrive where we started
> And know the place for the first time.[637]
> Or...
> A condition of complete simplicity
> (Costing not less than everything)
> And all shall be well and
> All manner of thing shall be well.[638]

In many ways, "Little Gidding" summed up various aspects of Van's life. Now, coincidentally enough, I lived on a street that constantly reminded him of this beloved poem. I was glad.

Van's letter of September 9 began with a request for forgiveness because the letter was handwritten instead of typed. He didn't need to ask, for I treasured his handwritten letters even more than the typewritten. Van explained that he had been suffering from weakness and the pen was easier for him to handle than the typewriter.

I had asked in my last letter about his physical condition so that I could, as I put it, "pray more intelligently." Van answered that he had a spot in the lung. The doctor wasn't sure what the spot was and was treating him first with antibiotics. Van felt like the antibiotics and prayers were working. Though he hadn't taken a shower for two or three weeks, he took one the day he wrote to me. He also mentioned that the Church had brought him the Eucharist.

Van asked me to pray that the spot on his lung would disappear. At the same time, he explained something about his prayer life as a Catholic. He said that Catholics often ask their friends to pray for their "intentions", which means praying without specific knowledge of what the requester is praying for. Van felt that such prayers as well as my "more intelligent" prayers would both be equally effective.

On September 4, Van received an advance copy of the *New Oxford Review* with his article "Man as Redeemer of Beast." The cover had the catchier title: Do Some Dogs Go to Heaven?[639] He asked Loring to lend me her copy, which she did. Van's thesis was that what Christ as Savior is to us, we can be, in Christ, to some individual animals. This was a development of C. S. Lewis' idea:

> Now it will be seen that, in so far as the tame animal has a real self or personality, it owes this almost entirely to its master.... it seems to me possible that certain animals may have an immortality, not in themselves, but in the immortality of their masters.... In other words, the man will know his dog; the dog will know its master and in knowing him, will *be* itself.[640]

This whole concept may sound strange to some. However, it has at least some justification in Scripture. In Romans 8:19-22, Paul talks about the redemption of *all* creation:

> For the creation waits in eager expectation for the children of God to be revealed. For the creation was subjected to frustration, not by its own choice, but by the will of the one who subjected it, in hope that the creation itself will be liberated from its bondage to decay and brought into the freedom and glory of the children of God. We know that the whole creation has been groaning as in the pains of childbirth right up to the present time.

Van's meditations in 1996 were, I think, very much in line with the Apostle Paul. However, that is not all Van was thinking about. He was waiting anxiously to hold in his hand a copy of his book, *The Little Lost Marion and Other Mercies*. In that hope, he was not disappointed.

On September 6, Hurricane Fran made landfall near Cape Fear, North Carolina. The result in Lynchburg was a night of heavy wind and rain. Van woke in the night to discover he had no electricity. He read by the light of an oil lamp and had a cold breakfast the next morning. The wind and rain continued until about two o'clock in the afternoon of September 7. Still, Van had no electricity. As evening approached, Van was ready to light his oil lamp again when there came a knock at his front door. It was the UPS man with a parcel—the first copy of *The Little Lost Marion*. Van looked at it in the dim light thinking what a pity it was he couldn't see it better, when soundlessly the electricity came on again. Van was very happy with the book—especially Davy's painting of *Ettarre* on the front cover.

Van wrote to me again on September 21. He related how he had come home the night before, around 5 pm, from seeing the doctor and having x-rays. Throughout the evening, he had ten or twelve people call from as far away as South Carolina and California; they all wanted to know the doctor's verdict about the spot on Van's lung. That verdict was: almost certainly not cancer. Rather, it was thought the spot was fibrosis and that it could be cured. Van closed this particular letter by saying that he felt a kinship with me as a believer and signed off: "Yours in the Faith."

The next letter, of October 10, brought sad news. Van told me that the doctor had spoken too hastily in pronouncing the lung spot "not cancer." He didn't know what would be next. He was seeing a specialist the next day and expected to undergo chemotherapy. He didn't want news of his illness spread abroad, though he had of course told Loring and others close to him.

Somewhere during this time of Van's illness, a blessed reconciliation occurred. I already knew from Loring that Van and Julian had a falling out. However, I knew little of the circumstances of this until Father Julian told me about it years later. What had happened was this: beginning in 1985, Julian spent a year undergoing psychotherapy at the House of Affirmation; Julian had battled for most of his life with depression. He told Van about this and Van had a rather strong reaction. He was leery of psychologists, psychiatrists and all the rest, and so he asked Julian, "Why are you doing this? What is happening with you that you feel you need to see a psychotherapist?" Julian refused to talk about the details of his therapy with Van; he felt that to do so would mean betraying certain confidences. Van simply could not accept this. He wrote long letters objecting to what Julian was doing.

After this, Julian went down to Lynchburg for a visit with Van in early 1986, before traveling to Rome for six months, followed by an extended stay at Downside Abbey in England. Julian's abbot in Rhode Island thought it would be better for him, emotionally and spiritually, to be in England for a time. Van had great difficulty accepting this. He didn't want Julian to move from Rhode Island, where he was more accessible, to England, where it might be difficult to reach him. Julian was like Van's North Star, and so Van simply didn't want him to move away.

When Julian moved to Downside, Van continued to write to him. He was still upset about Julian "keeping secrets" from him and told Julian that friends shouldn't do that. Julian found Van's letters disturbing and told his spiritual director about it. His director advised him to tell Van that he was not opening his letters. Thus, Van wrote to Julian's spiritual director and told *him* what he wanted to say to Julian. Eventually, in about 1990, Julian had to cut off all communication with Van.

In 1996, when Julian heard that Van was desperately ill he called his old friend on the telephone. Van thought Julian had never really loved him as a close friend. Julian told him he was mistaken. The two talked long and deep and patched up their relationship. It was a reconciliation coming none too soon.

On Friday, October 25, Van sent me a postcard saying he was in the midst of two and a half weeks of radiation treatment for his lung cancer. He was told that this would ease his breathing and leave him less weak, but such was not the case. Lynchburg friends, Bill and Mary Bell, as well as Dick Seymann, were caring for Van in his illness.

I had asked Van in whom or in what he was trusting for his salvation. In response he wrote: "I trust in Jesus, but I might say I trust in God the Father. I trust in my saying 'I believe' when I became a Christian. I trust I am a Christian. If we are to be judged, it is surely Judgment on all we are... Is there not a Judgment?"

I received Van's card on Monday, October 28. The next day, Loring called to tell me that Van had died that Monday morning at Lynchburg General Hospital.

POSTCARD WITH SKETCH BY VAN ANNOUNCING HIS PASSING

ETTARRE FIGUREHEAD

VAN'S FRIENDS GATHERED AT VANCOT

GLEN MERLE GOTHIC LAMP

EPILOGUE

> The term is over: the holidays have begun.
> The dream is ended: this is the morning.
>
> C. S. Lewis, *The Last Battle*

On Saturday, December 14, 1996, a number of Van's friends gathered at Vancot. I was there with Loring Ellis and a friend of hers from Hampton. Van's godson, Tracy Simmons was present, along with Marion, Jack Taylor and his family, and one surprise guest—Cal Thomas. After reminiscing for a bit, we all drove out to St. Stephen's for the memorial service, Marion rode with me in my car.

The service, conducted by the rector of the church, The Reverend Ronny Dower, followed the Burial Office from The Book of Common Prayer. In addition to readings from Van's works, Scripture, Creed and remembrances from Marion and Tracy, there was the Collect for Theologian and Teacher:

> O God who by thy Holy Spirit dost give to some the word of wisdom, to others the word of knowledge, and to others the word of faith: We praise thy Name for the gifts of grace manifested in thy servant, Sheldon Vanauken, and we pray that thy Church may never be destitute of such gifts. Through Jesus Christ our Lord, who with thee and the same Spirit liveth and reigneth, one God, for ever and ever. Amen.

Some of Van's ashes were scattered by the old stone cross where he and Davy had so often knelt to pray in the churchyard at St. Stephen's. The rest were scattered in the grounds of St. Margaret's Church in Binsey, England.

I believe Van died as he lived—ready, under the Mercy, to face his Creator, Redeemer and Judge. He died longing to see Davy again. I will always remember my last sight of Van in August 1996. As I walked away from Vancot, I turned back and saw him standing on the stoop in front of his house. He stood tall and straight, clear-eyed, looking not at me, but off into the distance. Sheldon Vanauken was indeed a man of vision who increased the clarity of my understanding of the Savior.

There is, perhaps, no better way to close this account of Van's earthly life than with these words written to him by one of the million readers of *A Severe Mercy*. In June of 1978, an Indonesian missionary child, just sixteen years old at the time, wrote to Van after reading his most famous book. What she wrote was not a letter, but a little "Afterword" to *A Severe Mercy* about Van's own death ... and arrival:

> Something in the air smelt very clear and sweet. It was the golden brightness, of course. He was sitting on the grass by the lily pond, Davy's hand in his. "Van," she said delightedly. "Welcome home!" He was just going to say, "But I've been here all along," when he remembered. "Oh, Davy!" he said, and he took her into his arms. "Why, it's spring," he said. "Of course," she said. "So it always is." Then, Aslan ... and Jack were there too.[641]

ACKNOWLEDGEMENTS

There are so many people who helped me along the way in the writing of this book, I am afraid I will forget some. However, I must make attempt to remember as many as I can.

First, I must thank all those who knew Van who granted interviews to me, some by telephone, some by letter or email, others in person, as well as those who shared their letters from Van. Among these were: David Bovenizer, Edmund Dews, Ken Eakins, Larry Farmer, Sandy Kellogg Grey, Geraint Gruffydd, Tom Hall, Tom Harpur, David Hartman, Walter Hooper, Ed Hopkins, Darrell Laurant, Joseph Nelson, Carroll Nicklaus, Clifton Potter, Norma & Bucky Reynolds, Betty Wright Smith and Dom Julian Stead. My debt of gratitude to each of you is beyond words, and so is my thankfulness to all the monks of Portsmouth Abbey who so warmly welcomed and hosted me during my visit there.

I am also deeply grateful to those who assisted me in research about Van's early life. It all started with a visit to the museum of Staunton Military Academy in Staunton, Virginia. Without the help of their welcoming archivist, Arlene Nicely, not only would I be impoverished in my knowledge of that great institution, and Van's brief experience there, I never would have discovered the name of the town in which Van grew up. What a thrill it was to read the name of Van's father on that student card, carefully saved in the archive, and to spot the name of Van's hometown: Carmel, Indiana. That was my first great discovery.

From Staunton, it was on to Indiana. I am grateful to God for guiding me to John Martin Smith, lawyer and historian in Auburn, Indiana, who showed me around Van's birthplace, treated me to lunch and assisted me in my research in northeast Indiana.

From Auburn, it was on to Steuben, Indiana, where I did research on Van's ancestry, assisted by the very capable hands of Carol Love in the Reference Department of the Carnegie Public Library of Steuben County. Thanks Carol for all your help. Much of what I know about Van's ancestors would not be available in this book if it were not for you.

Special thanks to Duwayne and Connie Hintz, as well as Ed and Pat Brown, for very graciously providing most comfortable accommodation for me in Indianapolis, in addition to assisting in a lot of the leg work of my research there. The pleasure of staying with these two lovely couples and enjoying their warm hospitality on numerous occasions will live in my memory for a long time to come.

The words "thank you" seem insufficient to express my gratitude to Alan Loehr for opening wide the archives of Culver Military Academy to my exploration, and for providing a delightful tour of the campus. Similar thanks are due to Beth Swift, Archivist at Wabash College, for pointing the way in my research there, helping me to follow the trails of various clues, unlocking the mysteries of Van's early life.

Perhaps the most exciting discovery in all of my research for this book, was finding the actual, specific location of Glen Merle. I could not have done that without the assistance of Tom Rumer, historian for the Carmel-Clay Historical Society. Tom was the one who took my meager description of Glen Merle and almost immediately determined the spot where the house must have been, based upon his almost encyclopedic knowledge of Carmel, Indiana. I will never forget the day Tom and I drove to see the former site of Glen Merle and walk the grounds, noticing every detail that fit perfectly with Van's description in *A Severe Mercy*.

Tom was also the one who put me in touch with Sister Barbara Lee McCormick, former resident of Glen Merle after the Van Aukens' time there. It is a joy to express my appreciation to Sister Barbara Lee, and all the Sisters of The Order of Saint Helena, for hosting me during my most memorable visit to their convent in Augusta, Georgia. Because of Sister Barbara Lee and the generous sharing of her time, memories and photographs, I now have a greater sense of not only what it looked like living at Glen Merle, but what it felt like too.

Gail and Ernie Mitchell played host to me in Lynchburg so many times they are practically like family now. However, that does not absolve me from saying "thank you from the bottom of my heart" for the countless, delicious meals and the endearing fellowship shared in their home. It was Gail who first took me on the tour of all the Vanauken "sites" around Lynchburg, many of which I had not seen before. She was also present with me when we "discovered" Elk Hill, the former home of Barney and Frances Hodges. Thanks for sharing so many fun times Gail.

My undying gratitude goes out to Father Chris Heying, of St. Stephen's Episcopal Church in Forest, Virginia, for revealing the exact location of "the old stone cross" in the churchyard, as well as sharing very valuable information about the history of the church and Van's membership there. Father Chris was also the one who graciously guided me to others who knew Van at St. Stephen's. I am especially thankful to Bill Hodges for sharing his memories of Van with me.

At the same time, I cannot go without expressing my appreciation to Father Kenneth Rush of Holy Cross Catholic Church in Lynchburg. I am grateful for Father Rush answering a number of questions by email.

Ariel Myers, Archivist at Lynchburg College, was of immense help in providing access not only to the many files related to Sheldon Vanauken, but also in making available high resolution digital copies of photographs of Van belonging to the College Archives. Thank you Ariel for making me feel so "at home" in the Knight-Capron Library and thanks to the college for permission to reproduce the photographs contained herein.

I am also very appreciative of the guidance and assistance received from Lewis Averett and the staff of Jones Memorial Library in Lynchburg, the second oldest public library in the state of Virginia. Not only did Lewis and his staff help in researching Van's life in Lynchburg, directing my search through newspaper archives, city directories and history books, but Lewis and his staff shared with me their own memories of Van as their teacher at Lynchburg College. For all of the above, I will be always thankful.

One of the joys of writing a book like this is spending time in some of the most wonderful libraries of the world, always a delight for a book-lover. Certainly one of the most beautiful of those is the Marion E. Wade Center at Wheaton College in Wheaton, Illinois. The Wade Center, for those who don't know, is the repository of a wealth of material on C. S. Lewis and six other British authors related to him in one way or another. It was to the Wade Center, as well as Lynchburg College, that Van donated many of his papers, long before his death. At the Wade, I was assisted on numerous occasions by the gifted hands and minds of Heidi Truty, Laura Schmidt, Marjorie Mead and Chris Mitchell. To all of you I extend my gratitude. I am thankful not only for your research assistance but for your friendship.

Another delight in writing this book was simply having the excuse to visit so many fascinating places. It should come as no surprise that the most wonderful of these was Oxford, England. I was blessed to share two days with Jim and Michele Belcher, touring Vanauken sites around that fair city. Thanks to you both for your hospitality and for taking the photo of me on the Rainbow Bridge included in this book. In the same breath, I should say thank you to the C. S. Lewis Foundation of Redlands, California for providing accommodation during my visits to Oxford in 2010 and 2012 at C. S. Lewis' former home, The Kilns. Debbie Higgins, then Warden of the Kilns, was a most gracious, engaging host, guide and friend during my stays in Oxford, making my trips there on those occasions some of the most memorable of the many I have enjoyed. I also wish to extend my gratitude to Colin Harris of the Bodleian Library Special Collections Reading Room for his assistance in allowing me to view the original letters of C.S. Lewis to Sheldon Vanauken.

There are countless other helpful folks I met along the way from Virginia, to Ohio, to Indiana, Illinois and beyond who helped in various ways, not to mention all the folks who have shared their memories with me via telephone and email. Though I may have forgotten your names or simply failed to mention you, there is Someone who never forgets even a cup of cold water given to a stranger: may He reward you richly for your kindness to me.

This book is dedicated to Marion (a.k.a. Elizabeth Rose). I am so grateful to you Liz for sharing the photographs of yourself, your mother Jean Palmer Davis Van Auken, and your grandparents. Even more than that, I am grateful for the joy of knowing you.

Finally, I must give my thanks and my love to my family. Without my wife Becky's encouragement, this book never would have been conceived, nor would it have grown to maturity. I am also grateful for the patience of my three sons. Every time we have visited Lynchburg and I have wanted to drive by Vancot, they have never once said, "Not again!" In fact, my eldest son spent his freshman year at Lynchburg College.

I must close this chapter of acknowledgements before it, too, turns into a book. However, I cannot finish without recording one other amazing "happening" which took place during the course of my research. It was while I was walking through the cemetery near Pleasant Lake, Indiana, where many of Sheldon Vanauken's ancestors are buried. The day had been a long one, filled with a great deal of driving, as well as much fruitful research in libraries, county court houses and other locations. However, I was tired and beginning to wonder just what I was doing all alone in a cemetery, far from home, as darkness was coming on. Then it began to rain. Still, I searched for more Vanauken graves. It was then that I heard, overhead, the call of a goose. I looked up, and there, flying directly over me, was not one, but two geese, only two. I could not tell for sure from such a distance, but they looked grey. This may sound strange to some, but at that moment, I felt the presence of Van and Davy with me there in that lonely cemetery. That one experience was worth the whole trip, and perhaps worth all the research put into this book.

THE NORMAN CHRIST THAT VAN GAVE TO C.S. LEWIS

AUTHOR PHOTO COURTESY OF WALTER HOOPER

ENDNOTES

1. As of the spring of 1996, Sheldon Vanauken had the following books in print: *A Severe Mercy, Gateway to Heaven, Under the Mercy, The Glittering Illusion*, and *Mercies: Collected Poems*. See the Bibliography for a full account of all of Vanauken's published books.
2. I shall refer to Sheldon Vanauken as "Van" throughout the rest of this book since that was his preferred appellation by which he invited me to call him early on in our acquaintance.
3. This insight was gleaned from my interview with Dr. Clifton Potter of Lynchburg College, Lynchburg, Virginia. Potter related how one of Van's colleagues at Lynchburg College, Ellis Shorb, was at a cocktail party with Van. A woman, one of Van's fans, asked Ellis, "What part of England is Mr. Vanauken from?" Ellis said, "He's from Indiana." Van was not happy when he heard that Ellis had revealed the location of his birth and upbringing.
4. Archives, Wabash College, Crawfordsville, Indiana
5. Vanauken, Sheldon, *A Severe Mercy*, New York: Bantam, 1979, p. 6.
6. Vanauken correspondence with Kenneth Eakin, Marion E. Wade Collection, Wheaton College, Wheaton, Illinois.
7. According to records at Culver Military Academy, Culver, Indiana, this change in spelling occurred at least as early as February 1961.
8. *A Severe Mercy*, p. 6.
9. See http://vanauken.org and http://ancestry.org.
10. Ancestry.org.
11. *A Severe Mercy*, p. 5.
12. *History of Steuben County, Indiana*, Chicago: Inter-State Publishing Co., 1885, pp. 796-797.
13. Ibid. p. 798.
14. Ibid. p. 799.
15. Ibid. p. 797.
16. Ibid. p. 799.
17. Ibid. p. 800.
18. Ibid. p. 794.
19. *A Severe Mercy*, p. 5.
20. Brown, Demarchus C., *State of Indiana Legislative Manual*, Indianapolis: William B Burford, 1913, p. 139.
21. Walsh, Justin E., General Editor, *A Biographical Directory*

of the Indiana General Assembly, Vol. 2, Indianapolis: Select Committee on the Centennial History of the Indiana General Assembly, 1984, p. 424.
22   Upton, Harriet Taylor, *History of the Western Reserve*, Vol. II, Chicago: The Lewis Publishing Company, 1910, pp. 1172-1173.
23   *A Severe Mercy*, p. 5.
24   1910 US Census.
25   See "Glenn Van Auken is the Nominee" in The Fort Wayne Sentinel, Saturday, August 17, 1912.
26   Interestingly enough, Glenn's father, Frank B. Van Auken, while being a Republican, wrote an article on the History of the Democratic Party of Steuben County. See Stoll, John B., editor, *History of the Indiana Democracy, 1816-1916*.
27   *A Severe Mercy*, p. 10.
28   See "Glenn Van Auken, Local Attorney, Democratic Leader, Dies Here", Indianapolis Star, September 1, 1943.
29   Ibid.
30   Walsh, p. 424.
31   1920 US Census.
32   For more information on The Christian Church (Disciples of Christ) visit www.disciples.org.
33   Sheldon Van Auken letter to C. S. Lewis, 12/12/1950, Wabash College Archives.
34   *A Severe Mercy*, p. 7.
35   Vanauken, Sheldon, *Encounter with Light*, Wheaton: Marion E. Wade Collection, 1961, pp. 1-3, in the public domain.
36   Glenn Van Auken Obituary, Indianapolis Star, September 1, 1943.
37   Microfilm R806-F6 and R807, Culver Military Academy Archives, Culver, Indiana.
38   *A Severe Mercy*, p. 10.
39   Vanauken, Sheldon, *Under the Mercy*, Nashville: Thomas Nelson, 1985, pp. 24-25.
40   See letter in Wabash College Archives.
41   Vanauken, Sheldon, *Bibliography*, Marion E. Wade Center Archives, Wheaton College, Wheaton, Illinois and Lynchburg College Archives, Lynchburg, Virginia.
42   This description of Glen Merle is based upon Van's description in the opening chapter of *A Severe Mercy* as well as extensive interviews with Barbara Lee McCormick who lived in the former Van Auken home from the 1940's through the early

1960's.
43　*A Severe Mercy*, pp. 8-9.
44　1930 US Census enumerated on April 10, 1930.
45　*Under the Mercy*, p. 37
46　Ibid.
47　Ibid.
48　Magee, John Gillespie Jr., "High Flight", http://en.wikipedia.org/wiki/John_Gillespie_Magee,_Jr
49　Van's Honors Manuscript in English was copied, bound and placed in the library at CMA. However, the manuscript is no longer extant. See reference in letter of March 26, 1935 from Charles C. Mather, instructor in English, to Frank Van Auken in the CMA Archives. The topic of Van's paper was "the group mind." See Van's annotated bibliography of his own works, held both at the Marion E. Wade Center, Wheaton College, Wheaton, Illinois, and at Lynchburg College, Lynchburg, Virginia.
50　See Sheldon Van Auken letter to the Headmaster of Culver Military Academy, June 15, 1956, Culver Archives.
51　*A Severe Mercy*, p. 16.
52　Transcript of interview with Sheldon Vanauken in Wabash College Archives.
53　http://www.wabash.edu/aboutwabash/history.cfm
54　Poletti, Jonathan, *Paths Trod by Sheldon Vanauken*, New Oxford Review, January-February 1997, Volume LXIV, Number 1, p. 25.
55　See letter of February 8, 1935, from J. H. Smith to Frank Van Auken, CMA Archives.
56　Poletti, p. 25.
57　Ibid. p. 26.
58　*A Severe Mercy*, p. 15.
59　Ibid.
60　Hyde, A. B., *The Story of Methodism Throughout the World*, Springfield, MA: Willey & Co, 1889, p. 410.
61　1930 Census.
62　Vanauken, Sheldon, *The Little Lost Marion and other Mercies*, Steubenville: Franciscan University Press, 1996, pp. 1-2, and 5.
63　*A Severe Mercy*, p. 15.
64　Indianapolis News, March 13, 1941.
65　Joslin, Frisbie & Ruggles, *A History of the Town of Poultney, Vermont*, Poultney: Journal Printing Office, 1875, p. 162.

66 Information accessed from http://www.butler.edu/orientation-programs/get-to-know-bu/brief-bu-history and http://en.wikipedia.org/wiki/Butler_University#History on 1/29/11.
67 In 1951, the conservatory officially became part of the university.
68 *A Severe Mercy*, p. 15.
69 Ibid. p. 16.
70 Davy's mother had a stone cottage built by Davy's father in the country, on Culver Lake in New Jersey.
71 Ibid. p. 19.
72 Ibid. p. 21.
73 *Encyclopedia of Indianapolis*, p. 767.
74 *A Severe Mercy*, p. 21.
75 According to Van's annotated bibliography of his own works, there were two copies made of this book, perhaps for he and Davy. Apparently, however, later on, Van did not consider *The Loveliest Lamp* to be up to the level of his best work; he burned both copies.
76 Le Gallienne, Richard, *The Junk Man and Other Poems*, New York: Doubleday, 1920, pp. 31-32.
77 Morris, William, *The Earthly Paradise*, London: F. S. Ellis, 1868, p. 216.
78 *A Severe Mercy*, p. 22.
79 Ibid. p. 23.
80 These statues are recreations of the ones that stood in the University Park in the 1930s.
81 *A Severe Mercy*, p. 30.
82 Since *A Severe Mercy* was a favorite book of mine, I asked my wife to read it early on in our marriage. She enjoyed the book greatly. However, when she got to this part, about reading all the books the other had read, even in childhood, she said to me something to the affect of: "If you think I'm going to read all the books you have ever read, then you are kidding yourself!" I think my wife's comment highlights the uniqueness of Van and Davy's relationship. They both met in college and already had much in common, even in terms of their reading. So perhaps to read all the books the other had read up to that point in time was not such a stretch. My wife and I met while I was in seminary and she had never been to college. So for her to read all the books I had ever read would be asking quite a lot, perhaps asking the impossible. Yet, our love has endured for over twenty-five years nonetheless, a longer time than that of

Van and Davy's relationship.
83 See transcript of a letter from Van to Dean George Kendall, 5 April 1942, in the Wabash College Archives.
84 *A Severe Mercy*, p. 35.
85 Ibid. p. 41.
86 De la Mare, Walter, *Motley and Other Poems*, New York: Henry Holt, 1918, p. 75. C. S. Lewis once noted to a friend that, as a Christian, he could not sympathize with de la Mare on this point. Lewis said the line should be: "Look thy *first* on all things lovely."
87 *A Severe Mercy*, p. 37.
88 Ibid.
89 This may have been Hoosier Airport or Stout Field; both were grass airstrips in the 1930s west of downtown Indianapolis.
90 *A Severe Mercy*, pp. 38-40.
91 This story is told in notes taken for an Alumni Interview in the Wabash College Archives. Jonathan Poletti relates the tale in his article "Paths Trod by Sheldon Vanauken" in the New Oxford Review. Finally, Van tells the story in *Under the Mercy*, pp. 37-38.
92 *A Severe Mercy*, pp. 40-41.
93 Thompson, Donald Eugene, *Indiana Authors and Their Books 1967-1980*, Crawfordsville: Wabash College, 1981, p. 400.
94 It is possible that Van and Davy married in Arizona or in Davy's home state of New Jersey. It seems likely that Van and Davy visited Davy's mother at her stone cottage on Culver Lake some time before Van graduated from Wabash. I say this because a note with Van's forwarding address at Culver Lake is contained in Van's Wabash College file. Therefore, it seems quite possible that Van and Davy travelled to New Jersey to elope.
95 *A Severe Mercy*, pp. 41-42.
96 Ibid. p. 42.
97 Davies, William Henry, *The Collected Poems of William H. Davies*, New York: Alfred A. Knoph, 1916, p. 18.
98 Poletti, "Paths Trod by Sheldon Vanauken"
99 Bodenhamer, David J and Barrows, Robert G, editors, *The Encyclopedia of Indianapolis*, Indianapolis: Indiana University Press, 1994, p. 1395.
100 All the facts fit this timeframe. In *A Severe Mercy* (p. 46), Van says, in the paragraph immediately following mention of Dunkirk, that he and Davy decided to announce their wedding

the following winter. The evacuation from Dunkirk took place in May and June of 1940. Therefore, the following winter would be that of 1940-41.
101 *A Severe Mercy*, p. 42.
102 I have yet to find their marriage announcement in any of the Indianapolis area newspapers before March 1941.
103 This was Grace Van Auken's sister. Marie and her husband Wallace lived at 449 S. Maple, Winchester, Kentucky.
104 *A Severe Mercy*, p. 48. According to Glenn's World War II draft registration card, filed April 27, 1942, he was six feet, two inches tall, weighed 195 pounds, had brown eyes, grey hair and dark complexion.
105 National Archives at College Park, College Park, Maryland; *Muster Rolls of U. S. Navy Ships, Stations, and Other Naval Activities, 01/01/1939-01/01/1949;* Record Group: *24, Records of the Bureau of Naval Personnel, 1798-2007;* Series ARC ID: 594996; Series MLR Number: A1 135.
106 See letter From Sheldon Van Auken to Dean Kendall, April 5, 1942, Wabash College Archives.
107 Callaham, Frank, "Eyewitness Recalls That Day Of Infamy Just 15 Years Ago", *Lynchburg News and Advance*, Lynchburg, VA, December 8, 1956.
108 *Indianapolis Star*, March 16, 1941. Pearl Harbor had just been named the permanent base of the United States Pacific Fleet on February 1, 1941. See Wels, Susan, *Pearl Harbor: America's Darkest Day*, Richmond, VA: Time-Life, 2001, p. 80.
109 Ship's manifest
110 http://wc.rootsweb.ancestry.com/cgi-bin/igm.cgi?op=GET&db=stiddemdavid&id=I11015, accessed 2/3/11
111 See *Indianapolis Star*, September 25, 1943, "Sirens, Unnoticed Here Electrify Hawaii, Pearl Harbor Veteran Says."
112 http://homepages.rootsweb.ancestry.com/~stiddem/photos/3256.htm, accessed 2/3/11
113 See *Indianapolis Star*, February 6, 1941.
114 http://homepages.rootsweb.ancestry.com/~stiddem/homepage/HonorRoll.htm, accessed 2/3/11
115 http://wc.rootsweb.ancestry.com/cgi-bin/igm.cgi?op=GET&db=stiddemdavid&id=I11015, accessed 2/3/11
116 *A Severe Mercy*, p. 52.
117 Ibid. pp. 50-54.
118 Letter from Van Auken to Kendall, Wabash Archives

119 Ibid. pp. 55-56. However, Van apparently incorrectly remembered screening the Arizona *to* the west coast. According to the Navy's history of the Perry, it was the other way around. See http://www.history.navy.mil/danfs/p5/perry-iii.htm.
120 Callaham, Frank, "Eyewitness Recalls That Day of Infamy Just 15 Years Ago", Lynchburg News & Advance, December 7, 1956.
121 *A Severe Mercy*, p. 55.
122 http://www.to-hawaii.com/oahu/beaches/kahanabay.php, accessed 2/4/11
123 http://www.wunderground.com/history/airport/PHNL/1941/12/7/DailyHistory.html?req_city=NA&req_state=NA&req_statename=NA, accessed 2/4/11
124 *A Severe Mercy*, p. 55.
125 See Callaham, Frank, "Eyewitness Recalls That Day", and http://corrdefense.nace.org/corrdefense_October_2005/feature.htm.
126 Vanauken, Sheldon, "Normalcy quickly shattered", Lynchburg News & Advance, December 7, 1991.
127 Indianapolis Star, September 25, 1943.
128 Van Auken letter to Kendall, Wabash Archives.
129 See http://www.ussperry.com/dms-17/pearlharbor.htm for the official report of the Perry's activities on December 7, 1941.
130 *A Severe Mercy*, p. 56.
131 "Eyewitness Recalls That Day"
132 *A Severe Mercy*, p. 56.
133 Van Auken letter to Kendall, Wabash Archives.
134 See letters from Van to Geraint Gruffydd, 17 December 1993 and 14 December 1994. Once the necessity of typing code was gone, Van reverted to typing with two fingers by the "hunt and peck" method!
135 Indianapolis Star, September 25, 1943.
136 Vanauken, Sheldon, "Islanders recount tale of Hawaiian heroism", Lynchburg News & Advance, February 9, 1992. Elizabeth Sinclair purchased Niihau from the Kingdom of Hawaii in 1864; private ownership of the island has passed to her descendants, the Robinsons, ever since that time. Other than the Robinsons, the island is inhabited, to this day, largely by native Hawaiians, Kanakas.
137 See also: Vanauken, *The Little Lost Marion*, pp. 18-19.
138 "Glenn Van Auken, Local Attorney, Democratic Leader, Dies

Here", Indianapolis Star, September 1, 1943.
139 *A Severe Mercy*, p. 57.
140 *Under the Mercy*, pp. 54-55
141 *A Severe Mercy*, pp. 57-58.
142 Ibid. p. 58.
143 Ibid.
144 Wels, Susan, *Pearl Harbor*, p. 282.
145 This account is based upon Van's article: "A Two-Reef Breeze in the Florida Keys", New York: Yachting Magazine, March 1947.
146 In *The Little Lost Marion* (p. 22), Van defines reefing for us landlubbers: "to lessen the area of a sail when wind is too strong. In the lower part of the sail are two rows of short ropes running through the sail. If sail is lowered and the ropes tied round the boom, the sail is reefed; lowered further and the upper row tied, it's double-reefed for strong wind."
147 *A Severe Mercy*, p. 59.
148 Van Auken, Sheldon, "Sun, Keys & Tropic Seas", New York: Yachting, September & October 1949.
149 *Ilikea Moana* means "the fair skin of the water."
150 *A Severe Mercy*, p. 60. See also Van's letter to Dr. Osborne of Wabash from Jesus College, Oxford, 29 September 1951, Wabash College Archives.
151 *A Severe Mercy*, p. 60.
152 This was probably the Winchester Repeating Arms Company headquartered at the time in New Haven. The factory closed in 2006.
153 *A Severe Mercy*, pp. 61-62.
154 Ibid. p. 62.
155 Johnson, Mary Lynn and Grant, John E. *Blake's Poetry and Designs*, New York: W.W. Norton & Company, 1979, p. 47.
156 *A Severe Mercy*, pp. 62-64.
157 According to Clifton Potter of Lynchburg College, William Webster Ferguson, head of the history department at the college in 1948, was originally from Indiana. Apparently, Ferguson wanted to hire Van because Van was a Hoosier and because he knew Van's father. Ferguson said that Glenn Van Auken was a fine man, a fine lawyer and one of the best shots in the United States Army. Potter also noted that Web Ferguson would call Van "Sheldon" just to irritate him.
158 http://www.lynchburg.edu/collegehistory accessed 2/16/11
159 *A Severe Mercy*, p. 19.

160 Ibid. p. 51.
161 See letter from Sheldon Van Auken to Dr. Osborne, 29 September 1951, in the Wabash College Archives.
162 *The Prism*, Lynchburg College, Lynchburg, VA, February 1950, p. 37.
163 Patterson, Helen Strange, *St. Stephen's Episcopal Church of Bedford County*, Lynchburg: Warwick House Publishing, 1998, pp. 9, 11.
164 *A Severe Mercy*, p. 66.
165 Ibid. pp. 66-67.
166 Van Auken, Sheldon, "A Boat on the Wave: The Design and Construction of *Ettarre*", New York: Yachting Magazine, August 1952.
167 "Dead-rise" refers to the angle the bottom rises from a horizontal when looking at the hull in cross-section. The centerboard is a pivoting keel that retracts into a case inside the sailboat. A gaff-rigged sailboat has a lower boom and an upper "mast" or boom that attaches to the mainmast. The sail is a quadrangle. This is an older style rig now used to give a boat a traditional look. A schooner uses fore and aft sails on two or more masts, with the forward mast no taller than the rear masts.
168 Van mistakenly refers to the location as Fishing Creek. See http://dickersonowners.org/history.html.
169 In addition to being a naval architect, Chapelle was later curator of maritime history at the Smithsonian.
170 *A Severe Mercy*, p. 64. The CSS *Virginia* battled the USS *Monitor* at Hampton Roads, Virginia, on March 9, 1862. Before her rebuilding as an ironclad, the *Virginia* was called the *Merrimack*; the name was and is often misspelled *Merrimac*. Federal sources about the conflict always referred to the ship as the *Merrimack*, whereas Confederate sources referred to her as the *Virginia*. Van, characteristically, refers to the ship as the *Virginia*. Van says that he "liberated" a sliver of wood from the CSS *Virginia* from a northern museum. I have not been able to trace what museum this was, nor how Van was able to "liberate" such a piece of history.
171 See "A Boat on the Wave." As Van notes in *A Severe Mercy* (p. 64), this ship was to be the last forerunner of the dreamed of deep-keel schooner. Van admits that this was not *Grey Goose*, for in fact her name was *Ettarre*. However, perhaps because this was their final ship, Van chose to call it *Grey Goose*, after the

fact, in *A Severe Mercy*.
172 *A Severe Mercy*, p. 65.
173 Ibid. p. 67.
174 The timing of this cruise is noted in *A Severe Mercy*, p. 68, as being just before Van and Davy's departure to Oxford, which was in August 1950. However, in Van's original telling of this tale, "Island and Creek in the Chesapeake" (Yachting, August 1956), he refers to this as their first cruise; if the latter is correct then it would have been in the summer of 1949, not 1950. Another difference is that Van does not mention in *A Severe Mercy* that his brother Paul joined them. Paul's company *is* mentioned in Van's "Island and Creek in the Chesapeake", both the Yachting Magazine version and the revised version in *The Little Lost Marion*, pp. 65-78. However, in *The Little Lost Marion* Van calls their ship *Grey Goose* whereas in the original magazine article he calls the ship by its correct name *Ettarre*.
175 Cunard chartered the Stratheden from the P&O line in 1950 for four voyages.
176 *A Severe Mercy*, pp. 71-73.
177 Arnold, Matthew, "Thyrsis", *Norton Anthology of English Literature*, Fourth Edition, Volume 2. New York: W. W. Norton, 1979, p. 1385.
178 http://www.asa3.org/ASA/topics/NewsLetter70s/APRMAY78.html accessed 2/19/11
179 Jesus College was founded in 1571 under the reign of Queen Elizabeth I. Jesus is known as the Welsh College because between the years 1571 and 1915 an almost unbroken succession of 24 Principals of the college came from Wales or were of Welsh descent. Up until 1859, most of the college fellows were also Welsh.
180 The B.Litt. is no longer awarded at Oxford. C. S. Lewis once said that there were three types of people at Oxford: the literate, the illiterate and the B Literati. Lewis also said that he preferred the first two to the third.
181 See "Van Auken Granted Leave, Will Study in England", Lynchburg News & Advance, August 13, 1950. Oxford University has three terms: Michaelmas (October-December), Hilary (January-March) and Trinity (April-June).
182 Van says he was paid twenty guineas. However, the guinea went out of circulation in 1816 and was replaced by the pound, or the sovereign in coinage. So why does Van refer to guineas?

Perhaps the payment offered to him by *History Today* was quoted in guineas since professional fees were often so quoted until decimalization in 1971.
183 In his annotated bibliography of his own works, Van refers to this essay as being written at Yale. However, in *A Severe Mercy*, p. 78, Van states that this paper was written at Oxford. It is certainly possible that the essay was begun during Van's time at Yale and completed at Oxford.
184 McMahon, Gail, "Van Auken Article Appears In English History Paper", Lynchburg News & Advance, August 18, 1951.
185 Vanauken, Sheldon, *The Glittering Illusion: English Sympathy for the Southern Confederacy*, Columbia, South Carolina: The Southron Press, 1985.
186 *A Severe Mercy*, p. 74.
187 Fanshawe, Reginald, *Corydon: An Elegy in Memory of Matthew Arnold and Oxford*, London: Henry Frowde, 1906, p. 1.
188 Also a favorite of Inspector Morse
189 Author interview with Edmund Dews
190 Carroll, Lewis, *Alice's Adventures in Wonderland and Through the Looking Glass*, New York: Macmillan, 1897, pp. 106-108. See also Bell, Brian, *Oxford Insight Guide*, Singapore: APA Publications, 1998, pp. 191-192 and http://www.friendsofbinsey.com.
191 *A Severe Mercy*, p. 78. The former Jesus College barge is now a restaurant on the Thames in Richmond.
192 Jesus College did not admit women until 1974. For a film of Jesus College made in 1948, see http://www.jesus.ox.ac.uk/videos/jesus-college-1948-a-film-impression-video.
193 *A Severe Mercy*, pp. 76-78. From 1947-1954 Studley Priory was run as a country club to which C. S. Lewis belonged, among others. It subsequently became a hotel and restaurant. Since 2004, Studley Priory has been a private home.
194 From 1947-50 Peter Campion was reading for his first degree in Physics. In the autumn of 1950 he married Beryl and returned to Oxford for a DPhil course (1950-1954). It was sometime after that, probably in 1951, that the Campions were introduced to Davy and Van through Lewis and Mary Ann Salter.
195 Peter Campion related the following to me in an email on June 30, 2011: "My wife was the eldest of three daughters and her mother was determined to give them names that couldn't be shortened; she named them Beryl, Audrey and Velma. They eventually became known to everybody as B., A., and V.—much

to her annoyance!! So my wife was not put out but would have preferred to have been called Beryl or just "B" rather than "Bee" in A Severe Mercy. From which you can deduce that we did not see it in manuscript."

196 *A Severe Mercy*, p. 73-75.
197 If Van was standing in front of Jesus College, collecting his bicycle, when he looked up he could not have seen the spire of St. Mary the Virgin. Rather, he would have seen the eighteenth century spire of All Saints Church (now the Lincoln College Library). Perhaps Van, when writing *A Severe Mercy* years later, mistook which spire he had seen, or maybe he was standing in a different spot when he looked up. To see the spire of St Mary the Virgin, and then turn around to walk to Blackwell's, Van would probably have been standing somewhere on Catte Street or in Radcliffe Square.
198 *A Severe Mercy*, p. 81.
199 See Van Auken letter to C. S. Lewis (12/12/50) in the Wabash College Archives.
200 See *Encounter with Light*, p. 8, and Van's notes on his letters from C. S. Lewis where he says he "read much of C. S. Lewis (instead of working)." Van's notes on the Lewis letters are at The Bodleian Library, Oxford and at the Wade Center, Wheaton College, in Wheaton, Illinois.
201 *A Severe Mercy*, p. 84.
202 See Van Auken letter to Lewis (12/12/50) in Wabash College Archives. Note: that the letters as they appear in *Encounter with Light* and *A Severe Mercy* are edited by Vanauken.
203 See Lewis, C. S., *The Problem of Pain*, London: Geoffrey Bles, 1946, pp. 57-76. In this chapter, Lewis relates his "myth" of what may have happened when Man fell. Apparently, Van found Lewis' theistic evolutionary approach very compelling.
204 See *The Problem of Pain*, p. 12 and Van's 12/12/50 letter to Lewis in the Wabash College Archives.
205 This letter was first published in Vanauken's booklet *Encounter with Light* at which time it was placed in the public domain.
206 *A Severe Mercy*, p. 93. I say that this happened during the week of December 14-21, 1950 because Van notes that Davy committed her life to Christ during Advent (ASM, p. 94). Furthermore, Van notes that a few nights later he was reading *Miracles* and his letter of 12/21/50 to Lewis says he had read *Miracles* by that time.

207 *A Severe Mercy*, pp. 90-92.
208 Ibid. p. 67.
209 Postcard from Van to Geraint Gruffydd, Boxing Day 1992
210 *Encounter with Light*, p. 20.
211 See Van's letter of 12/21/50 to Lewis in the Wabash College Archives.
212 Pope, Alexander, "An Essay on Criticism", (line 475), *The Norton Anthology of English Literature*, Fourth Edition, Volume I, 1979, p. 2205.
213 See *A Severe Mercy*, pp. 102-103.
214 See *A Severe Mercy*, pp. 94-95 and *Encounter with Light*, pp. 20-21.
215 Mark 9:24 King James Version. Van says that he read this statement in one of Dorothy Sayers short plays on the life of Jesus (ASM, p. 95), but I have yet to find this scene in any of Sayers' plays.
216 Van wrote the date in his Notes on the Letters from C. S. Lewis now at the Bodleian Library, Oxford, with copy at the Wade Center, Wheaton, Illinois.
217 *A Severe Mercy*, p. 96.
218 *A Severe Mercy*, p. 97. See also Vanauken, Sheldon, *Mercies: Collected Poems*, Front Royal, Virginia: Christendom College Press, 1988, p. 11.
219 Hooper, Walter, editor, *The Collected Letters of C. S. Lewis*, Volume III, New York: HarperCollins, 2007, p. 106.
220 *A Severe Mercy*, p. 99.
221 http://en.wikipedia.org/wiki/St_Ebbe's_Church,_Oxford accessed 2/24/11. There have been many changes in the church and the St Ebbe's parish since Van and Davy's time there. Part of the parish was demolished to make way for the rather hideous looking Westgate Shopping Center in the 1970s. St Ebbe's Church has moved in an increasingly contemporary direction in terms of its worship style. If Van were to re-visit the church today, I believe he would be quite encouraged by St Ebbe's continued efforts at evangelism. However, he would probably not care for the style of the service, the use of chairs instead of pews, and the recent re-orientation of the direction in which the congregation sits, no longer facing east toward the original altar of the church, but now facing south.
222 http://www.timesonline.co.uk/tol/comment/obituaries/article1996358.ece accessed 2/24/11

223 *A Severe Mercy*, p. 139.
224 Ibid. pp. 99-100. See also *The Book of Common Prayer*, Cambridge: University Press, 2003, pp. 6-7. The arrangement of the *Te Deum* sung at St. Ebbe's may have been the one composed by Henry Purcell in 1693 since that one fits Van's description.
225 *A Severe Mercy*, p. 101.
226 Ibid. pp. 103-105.
227 "Long Vacation" is the terminology used at The University of Oxford for what American students would otherwise call "summer vacation." At Oxford the "Long Vacation" or "Vac" usually includes the entirety of the months of July and August.
228 Tom Harpur remembered Van often sitting or lying down on a day bed at The Studio, even when a number of visitors had come to call. Van also worked from the day bed, researching and writing his thesis. This habit of working from bed, that Van perhaps picked up while in Oxford, continued for the rest of his life.
229 See Van Auken letter to Dr. Osborne, 29 September 1951 in the Wabash College Archives.
230 Coincidentally, Roger Lancelyn Green, a student, friend and later biographer of C. S. Lewis, had also lived in The Studio before the Van Aukens. (See letter from Van to Geraint Gruffydd, 8 August 1995.)
231 *A Severe Mercy*, p. 109.
232 Van refers to the flat being on cobblestoned, gas-lit, Pusey *Lane* and that the entrance opened on to an alleyway (ASM, p. 109). That "alleyway" was and is Pusey *Place*. Pusey Place is no longer cobblestoned, while Pusey Lane still is. Furthermore, Pusey Place, near the former location of The Studio, no longer has any gas-lamps or traditional lampposts of any kind. However, Pusey Lane does have some traditional lamps and lampposts remaining, though they are no longer gas-lit, but rather, electric.
233 Great Tom is the loudest bell in Oxford, weighing some six and a half tons. The bell had hung in Osney Abbey until 1545 when it was moved to St. Frideswide's Church. Part of this church was demolished, but what remains is now incorporated into the chapel of Christ Church that also functions as the cathedral for the Diocese of Oxford. Great Tom has hung, since the late 1600s, in Tom Tower, designed by Sir Christopher Wren. The bell is rung at 9:05 every night, which corresponds roughly to the, now antiquated, 9 pm Oxford time. It is rung 101 times

for the original 100 scholars of the college, plus one added in 1663. The 101 booms originally signaled the time for all Oxford colleges to close their gates.

234 Peter Campion wrote the following to me: "But certainly I remember the Studio which was quite close to our second flat, in Little Clarendon Street. (It was over a communist bookshop—which caused some mirth amongst our friends! The building no longer exists). The flat itself was on the 3rd floor, UK terminology, (4th floor US terminology) so it was quite high and I well remember the singing as recorded in A Severe Mercy.... There were no regular meetings of Christians in the Studio,--at least none that we attended. Such meetings as happened were very much on an ad hoc basis and numbers varied enormously. In fact in one sense the word 'meeting' gives the impression of a pre-arranged event but the reality was that somebody might drop by just for a chat, then maybe somebody else would turn up later…and so on. Because we had a spacious flat there were probably almost as many gatherings at our place."

235 Geraint was a postgraduate student, reading Celtic Studies, at Jesus College, Oxford between October 1948 and December 1952, although he was not always in residence between those dates.

236 Letter from Geraint Gruffydd to the author, 13 May 2011

237 Ibid.

238 *A Severe Mercy*, p. 110.

239 Waugh, Evelyn, *Brideshead Revisited*, New York: Knoph, 1993, p. 73.

240 See http://www.prattlibrary.org/uploadedFiles/www/locations/central/special_collections/finding_aids/MS%2023%20William%20Force%20Stead%20Papers.pdf accessed 2/25/11 and Stead, Julian, *There Shines Forth Christ*, Portsmouth, Rhode Island: Portsmouth Abbey, 1983, p. 185.

241 See Hooper, Walter, editor, *The Collected Letters of C. S. Lewis*, Volume I, London: HarperCollins, 2000, p. 529, n. 35. William Force Stead was responsible for introducing C. S. Lewis to the Irish poet William Butler Yeats.

242 Years later Van recalled his acquaintance with Father Christopher Fullman in a letter to Geraint Gruffydd on 22 December 1995. Fr. Christopher was a Benedictine monk as was Julian Stead. One day he was reading Charles Williams in the Bodleian Library when Geraint Gruffydd struck up a conversation with

him. As a result, Fr. Christopher was introduced to the Van Aukens and their Christian circle. One night at the Studio Fr. Christopher and Catholicism were "under attack" by Mary Ann Salter and Beryl Campion. Van said that Fr. Christopher replied gently and peaceably, like a saint. Van later thought he became a little bit of a Catholic that night and he never liked Fr. Chris more than then. Fr. Christopher was later laicized and became a college professor. He and Van stayed in touch by letters through the years. Christopher Fullman died in 1994.

243 Tom Harpur confirmed Julian's perspective on Van and Davy in a telephone interview with the author. Tom remembered Davy as a very sweet person, diminutive and not assertive. While Tom was forever grateful for Van and Davy's hospitality and the center of warmth they provided at the Studio, he couldn't help but notice that Van, in relation to Davy, was often domineering. He was later surprised at what a different picture Van portrayed of his relationship with his wife than what he, Tom, had perceived in the 1950s in Oxford.

244 Author interview with Father Julian Stead

245 See *A Severe Mercy*, p. v, and Stead, Dom Julian, *There Shines Forth Christ*, p. 86.

246 *A Severe Mercy*, p. 108.

247 Ibid. p. 112.

248 Introduction by Dom Julian Stead, OSB in Vanauken, Sheldon, *Mercies: Collected Poems*, pp. x-xi

249 Tom Harpur was a good friend of Peter and Bee (Beryl) Campion, and was introduced to the Van Aukens through them. Among other things, Tom played ice hockey at Oxford. Davy and Bee travelled to Harringay Arena in London on at least one occasion to watch him play.

250 *A Severe Mercy*, p. 111.

251 Ibid. p. 117.

252 Ibid. pp. 113-114. While Van may have thought his illustration of the Incarnation to be original, similar illustrations can be found in the work of C. S. Lewis, and perhaps other writers.

253 Peter Campion related the following to me regarding his first impressions of the Van Aukens: "They were a charming but slightly odd couple, but then Oxford was full of interesting characters. If Van represented the upper crust of Southern society then we well understood how some of the characters in the novels about that region came into being. I got on well with

him—we were both ex destroyer men, he from the US Navy, I from the Royal Navy, so we had much in common. Beryl (an ex nurse) took to Davy immediately, seeing her as a warm caring person, perhaps dominated somewhat by Van."

254 *A Severe Mercy*, pp. 114-115. Information here is also based upon author interview with Edmund Dews.

255 Postcard from Lewis to Van Auken, 11/5/51, Wade Center Archives.

256 *A Severe Mercy*, p. 106. John Bull was a sort of national personification of Great Britain (something akin to the American Uncle Sam) created by John Abruthnot in 1712 and popularized by British illustrators and cartoonists. Bull was usually portrayed as a stout, portly man in tailcoat and breeches.

257 *A Severe Mercy*, p. 106. Van mistakenly thought the vote for Professor of Poetry came after his first face-to-face meeting with Lewis. It actually happened a few months before. See Griffin, William, *Clive Staples Lewis: A Dramatic Life*, San Francisco: Harper & Row, 1986, pp. 318-320.

258 *A Severe Mercy*, p. 106.

259 Ibid. p. 107. Addison's Walk, dating to 1710, is part of a somewhat lengthy, circular pathway within the grounds of Magdalen College, named for Joseph Addison, former undergraduate and then Fellow of the college. Lewis would go for a stroll along Addison's Walk every morning before chapel in good weather. It was on this pathway in September 1931 that C. S. Lewis had a very important conversation with his friends, Hugo Dyson and J. R. R. Tolkien, which led to Lewis' own return to Christian faith.

260 The Examination Schools, built in the late 1800s, is the building where thousands of Oxford undergraduates sit for their exams every year. Located not far from Magdalen College and across the street from the Eastgate Hotel, the Examination Schools offer the largest lecture halls (seating some 450 people) at the university. By the 1950s, Lewis had become one of the most popular lecturers in Oxford and thus his lectures had to be held in the Examination Schools.

261 The Socratic Club was formed at Oxford University in 1941 as an "open forum for the discussion of the intellectual difficulties connected with religion and with Christianity in particular." Lewis served as President until 1954. Lewis served as speaker on only eleven occasions during his years as president. However,

it often fell to Lewis to open the discussion. Many students would come along to these meetings just to watch Lewis "make mincemeat of those atheists who were intrepid enough to step into the ring with him." See Como, James T. *C. S. Lewis at the Breakfast Table*, San Diego: Harcourt Brace & Company, 1992, pp. 137-185.
262 *A Severe Mercy*, p. 107.
263 See Wade Center Archives for dates of the correspondence.
264 *A Severe Mercy*, pp. 107-108.
265 A punt is a flat-bottomed boat with a square bow and stern. The punt is designed for use in small rivers where the water is shallow. The punter propels the boat by pushing against the bottom of the riverbed with a rather long pole. When in Cambridge, one punts from the flat deck at the stern of the punt. In Oxford, the tradition is to punt while standing inside the boat with the stern, or "till", facing forward.
266 *A Severe Mercy*, p. 119. A musical celebration has taken place on the first morning of May ever since Magdalen Tower was built over five hundred years ago. Since the 1770s, the choirboys have sung, as their first piece, the college hymn: *Hymnus Eucharisticus*, composed by Benjamin Rogers in 1660. More recently, two other pieces have been added to the performance: the sixteenth century tune—*Now is the month of Maying*, and the thirteenth century, *Sumer is icumen in*.
267 Peter Campion related the following story to me: "One amusing incident that sticks in my memory concerned a plan for an early morning start (early by student standards!). It might even have been the trip to Binsey church, but whatever, Davy claimed that she would not be up at the proposed time. Whereupon I said that I would pop round and knock her up (a perfectly acceptable UK expression at the time—meaning that I would rattle or bang on the door of the Studio until someone responded). You can guess the consequences."
268 *A Severe Mercy*, p. 119-120.
269 See Wade Center Archives.
270 *A Severe Mercy*, pp. 118-119. The Martyrs' Memorial is dedicated to the memory of three Protestant martyrs of the sixteenth century: Thomas Cranmer, Hugh Latimer and Nicholas Ridley. The actual site of their execution is in nearby Broad Street: marked by a cross in the midst of the road.
271 *There Shines Forth Christ*, p. 84.

272 St John's College bought the property at 12 St Giles from Godstow Abbey, opening a tavern there in 1695. The pub was named for a symbol often associated with St John the Baptist who said of Jesus: "Behold the Lamb of God who takes away the sins of the world." (John 1:29) The flag on the pub sign is that of England: a red cross with white background. St John's College leased the pub to Halls Brewery from 1829 to 1963.
273 *A Severe Mercy*, pp. 121-122.
274 Arnold, Matthew, *Essays in Criticism*, London: Macmillan, 1875, p. xiv.
275 *A Severe Mercy*, p. 123.
276 Ibid. p. 122.
277 Ibid. p. 124.
278 Ibid. p. 127.
279 *Lynchburg College: more than books and bricks*, p. 54. According to Clifton Potter of Lynchburg College, Shirley Rosser once said, "Davy was the sweetest lady but she always walked in Van's shadow."
280 *A Severe Mercy*, p. 128.
281 See *A Severe Mercy*, p. 128. See also *The Book of Common Prayer*, New York: The Church Hymnal Corporation, 1945, pp. 587-600. The 1928 Book of Common Prayer, used in the Protestant Episcopal Church until the revised edition of 1979, contained a section entitled "Forms of Prayers to be used in Families." This is what Van and Davy utilized for their prayer time together at home. This section had a series of prayers to be said in the morning and a series of prayers to be said in the evening. There was also a Shorter Form for Morning and Evening Family Prayer consisting of The Lord's Prayer, a Collect, and The Grace. There were also Additional Prayers for Morning and Night and for specific needs. Many of the prayers in this Family Prayer section were taken from the longer church services for Morning and Evening Prayer in the Anglican 1662 Book of Common Prayer.
282 *A Severe Mercy*, pp. 128-132.
283 *The Collected Letters of C. S. Lewis*, Volume III, pp. 324-325
284 See "Van Aukens to Discuss Sojourn in England", *The Daily Advance*, April 23, 1953.
285 *A Severe Mercy*, p. 133-134
286 Ibid. pp. 134-136.
287 Ibid. p. 137.
288 See "Lynchburg College Professor Back at Desk", *The Daily*

Advance, February 5, 1953.
289 *A Severe Mercy*, pp. 137-138.
290 Ibid. p. 138.
291 Ibid. pp. 138-139.
292 Ibid. p. 139.
293 The MG TD was a standard transmission, rear wheel drive convertible roadster manufactured by the Morris Garage (thus the MG) in Oxford from 1950 to 1953.
294 *A Severe Mercy*, pp. 140-141.
295 Ibid. pp. 142-143.
296 Author interview with Dr. Joseph Nelson
297 *A Severe Mercy*, pp. 143-144.
298 Ibid. p. 145.
299 Ibid.
300 Ibid. pp. 147-148.
301 *A Severe Mercy*, p. 148.
302 Chambers, S. Allen Jr., *Lynchburg: An Architectural History*, Charlottesville: University Press, 1981, p. 423.
303 Grahame, Kenneth, *The Wind in the Willows*, New York: Dell Publishing, 1984. This was a book Van and Davy read often at Oxford as they sat in the grass beside the Cherwell on lazy summer days. Kenneth Grahame was born in Edinburgh, Scotland on 8 March 1859 and was later raised in southern England by his grandmother. In his adult years, he worked for the Bank of England. However, more than anything else, he loved telling stories of Mole, Toad, Ratty and Badger to his only son, Alastair. He and his son are buried in a joint grave in Holywell Cemetery beside St Cross Church, Oxford, just up the street from Magdalen College. Grahame was educated at St. Edward's Boys School, Oxford and his son was a student at Christ Church at the time of his death. Oxford was one of Grahame's favorite places; he modeled Toad Hall on a large house called Holywell Ford, not far from Holywell Cemetery. One can see the exterior of the house when making the circuit of Addison's Walk within the grounds of Magdalen College. A number of C. S. Lewis' friends are also buried at Holywell Cemetery, including: Charles Williams, Hugo Dyson and Austin Farrer.
304 *A Severe Mercy*, p. 150.
305 Ibid.
306 Author interview with Betty Wright Smith

307 *A Severe Mercy*, pp. 151-152. Davy's *Wave of God* painting is now part of the Vanauken collection at the Wade Center, Wheaton College, in Wheaton, Illinois.
308 *A Severe Mercy*, p. 152, and author interview with Father Julian Stead
309 Also known as Judas Tree
310 *A Severe Mercy*, pp. 145-146.
311 See Van Auken's Notes on his letters from C. S. Lewis, Wade Center and Bodleian Library.
312 Vanauken, Sheldon, *Gateway to Heaven*, San Francisco: Harper & Row, 1980.
313 See Van Auken letter to Dean Kendall, 21 June 1954, Wabash College Archives.
314 Thomas Jefferson founded the tenth medical school in the USA at Charlottesville in 1825. Recently, the University of Virginia Medical School was ranked tenth in the nation, and the attached medical center consistently ranks as one of the best in the country, providing the most advanced care available in the State of Virginia.
315 *A Severe Mercy*, pp. 154-155. See also Van Auken letter to Dean Kendall, 29 July 1954, Wabash College Archives.
316 *A Severe Mercy*, pp. 155-156.
317 Ibid. p. 157.
318 Ibid. p. 159.
319 See Van Auken letter to Dean Kendall, 29 July 1954, Wabash College Archives.
320 *A Severe Mercy*, p. 160.
321 Ibid.
322 Ibid. pp. 161-162.
323 Ibid. p. 163.
324 Stead, Julian, *There Shines Forth Christ*, p. 85. All poetry and prose by Dom Julian Stead quoted herein is by permission of the author.
325 See notes that Van copied from Davy's old Bible into their new King James Bible picked up in Oxford (Vanauken Archives, Wade Center, Wheaton College).
326 *A Severe Mercy*, pp. 162-163.
327 Ibid. p. 164.
328 Vanauken Papers, Wade Center, Wheaton College
329 The hospital has since been remodeled and thus the veranda no longer exists.

330 *A Severe Mercy*, pp. 166-168.
331 *Collected Letters of C. S. Lewis*, Volume III, p. 531.
332 *A Severe Mercy*, pp. 169-170.
333 Author interview with The Reverend Joseph Nelson
334 See *A Severe Mercy*, pp. 165-166 & 171. See also the chapter on "The Practice of Substituted Love" in Williams, Charles, *He Came Down from Heaven*, Grand Rapids: Eerdmans, 1984, pp. 114-133.
335 *A Severe Mercy*, pp. 171-173.
336 Ibid. p. 173.
337 Ibid. pp. 173-174.
338 Ibid. p. 174.
339 This is The Third Collect, for Aid against all Perils, taken from The Order for Evening Prayer, *Book of Common Prayer*, Cambridge University Press, p. 24.
340 *A Severe Mercy*, p. 175.
341 Clifton Potter once told me that a former Lynchburg College student who became a doctor had occasion to look at Davy's medical records. He said, "Davy had so many things wrong with her I am surprised she survived as long as she did."
342 Shakespeare, William, *The Tempest*, Act I, Scene ii.
343 Browning, Robert, *The Poetical Works*, Volume V, London: Smith, Elder & Co, 1888, p. 101.
344 *A Severe Mercy*, pp. 23 & 178
345 This "newer" annotated, Oxford University Press, King James Bible belonging to Davy contains a loose insert near the title page with passages from Matthew written on it, as well as several glued inserts, and many marginal notes. This Bible is now part of the Vanauken collection at the Wade Center, Wheaton, Illinois.
346 *A Severe Mercy*, p. 179. See also Julian of Norwich, *Revelations of Divine Love*, London: Penguin, 1998, p. 22.
347 *A Severe Mercy*, pp. 164-165.
348 George Kendall letter to Van, 22 January 1955, Wabash College Archives
349 This poem originally appeared in Welsh in the following publication: E. WYN JAMES (ed) (2008) <u>Y FFORDD GADARN'S YSGRIFAU AR LÊN A CHREKYDD GAN R. GERAINT GRUFFYDD</u>, PEN Y BONT AR OGLIER: GWASG BRYNTIRION, p. 309. The poem is reprinted here by permission of the author.

350 Author interview with Betty Wright Smith
351 *A Severe Mercy*, p. 180.
352 Ibid. p. 182.
353 Ibid. p. 183. This information is based also upon the author's interview with Edmund Dews.
354 *Collected Letters of C. S. Lewis*, Volume III, p. 560.
355 Lewis wrote an entire chapter on the word "Sad" in his book, *Studies in Words*, Cambridge: University Press, 1991, pp. 75-85.
356 *A Severe Mercy*, pp. 184-185.
357 *Collected Letters of C. S. Lewis*, Volume III, pp. 565-566.
358 *A Severe Mercy*, p. 188.
359 *Collected Letters*, pp. 592-593.
360 *A Severe Mercy*, pp. 192-193.
361 Ibid. p. 194.
362 Ibid. pp. 195-196.
363 Ibid. p. 196.
364 Ibid. p. 210.
365 Augustine first used this phrase in his *Confessions* (VIII, 11). "And you, O Lord, never ceased to watch over my secret heart. In your stern mercy [severa misericordia] you lashed me with the twin scourge of fear and shame in case I should give way once more and the worn and slender remnant of my chain should not be broken but gain new strength and bind me all the faster." Saint Augustine, *Confessions*, translated by R. S. Pine-Coffin, Middlesex, England: Penguin, 1984, p. 175.
366 *Collected Letters*, pp. 605-606.
367 *A Severe Mercy*, p. 212.
368 Ibid. pp. 213-215.
369 Ibid. pp. 216-218.
370 Ibid. pp. 197-198.
371 Dante, *Paradiso*, XXXI, 93.
372 Lewis concludes his own *A Grief Observed* with this same quote: *Poi si tornò all'eterna fontana*. See Clerk, N. W. *A Grief Observed*, Greenwich, CT: The Seabury Press, 1961, p. 60.
373 *Collected Letters*, p. 617.
374 The sonnets were, perhaps, written after the death of Lewis' beloved friend Charles Williams. See Lewis, C. S. *Poems*, San Diego: Harcourt Brace & Company, 1992, pp. 125-127.
375 See Van Auken's Notes on Letters from C. S. Lewis both in the Bodleian Library collection and at the Wade Center, Wheaton College.

376 Author interview with Tom Harpur.
377 *A Severe Mercy*, p. 221. In ASM Van says he visited Glen Merle in June 1955. According to his letter to George and Yvonne Kendall, the visit to Indiana took place later that summer. See Van Auken letter to Dean and Mrs. Kendall, Wabash College Archives.
378 *A Severe Mercy*, p. 190.
379 Ibid. p. 222.
380 Ibid. p. 191.
381 *Collected Letters*, pp. 783-784.
382 According to Edmund Dews, Van had been invited to make changes to his thesis and resubmit it.
383 Teller was Hungarian. Betty Wright Smith (Class of 1956) remembered that in the 1950s Lynchburg College employed a number of professors from Europe. She also remembered Teller's pronunciation of the word mysticism as "moosticism." Norma Reynolds, another Lynchburg College student in the late 50s and early 60s remembers Teller driving a large car. She would always pull up behind Hopwood Hall right before her lecture time. Then she would ask a student to park her car for her. She would often forget whom she had asked to park her vehicle and she would count that student late to class.
384 The basis of my information is the HMS Newfoundland manifest. In ASM Van refers to "a friend" being on the ship with him but does not say whether this "friend" was male or female. See *A Severe Mercy*, p. 226.
385 *A Severe Mercy*, pp. 225-226.
386 Ibid. pp. 223-225.
387 Ibid. p. 226.
388 Ibid. pp. 226-227.
389 See Davidman, Joy, *Smoke on the Mountain*, London: Hodder & Stoughton, 1955. The book was dedicated to C. S. Lewis and contained a Foreword by him.
390 Lewis called the facility by its old name, the Wingfield; it was renamed the Nuffield Orthopedic Center in 1956. It was and is located in Headington, a couple of miles east of the center of Oxford, not far from Lewis' home, The Kilns, then in Headington Quarry, now Risinghurst.
391 *Collected Letters*, pp. 838-839.
392 *A Severe Mercy*, p. 227.
393 Ibid. pp. 227-228.

394 Samuel Pepys was a student at Magdalene College, Cambridge from 1651-1654. Upon his death, he bequeathed to the college his 3000 volume library, including his extensive diary that contained first-hand accounts of the Great Fire of London and the coronation of Charles II.
395 *A Severe Mercy*, p. 228.
396 Ibid. p. 229.
397 Ibid. pp. 232-233.
398 *Under the Mercy*, pp. 13-14
399 *Collected Letters*, p. 1721. Some readers have, perhaps, wondered why it took Van several years to complete his B.Litt. degree at Oxford. What had happened was this: Van had a rather triumphant viva voce examination in the autumn of 1952. Then, rather shockingly and unexpectedly, Van's thesis on English sympathy for the Confederacy was rejected, not even referred back for further work. The Examiners were Henry S. Commager, Sr., visiting professor at Queen's College and holder of the first Harmsworth Professorship at Oxford, and Baron Max Beloff, then a Fellow of Nuffield College, Oxford. Van thought that the rejection of his thesis was largely due to Commager being a Yankee without any sympathy for his thesis. Van confronted Commager saying, "I have heard that you are a man who has left scholarship behind; now I know that you are a man who has left honour behind as well." Then Van stalked off, literally leaving Commager with his mouth open. Everyone told Van there was no hope of the Board of Modern History at Oxford reconsidering his case. Nonetheless, Van argued with the Board for five years, offering information about Commager and appeals to "English fair play." Finally, the Board of Modern History at Oxford University invited Van to revise and resubmit his thesis. Max Beloff had virtually admitted that he had deferred to the distinguished Visiting Professor Commager and, perhaps, trying to salve a guilty conscience, volunteered to be Van's supervisor. In revising his thesis Van changed almost nothing except for removing his "If the South had Won" section. It sailed through examination and Van was finally awarded the B.Litt. Van's thesis was later published under the title, *The Glittering Illusion*, with the "If the South had Won" section restored and a Foreword by Max Beloff in the English edition. (This information is based upon Van's own account in a letter to his friend Geraint Gruffydd, 2nd April 1988.)
400 See Van Auken notes on letters from C. S. Lewis in Bodleian and Wade Center.
401 "Nevertheless I tell you the truth, it is expedient for you that I

go away: for if I go not away, the Comforter will not come unto you; but if I depart, I will send him unto you." John 16:7 KJV
402 *Collected Letters*, p. 901.
403 *A Severe Mercy*, p. 234.
404 *Under the Mercy*, pp. 9-14
405 Hartman, David, "Remembering Van", New Oxford Review, October 1997.
406 Author interview with Betty Wright Smith
407 Author interview with Bucky Reynolds
408 *Under the Mercy*, pp. 12-13
409 Ibid. p. 21. Van does not reveal the name of this "lady indeed."
410 Betty Wright Smith
411 Both Larry Farmer and Clifton Potter, friends of Van, made this comment in interviews with the author.
412 *Under the Mercy*, pp. 21-22
413 Betty Wright Smith
414 See Van's Notes to the Letters from CSL, Bodleian and/or Wade Center.
415 *Collected Letters*, pp. 940-941.
416 *Under the Mercy*, p. 40
417 See Lewis' letter of December 15, 1958 in *Collected Letters*, p. 1000.
418 *Under the Mercy*, p. 41
419 *Collected Letters*, p. 1146. This letter is dated May 16 in the *Collected Letters*. However, Van notes that Lewis' date on the letter was May 10 while the postmark on the envelope was April 18. Therefore, Van assumed, years later when writing his notes on the letters, that Lewis wrote the letter on April 10.
420 See Van's note on Lewis' letter #172. See also Walter Hooper's comment in *Collected Letters*, p. 1146, Note 46. After Lewis' death, his brother Warren gave this Norman Christ to Hooper.
421 See Van's Notes on the C. S. Lewis Letters.
422 *Collected Letters*, p. 1187.
423 The following narrative is based upon the author's interview with Dr. Potter.
424 http://www2.newsadvance.com/news/2010/dec/14/drug-store-sit-changed-city-ar-714198/ accessed 3/11/11
425 *Under the Mercy*, p. 44
426 Vanauken, Sheldon, "The Question of Justice", *The Prism*, Lynchburg College, February 1961, p. 9.
427 Interview with Clifton Potter

428 *Encounter with Light*, p. 30.
429 *Under the Mercy*, p. 47
430 "Vanauken Finds Car in Knight", *Critograph*, Lynchburg College, Friday, May 26, 1961, p. 1.
431 *Under the Mercy*, p. 49
432 Ibid.
433 Church of the Covenant was originally part of the Congregational Church. It is now part of the United Church of Christ and the Christian Church (Disciples of Christ).
434 Van was difficult if not impossible to pigeonhole on some issues. It is important to note that while he stood firmly against segregation in church, he was not in favor of erasing the Southern past. Sometime in this period, he wrote a letter to the editor, presumably of the Lynchburg newspaper, against the banning of "Dixie." (See *Under the Mercy*, pp. 55-56.)
435 See *Under the Mercy*, p. 33 and *Encounter with Light*, p. 27.
436 *Under the Mercy*, p. 34
437 Ibid. pp. 49-53.
438 Ibid. p. 47.
439 http://www.capecodtoday.com/blogs/index.php/2010/08/10/simone-reagor?blog=210 accessed 3/11/11
440 *Under the Mercy*, p. 54
441 Vanauken, Sheldon, *Gateway to Heaven*.
442 Simone may have provided the inspiration for the central crisis of the novel. Simone was a lesbian and, as noted in her obituary, she lived for many years with her partner, first in Boston, then in Wellfleet, Massachusetts. See http://www.capecodtoday.com/blogs/index.php/2010/08/10/simone-reagor?blog=210.
443 *Collected Letters*, p. 1354.
444 Shelly, Percy Bysshe, "Ode to the West Wind", *Norton Anthology of English Literature*, Volume II, p. 704.
445 *Under the Mercy*, pp. 59-63
446 *Under the Mercy*, p. 65
447 Ibid. p. 66. The photo by Kyoichi Sawada won the World Press Award for photography in 1966.
448 Ibid. pp. 68-69.
449 Ibid. pp. 78-79.
450 Ibid. pp. 79-80.
451 Santos, Michael, editor, *Through the Years: Essays in Lynchburg College History, 1903-1984*, Lynchburg: Alpha Beta Upsilon Chapter of Lynchburg College, H. E. Howard, Inc. Printers, p.

88.
452 Molfase resigned from his teaching position by mutual agreement with officials of Lynchburg College directly following his involvement in this protest march.
453 *Under the Mercy*, p. 80
454 See "LC Students and Professor to March in War Protest", Lynchburg News & Advance, October 18, 1967 and "LC President Opposed to 'Peacenick' Protests", Lynchburg News & Advance, October 21, 1967.
455 http://www.jofreeman.com/photos/Pentagon67.html accessed 3/22/11
456 *Gateway to Heaven*, p. 239.
457 http://www.jofreeman.com/photos/Pentagon67.html
458 *Gateway to Heaven*, p. 240.
459 http://www.jofreeman.com/photos/Pentagon67.html
460 *Under the Mercy*, p. 76
461 http://www.nyu.edu/library/bobst/collections/exhibits/arch/1968/Index.html#Journal accessed 3/22/11
462 *Under the Mercy*, pp. 80-81
463 *Gateway to Heaven*, pp. 248-252.
464 *Under the Mercy*, p. 14
465 "LC Professor Named Gregory-Spock Elector", Lynchburg News & Advance, September 7, 1968.
466 Santos, *A Beacon through the Years*, p. 391.
467 "Leftwing Group Chartered at LC", Lynchburg News & Advance, November 2, 1968.
468 "Leftwing Group will show Controversial Film on Riots", Lynchburg News & Advance, February 3, 1969
469 *Under the Mercy*, p. 66
470 See *Under the Mercy*, pp. 81-85 for the text of Van's sermon.
471 Sayers, Dorothy, *Creed or Chaos?* Manchester, New Hampshire: Sophia Institute Press, 1995, p. 7.
472 Hartman, David, "Remembering Van."
473 Ibid.
474 *Under the Mercy*, p. 85-86
475 Ibid. p. 86.
476 Vanauken, *Freedom for Movement Girls—Now*, Nashville: SSOC, 1969. Available online at http://scriptorium.lib.duke.edu/wlm/vanauken/
477 *Under the Mercy*, p. 88
478 http://dictionary.reference.com/browse/sexist and http://

finallyfeminism101.wordpress.com/2007/10/19/feminism-friday-the-origins-of-the-word-sexism/ accessed 3/23/11
479 http://www.time.com/time/magazine/article/0,9171,902933,00.html accessed 3/23/11
480 *Under the Mercy*, p. 89
481 Ibid. p. 79
482 http://libcom.org/library/ending-war-inventing-movement-mayday-1971 accessed 3/23/11
483 *Under the Mercy*, p. 79
484 Ibid. p. 90.
485 These details are based upon my interview with Dr. Clifton Potter. See also *Under the Mercy*, p. 96.
486 *Under the Mercy*, p. 93
487 Ibid. p. 94.
488 Interview with Dr. Clifton Potter
489 *Under the Mercy*, p. 94
490 Ibid.
491 Interview with Rev. Dr. Joseph Nelson, Jr.
492 In 1966, the Episcopal Church USA published "The New Liturgy." This was just the beginning of the process of revision that finally produced the 1979 Book of Common Prayer. While this liturgy retained some traditional language, it incorporated a number of significant changes that distinguished it from its 1928 predecessor.
493 Van's mentor, C. S. Lewis, had preached a sermon in 1946 on the meaning of this important word in the General Confession, advocating retention of the original prayer book language. That sermon was entitled "Miserable Offenders." Saint Matthew's Church, Northampton, England and Forward Movement Publications of Cincinnati, Ohio, both published this sermon during Lewis' lifetime. Van may have encountered the sermon in one of these editions or in the anthology edited by Walter Hooper—*God in the Dock*, Grand Rapids: Eerdmans, 1970, pp. 120-125.
494 *The 1662 Book of Common Prayer*, p. 3.
495 Interview with the Rev. Dr. Joseph Nelson, Jr.
496 *Under the Mercy*, p. 94
497 Ibid. p. 95.
498 This information was acquired from the National Register of Historic Places Inventory Nomination Form.
499 *Under the Mercy*, p. 96

500 Ibid. pp. 96-97.
501 Gilbert, Douglas & Kilby, Clyde, *C. S. Lewis: images of his world*, Grand Rapids: Eerdmans, 1973.
502 Ibid. p. 12.
503 *Under the Mercy*, p. 97
504 Ibid. p. 98.
505 Ibid. p. 99.
506 Ibid. p. 100.
507 Lewis, C. S., *Out of the Silent Planet*, London: John Lane The Bodley Head, 1943, p. 1.
508 *Under the Mercy*, p. 101
509 Bodleian Library, Oxford, Catalogue of C. S. Lewis Papers.
510 *Under the Mercy*, p. 124
511 Author interview with Dom Julian Stead
512 Communicants List, St. Stephen's Episcopal Church, Forest, Virginia.
513 *Under the Mercy*, p. 102
514 Phillips, J. B., *Ring of Truth*, New York: Macmillan, 1967.
515 *Under the Mercy*, p. 102
516 Ibid. p. 104.
517 Ibid.
518 See The Nicene Creed in *The Book of Common Prayer of the Protestant Episcopal Church*, p. 71.
519 See *Under the Mercy*, p. 106 and *Southern Episcopalian*, June 1976.
520 *New Oxford Review*, September 1978.
521 *Mercies: Collected Poems*, p. 54.
522 *New Oxford Review*, March 1983.
523 *Eternity*, December 1978.
524 *Under the Mercy*, pp. 106-111
525 Ibid. p. 111 and *A Severe Mercy: Davy's Edition*, p. 236.
526 *Under the Mercy*, p. 112
527 Vanauken, Sheldon, letter to Will Vaus, 17 August 1996.
528 *Under the Mercy*, p. 113
529 *There Shines Forth Christ*, p. 86.
530 *Under the Mercy*, p. 113
531 Ibid. p. 112
532 Peter Campion confirmed this impression when he wrote the following to me: "My late wife and I read 'A Severe Mercy' with great interest. I cannot comment on that which concerns C. S. Lewis but our overall impression was that it recounted the

gist of the time Davy and Van spent in Oxford seen, perhaps, through slightly rose tinted spectacles."
533 Author interview with Edmund Dews
534 See *Under the Mercy*, pp. 114-115 and Van's notes on the proposed dust jacket for ASM in the Vanauken papers at the Wade Center, Wheaton College.
535 See *Under the Mercy*, pp. 115-116 and *A Severe Mercy, Davy's Edition*, p. 237.
536 *Under the Mercy*, p. 116
537 See Sheldon Vanauken Collection, The Marion E. Wade Center, Wheaton College, Series 2, Folders 11 & 13.
538 *Under the Mercy*, p. 116
539 Originally "It Was God's Will", *The Living Church*, 21 June 1981. It was later included in *Intellectuals Speak Out About God*, Regnery Gateway, 1984.
540 See Vanauken, Sheldon, "Women's 'Ordination' Denies the Incarnation", *New Oxford Review*, March 1978.
541 *Christianity Today*, January 1978, and in the *New Oxford Review*, March 1981. See also *Under the Mercy*, p. 123 and *Mercies: Collected Poems*, p. 52.
542 *Under the Mercy*, p. 125
543 Van mentioned this reason for burning his diaries and photos in a letter to correspondent Kenneth J. Eakins, now in the Vanauken Collection at the Wade Center.
544 *Time*, December 5, 1977, p. 92.
545 See Hooper, Walter, editor, *The Dark Tower & Other Stories*, New York: Harcourt Brace Jovanovich, 1977 and Lewis, C. S., *The Joyful Christian*, New York: Macmillan, 1977.
546 *Church of England Newspaper*, 25 November 1977
547 Forbes, Cheryl, assistant editor, *Christianity Today*, 13 January 1978, p. 38.
548 Kennedy, John S. "A Journey Beyond Death", *The Catholic Transcript*, 25 November 1977, p. 5.
549 See *The Wittenburg Door*, June-July 1979, pp. 8-9 and *Under the Mercy*, pp. 128-129.
550 *Under the Mercy, p. 130*
551 Ibid. p. 131
552 Ibid. p. 126
553 Vanauken, Sheldon, *Letter Log*, Lynchburg College Archives, November 1977, p. 1.
554 Ibid. February 1978, p. 4.

555 Ibid. The minister was the Rev. Earl F. Palmer then pastor of First Presbyterian Church, Berkeley, California.
556 Ibid. p. 5.
557 Ibid. March 1978, p. 5.
558 Ibid. May 1978, p. 9.
559 *Under the Mercy*, p. 137
560 Ibid. pp. 132-136.
561 Ibid. p. 137
562 Ibid. p. 138.
563 Letter Log, p. 26.
564 *Wittenburg Door*, June-July 1979.
565 *The News*, Lynchburg, Virginia, Wednesday, May 30, 1979, B-6
566 Interview with Clifton Potter.
567 To listen to Van reading the first chapter of ASM visit: www.willvaus.com/sheldon_vanauken.
568 St. Stephen's Episcopal Church Cemetery Records, p. 291 and email to author from Lady Frances' son, Bill Hodges.
569 Letter Log, p. 44.
570 *New Oxford Review*, December 1979.
571 *Eternity*, April 1980, p. 38.
572 *Christianity Today*, 18 April 1981.
573 *Hillsdale Review*, Fall 1981, pp. 46-48.
574 *The American Oxonian*, Fall 1980.
575 Author interview with Clifton Potter
576 *Richmond News Leader*, Wednesday, June 25, 1980, p. 11.
577 Author interview with Clifton Potter
578 *Lynchburg News & Advance*, April 27, 1980.
579 See also *Under the Mercy*, pp. 219-236.
580 Ibid. p. 221. This information is also based upon the author's interview with Edmund Dews.
581 Author interview with Father Julian Stead
582 *Under the Mercy*, p. 228.
583 Ibid. pp. 232-233.
584 Ibid. pp. 217-218, 221-222.
585 Genesis 22
586 See also *Under the Mercy*, pp. 57-59.
587 See Van's annotated bibliography of his own works in the Lynchburg College Archives and at the Wade Center, Wheaton College.
588 Author interview with Dr. Clifton Potter
589 See *Under the Mercy*, pp. 152-162.

590 Letter Log, p. 96.
591 Letter Log, p. 104.
592 See *Under the Mercy*, pp. 248-256 and Lewis, C. S., *The Last Battle*, New York: HarperCollins, 1994, chapter fifteen.
593 See Van's bibliography of his own works in the Lynchburg College Archive and at the Wade Center, Wheaton.
594 Stickley, Dave, "Local author writes sequel to 'Severe Mercy'", Lynchburg News & Advance, 4/7/85.
595 Letter Log, p. 170.
596 Letter Log, p. 178.
597 Ignatius published a second edition of *Under the Mercy* in 1988.
598 Rice, Pat, "Sequel to best seller tells of author's healing", Lynchburg News & Advance, 5/26/85.
599 Comments on *Under the Mercy*, part of Letter Log, pp. 1-2, Vanauken Archive, Lynchburg College
600 Letter Log, p. 173.
601 Ibid. p. 176.
602 Ibid. p. 177.
603 Ibid. p. 163.
604 See *The Little Lost Marion*, pp. 173-182.
605 Ibid. pp. 243-246.
606 Letter Log, p. 140.
607 Ibid. See also Vanauken, Sheldon, *Gateway to Heaven*, p. 272.
608 See *The Little Lost Marion*, pp. 79-86.
609 This title was taken over by Regnery Gateway in 1989.
610 Phillips, Susan, "Book documents British support of Confederacy", *The News & Daily Advance*, Lynchburg, VA, September 21, 1986, p. D-4.
611 Ibid.
612 Van had originally planned to travel with his friend Belle Hill to Nepal and Kashmir in the spring of 1986. However, that trip had to be cancelled due to illness contracted by Belle. The two friends shifted gears and planned to visit New Zealand and Australia in November 1986 instead. However, that trip had to be postponed due to the illness and subsequent death of Belle's brother. The two finally made their jaunt down under in the spring of 1987. (This information is based upon a letter from Van to Geraint Gruffydd, October 5, 1986.)
613 *The Little Lost Marion*, p. 8.
614 *Ibid*, pp. 5-10.
615 Van first published the story of Marion under the title

"Discovery" in the June 1990 issue of the *New Oxford Review*.
616 St. Stephen's Episcopal Church, Cemetery Records, p. 305.
617 *Under the Mercy*, p. 260
618 http://www.people.com/people/archive/article/0,,20099677,00.html accessed 4/13/11.
619 Baradell, Scott, "Author is puzzled by what book has wrought", Lynchburg News & Advance, 8/26/88.
620 Sayer, George, "A Poet in the Great Tradition", *Crisis*, June 1989.
621 Sayer, George, *Jack: A Life of C. S. Lewis*, San Francisco: Harper & Row, 1988.
622 It is my hope and desire that Van would feel the same way about this biography, were he able to read it.
623 The same could be said of Van himself.
624 Again, I would hope Van would feel a similar appreciation for the space devoted in this biography to his ancestry, childhood in Indiana, and family background, with a particular focus on his father.
625 Letter from Van to Geraint Gruffydd, 11 December 1989.
626 See Kirsh, Diane, "Author's book gets second life in world of publishing", *The News & Daily Advance*, Lynchburg, Virginia, Sunday, October 14, 1990, C-4.
627 See Van's letters to Geraint Gruffydd, 8 August 1995 and 22 December 1995.
628 Vanauken, Sheldon, "There's no conflict", Lynchburg, Virginia: The News & Advance, Saturday, February 3, 1996.
629 *Under the Mercy*, pp. 215-242
630 In fact, Van was so determined to develop a believable female persona for the purpose of his novel that he practiced by writing letters under a fabricated female name, pretending to be a woman, to Walter Hooper, C. S. Lewis' last secretary.
631 Lynchburg News & Advance, June 30, 1996.
632 "Will you also go away?" *This Rock*, April 1996 and "Christians R Us", *This Rock*, May 1995
633 See letter from Van to Geraint, 20 August 1996.
634 Alfred, Lord Tennyson, "Ulysses", *Norton Anthology of English Literature*, Vol. II, p. 1111.
635 Eliot, T. S., From *Four Quartets*, "Little Gidding", *Norton Anthology of English Literature*, Volume II, p. 2291.
636 Ibid. p. 2287.
637 Ibid. p. 2292.

638 Ibid.
639 Vanauken, Sheldon, "Man as Redeemer of Beast", *New Oxford Review*, September 1996, pp. 16-20.
640 Lewis, *The Problem of Pain*, pp. 127-128.
641 Letter Log, June 1978, p. 12.

BIBLIOGRAPHY

Abrams, M. H., General Editor, *The Norton Anthology of English Literature*, Fourth Edition, Volume 2. New York: W. W. Norton, 1979.

Arnold, Matthew, *Essays in Criticism*, London: Macmillan, 1875.

Bell, Brian, *Oxford Insight Guide*, Singapore: APA Publications, 1998.

Bodenhamer, David J and Barrows, Robert G, editors, *The Encyclopedia of Indianapolis*, Indianapolis: Indiana University Press, 1994.

Brown, Demarchus C., *State of Indiana Legislative Manual*, Indianapolis: William B Burford, 1913.

Browning, Robert, *The Poetical Works*, Volume V, London: Smith, Elder & Co, 1888.

Callaham, Frank, "Eyewitness Recalls That Day Of Infamy Just 15 Years Ago", *Lynchburg News and Advance*, Lynchburg, VA, December 8, 1956.

Carroll, Lewis, *Alice's Adventures in Wonderland and Through the Looking Glass*, New York: Macmillan, 1897.

Chambers, S. Allen Jr., *Lynchburg: An Architectural History*, Charlottesville: University Press, 1981.

Clerk, N. W., *A Grief Observed*, Greenwich, CT: The Seabury Press, 1961.

Como, James T. *C. S. Lewis at the Breakfast Table*, San Diego: Harcourt Brace & Company, 1992.

Davidman, Joy, *Smoke on the Mountain*, London: Hodder & Stoughton, 1955.

Davies, William Henry, *The Collected Poems of William H. Davies*, New York: Alfred A. Knoph, 1916.

De la Mare, Walter, *Motley and Other Poems*, New York: Henry Holt, 1918.

Eubank, Carolyn Austin & McKinney, Betty Cooper, *Lynchburg College: more than books and bricks*, Virginia Beach: The Donning Company Publishers, 2006.

Fanshawe, Reginald, *Corydon: An Elegy in Memory of Matthew Arnold and Oxford*, London: Henry Frowde, 1906.

Gilbert, Douglas & Kilby, Clyde, *C. S. Lewis: Images of his World*, Grand Rapids: Eerdmans, 1973.

Grahame, Kenneth, *The Wind in the Willows*, New York: Dell Publishing, 1984.

Griffin, William, *Clive Staples Lewis: A Dramatic Life*, San Francisco: Harper & Row, 1986.
History of Steuben County, Indiana, Chicago: Inter-State Publishing Co., 1885.
Hooper, Walter, editor, *The Collected Letters of C. S. Lewis*, Volume I, London: HarperCollins, 2000.
____, Editor, *The Collected Letters of C. S. Lewis*, Volume III, New York: HarperCollins, 2007.
____, Editor, *The Dark Tower & Other Stories*, New York: Harcourt Brace Jovanovich, 1977.
Hyde, A. B., *The Story of Methodism Throughout the World*, Springfield, MA: Willey & Co, 1889.
Johnson, Mary Lynn and Grant, John E. *Blake's Poetry and Designs*, New York: W.W. Norton & Company, 1979.
Joslin, Frisbie & Ruggles, *A History of the Town of Poultney, Vermont*, Poultney: Journal Printing Office, 1875.
Julian of Norwich, *Revelations of Divine Love*, London: Penguin, 1998.
Le Gallienne, Richard, *The Junk Man and Other Poems*, New York: Doubleday, 1920.
Lewis, C. S. *God in the Dock*, Grand Rapids: Eerdmans, 1970.
____, *Out of the Silent Planet*, London: John Lane The Bodley Head, 1943.
____, *Poems*, San Diego: Harcourt Brace & Company, 1992.
____, *Studies in Words*, Cambridge: University Press, 1991.
____, *The Joyful Christian*, New York: Macmillan, 1977.
____, *The Last Battle*, New York: HarperCollins, 1994
____, *The Problem of Pain*, London: Geoffrey Bles, 1946.
McMahon, Gail, "Van Auken Article Appears In English History Paper", Lynchburg News & Advance, August 18, 1951.
Morris, William, *The Earthly Paradise*, London: F. S. Ellis, 1868.
Patterson, Helen Strange, *St. Stephen's Episcopal Church of Bedford County*, Lynchburg: Warwick House Publishing, 1998.
Phillips, J. B., *Ring of Truth*, New York: Macmillan, 1967. Poletti, Jonathan, *Paths Trod by Sheldon Vanauken*, New Oxford Review, January-February 1997, Volume LXIV, Number 1, p. 25.
Saint Augustine, *Confessions*, translated by R. S. Pine-Coffin, Middlesex, England: Penguin, 1984.
Santos, Michael, editor, *Through the Years: Essays in Lynchburg College History, 1903-1984*, Lynchburg: Alpha Beta Upsilon Chapter of Lynchburg College, H. E. Howard, Inc. Printers, 1988.

Sayer, George, *Jack: A Life of C. S. Lewis*, San Francisco: Harper & Row, 1988.
Shakespeare, William, *The Tempest*, New York: Penguin, 1987.
Stead, Julian, *There Shines Forth Christ*, Portsmouth, Rhode Island: Portsmouth Abbey, 1983.
The Book of Common Prayer, Cambridge: University Press, 2003.
The Book of Common Prayer, New York: The Church Hymnal Corporation, 1945.
Thompson, Donald Eugene, *Indiana Authors and Their Books 1967-1980*, Crawfordsville: Wabash College, 1981.
Upton, Harriet Taylor, *History of the Western Reserve*, Vol. II, Chicago: The Lewis Publishing Company, 1910.
Van Auken, Sheldon, "A Boat on the Wave: The Design and Construction of *Ettarre*", New York: Yachting Magazine, August 1952.
Vanauken, Sheldon, *A Severe Mercy*, New York: Bantam, 1979.
____, "A Two-Reef Breeze in the Florida Keys", New York: Yachting Magazine, March 1947.
____, *Encounter with Light*, Wheaton: Marion E. Wade Collection, 1961.
____, *Freedom for Movement Girls—Now*, Nashville: SSOC, 1969.
____, *Gateway to Heaven*, San Francisco: Harper & Row, 1980.
____, Contributor, *Intellectuals Speak Out About God*, Regnery Gateway, 1984.
____, "Islanders recount tale of Hawaiian heroism", Lynchburg News & Advance, February 9, 1992.
____, "Man as Redeemer of Beast", *New Oxford Review*, September 1996, pp. 16-20.
____, *Mercies: Collected Poems*, Front Royal, Virginia: Christendom College Press, 1988.
____, "Normalcy quickly shattered," Lynchburg News & Advance, December 7, 1991.
____, "Sun, Keys & Tropic Seas", New York: Yachting, September & October 1949.
____, *The Glittering Illusion: English Sympathy for the Southern Confederacy*, Columbia, South Carolina: The Southron Press, 1985.
____, *The Little Lost Marion and other Mercies*, Steubenville: Franciscan University Press, 1996.
____, "The Question of Justice", *The Prism*, Lynchburg College, February 1961.

___, *Under the Mercy*, Nashville: Thomas Nelson, 1985.

___, "Women's 'Ordination' Denies the Incarnation", *New Oxford Review*, March 1978.

Walsh, Justin E., General Editor, *A Biographical Directory of the Indiana General Assembly*, Vol. 2, Indianapolis: Select Committee on the Centennial History of the Indiana General Assembly, 1984.

Waugh, Evelyn, *Brideshead Revisited*, New York: Knoph, 1993.

Wels, Susan, *Pearl Harbor: America's Darkest Day*, Richmond, VA: Time-Life, 2001.

Williams, Charles, *He Came Down from Heaven*, Grand Rapids: Eerdmans, 1984.

INDEX

A Grief Observed, 4, 155, 187, 267, 281
A Severe Mercy, 1-2, 4-6, 11-12, 15, 23-25, 43, 52-53, 55, 59, 61, 76, 107, 144-145, 178, 181-185, 187, 189-193, 199, 204, 206-207, 209-213, 215-217, 220, 223, 228, 237-238, 240, 245-270, 274-275, 277, 283
Ambler, Preston, 117-118, 129
Anglican Church, 7, 78, 91- 92, 103, 106, 111, 121, 149, 159, 191, 192, 195-199, 263
Anglo-Catholic, 88, 103, 111, 121, 226
Apostolic succession, 7, 159, 225
Arnold, Matthew, 87, 99, 254, 255, 263, 281
Auburn, Indiana, 14-16, 239
Auden, W. H., 75, 223
Augustine, 91, 185, 209, 267, 282
Awards, 186, 187, 190
Bachelor of Letters Degree, B.Litt., Oxford, 88, 91, 92, 100, 104, 148, 150, 254, 269

Binsey, England, 86, 89, 112, 113, 141, 148, 237, 255, 262
Birdhouse, the, 2-3, 150, 152-153, 156, 164, 166, 169, 173
Blake, William, 75, 126, 252, 282
Bodleian Library, 5, 115, 148, 178, 242, 256, 257, 259, 265, 267, 269, 270, 274
Book of Common Prayer, 118, 131, 174, 196, 237, 258, 263, 266, 273, 274, 283
Brewer, Carey, 164, 168
Brideshead Revisited, 106, 196, 205, 225, 228, 259, 284
Browning, Robert, 41, 47, 139, 266, 281
Butler University, 14, 45-46, 54-55, 60, 248
Cabell, James Branch, 81-82
Cambridge, England, 5, 73, 149, 212, 213, 262, 269
Cambridge, Maryland, 81-83
Campion, Beryl, 90, 111, 113, 145, 220, 255, 260
Campion, Peter, 90, 111, 113, 145, 220, 255, 259, 260, 262, 274

285

Carmel, Indiana, 23-24, 29-30, 32, 59, 64, 239, 240
Catholic Answers, 226-227
Catholic Church, 7, 103, 106-108, 178, 185, 195-200, 202, 203, 205, 206, 210, 211, 213, 218, 219, 224-228, 232, 241, 260, 275
Chapelle, Howard, 81-83, 253
Chesterton, G.K., 91, 96, 98, 173, 198, 199
Christian Church, the (Disciples of Christ), 14, 19-20, 45, 76, 118, 246, 271
Christian student group, 119, 121, 123, 126, 128, 141, 152, 155, 156
Christianity Today, 185, 192, 205, 206, 275, 276
Church of the Covenant, 159-160, 167, 173-174, 271
Civil Rights Movement, 156-157, 163-164
Cocking, Jim & Margery, 177, 187
Confederacy, 3, 11, 22, 81, 88, 163, 212, 219, 228, 253, 255, 269, 277, 283
Cosby, Bev, 159
Crane, Peter, 111, 187
Critograph, 156, 158, 166, 271

Culver Lake, New Jersey, 73, 248, 249
Culver Military Academy, 21, 29-39, 44, 55, 240, 245, 246, 247
Davidman, Joy, 5-6, 149-151, 153, 155, 161, 268, 281
Davis, Helen Larter Fredericks, 44-45, 49
Davis, Staley Franklin, 44-45, 49
Davy's Sin Picture, 6, 78, 193
Derrick, Christopher, 203-204, 224
Dews, Edmund, 89, 112, 115, 141, 183, 196, 239, 255, 261, 267, 268, 275, 276
Dickerson, William, 81-82, 253
Eastgate Hotel, 6, 110, 113, 115, 161, 207, 261
Eliot, T. S., 59, 91, 106, 111, 121, 231, 278
Ellis, Loring, 190, 223, 227, 228, 229, 232, 233, 234, 237
Elk Hill, 175, 178, 180, 182, 183, 187, 240
Encounter with Light, 20, 159, 161, 167, 177, 246, 256, 257, 271, 283
English Civil War, 151
Episcopal Church, 117, 157, 158, 174, 175, 178, 181, 184, 196, 263, 273, 274
Eros, 74, 155, 205, 207

Eternity Magazine, 187, 191, 192, 193, 274, 276
Ettarre, 80-85, 121, 147, 153, 190, 223, 233, 236, 253, 254, 283
Eucharist, 7, 196, 225, 232
Evans, Don, 153, 173-174, 192
Falwell, Jerry, 205-207, 220
Farrer, Austin, 104, 264
Feminism, 1, 143, 157, 164, 168, 184, 203, 217, 273
Fidelity Magazine, 205, 211
Flurry, 81-85, 117, 119, 122, 129, 133-135, 147
flying, 37, 53-54, 135
Ford, Allene, 60-61, 206
Ford, Jack, 60-61, 63
Fullman, Christopher, 106, 259-260
Gateway to Heaven, 112, 160, 165, 166, 170, 181, 187, 191-193, 203, 211, 217, 219, 220, 223, 224, 225, 226, 227, 228, 245, 265, 271, 272, 277, 283
Glen Merle, 3, 5, 11, 18-19, 23-26, 29-30, 37, 43, 46, 51, 55-56, 59, 64-65, 67, 74, 82, 125, 132, 134, 145, 173, 175, 182, 228, 236, 240, 246, 268
Glittering Illusion, The, 88, 212, 219, 226, 245, 255, 269, 283
Grace Memorial

Episcopal Church, 117, 118, 122, 126, 128, 140, 157-159, 178
Grahame, Kenneth, 125, 264, 281
Grey Goose, 4, 55-56, 65, 67, 71, 81, 82, 121, 122, 135, 147, 148, 153, 176, 253, 254
Griffiths, David, 111, 187
Gruffydd, Geraint, 105-106, 111, 140, 218, 220, 229, 239, 251, 257, 258, 259, 266, 269, 277, 278
Gull, 67-71, 74, 81, 223
Gypsy, 74, 81, 83, 119
Hanselman, Sheldon Fitch, 14-15
Harper & Row (HarperCollins), 184, 185, 191, 193, 257, 259, 261, 265, 277, 278, 282, 283
Harpur, Tom, 111, 145, 220, 239, 258, 260, 268
Hawaii, 2, 58, 60-61, 63-65, 69, 90, 129, 176, 191, 223, 250-251, 283
Hawthorne, Nathaniel, 73-74
Hill, Belle, 118, 119, 129, 152-153, 155, 173, 174, 187, 203, 216, 277
Hodder & Stoughton, 183, 184, 190, 209, 268, 281
Hodges, Barney & Frances, 175, 182, 190, 240, 276

Holy Cross Catholic
    Church, 200, 202,
    241
Homosexuality, 127, 168,
    169, 191-192, 196,
    204, 210-211, 219,
    227, 271
Hooper, Walter, 239, 243,
    257, 259, 270, 273,
    275, 278, 282
Howard, Thomas, 183,
    199, 210
Horsebite Hall, 76-78
Ilikea Moana, 69, 82, 153,
    252
Illumination of the Past,
    142-145, 148, 204
Indianapolis, 10, 19-21,
    24, 30, 32, 35, 37-38,
    43-47, 51, 54, 56, 59-
    60, 64, 128, 176, 206,
    240, 245, 246, 247,
    248, 249, 250, 251,
    252, 281, 284
Integration, 156, 158-159
Jeffery, L. Stanley, 117,
    118, 126, 127, 129,
    132, 134, 158
Jesus College, Oxford, 87-
    90, 105, 151, 187, 252,
    254, 255, 256, 259
Julian of Norwich, 140,
    150, 266, 282
Just War Theory, 210
Kendall, George, 54, 127-
    128, 131, 140, 145,
    249, 250, 251, 265,
    266, 268
Kilby, Clyde, 175, 176, 177,
    183, 187, 209, 274, 281
Kilns, the, 5, 6, 106, 149,
    160, 161, 241, 268
King, Johnny, 35-36, 44
Knox, Ronald, 197-198
Kreeft, Peter, 199, 205,
    209, 210
Laddie, 55, 134
Ladywood, 122, 144
Letter Log, 189, 223, 275,
    276, 277, 279
Lewis, C. S., 1-7, 19, 20,
    23, 91-93, 95-100,
    103-104, 106, 111-
    115, 119, 127, 129,
    134-135, 141-145, 147,
    149-151, 153, 155, 157,
    159-161, 167, 176-178,
    183-186, 189-191, 197-
    198, 203-204, 207,
    210, 212-213, 217-219,
    223-224, 228, 232,
    237, 241-242, 246,
    249, 254-270, 273-
    275, 277-279, 281-282
Lewis, Warren, 6, 104,
    145, 270
Li'l Dreary, 116-123, 125,
    152
*Little Lost Marion & Other
    Mercies, The*, 215, 220,
    224, 233, 247, 251,
    252, 254, 277, 283
Lynchburg, 2-4, 50, 76-77,
    82, 87, 104-105, 114,
    117-123, 125, 127-
    128, 131, 134, 141,
    143, 146-148, 150,
    153-160, 162-170, 173,
    175-177, 183, 185, 187-
    193, 199-200, 202,
    205-207, 210, 216,
    219-220, 223, 226,

228, 230, 233-234, 240-242, 245-247, 250-255, 263-264, 266, 268, 270-272, 275-278, 281-284
Lynchburg College, 2-3, 50, 76-77, 87, 104-105, 114, 117-119, 121-123, 125, 128, 131, 134, 141, 143, 146-148, 150, 153—154, 156-158, 160, 162-164, 166-170, 173, 175-177, 183, 185, 187, 190-193, 210, 230, 241-242, 245-247, 252-253, 263, 266, 268, 270-272, 275-277, 281-282, 284
Lynchburg News & Advance, 87, 219, 220, 251, 254, 255, 272, 276, 277, 278, 282, 283
Magdalen College, Oxford, 90, 91, 103, 112-115, 261, 262, 264
Magdalene College, Cambridge, 5, 149, 269
March on the Pentagon, 8, 164-165, 191, 272
Marion, iii, 45, 214, 215, 216, 223, 237, 277-278
Marsh, Thad, 90, 111, 112, 218
Marvell, Andrew, 35, 218
Mayday Demonstration, 169-170, 273
Mercies: Collected Poems, 181, 217, 245, 257, 260, 274, 275, 283
Mere Christianity, 4, 19
MG, "The Trout", 121, 122, 126, 129, 133, 135, 139, 141, 143, 145, 158, 264
Miami, Florida, 30, 31, 37, 67, 68, 70, 71
Miami Military Academy, 30
Mole End, 124-126, 128, 129, 131, 141, 143, 144, 152
Morgan, 162-163, 169, 170, 175, 228
Navigator Councils, 53, 65, 120
Navy, U.S., 3, 11, 59-63, 65, 83, 103, 176, 250, 251, 261
Nelly Dean Watergate, 173, 175, 178
Nelson, Joseph, 118, 122, 134, 239, 264, 266, 273
Newman, John Henry, 91, 197, 198, 209
New Oxford Review, 181, 191, 195, 198, 203, 204, 210, 218, 232, 247, 249, 270, 274, 275, 276, 278, 279, 282, 283, 284
Norman Christ, 4, 155, 243, 270
O'Neill, Jane, 111, 121-122
Osborne, Dr., 11, 104-105, 128, 210, 252, 253, 258
Oxford, 1-3, 5-6, 71, 73, 86-90, 92, 97, 103-107,

111-115, 117, 119-122,
126, 128, 140-142,
145, 148-150, 157-161,
178, 181, 183, 186-
187, 191-193, 195-196,
198-199, 205, 207,
212, 218, 224, 229,
241, 252, 254-262,
264-266, 268-269,
274-275, 281
Oxford & Cambridge Club, 105, 115
Palmer, George, 176, 205
Paul, the Apostle, 4, 120, 192, 232
Pearl Harbor, 8, 59-62, 64, 219, 250-252, 284
Perch Pub, 86, 89
Peter Ibbetson, 51, 90, 141, 143
Pope John Paul II, 7, 198
Portsmouth Abbey, 106, 114, 129, 178, 194, 198-199, 239, 259, 283
Potter, Clifton, 155, 156, 192, 193, 203, 239, 245, 252, 263, 266, 270, 273, 276
Prism, the, 76-77, 147, 156-157, 253, 270, 284
Protest marches, 8, 163-165, 191, 272
Reagor, Simone, 157-160, 183, 193, 271
Romanticism, 47, 183, 185, 192
Rosser, Shirley, 118, 126, 129, 131, 175, 216, 263
Salter, Lewis, 87, 90, 128, 131, 140, 187, 218, 219, 255

Salter, Mary Ann, 87, 90, 128, 131, 218, 220, 255, 260
Salvation, of animals, 232
Sayer, George, 1, 217, 218, 278, 282
Sayers, Dorothy, 91, 119, 167, 225, 257, 272
Segregation, 65, 158, 271
Sexism, 168-169, 203, 272-273
Seymann, Dick, 216, 234
Shadowlands, 5-6
Shakespeare, William, 39, 47, 48, 139, 266, 283
Shelley, Percy Bysshe, 47, 160
Shining Barrier, the, 52-53, 122, 143-144, 153, 217
Shortridge High School, 37
Simmons, Tracy Lee, 204-205, 209, 229, 237
South, Old, 2, 5, 11, 12, 22, 35, 70, 76, 88, 89, 175, 190, 206, 210, 212, 213, 223, 227, 255, 260, 269, 271, 283
Southern Partisan, 206, 212
Southern Students Organizing Committee (SSOC), 164, 166, 167, 168, 169, 272, 283
St. Ebbe's Church, 102-104, 107, 111, 257, 258
St. Margaret of Antioch Church, 89, 113, 141,

148, 237,
St. Stephen's Episcopal
Church, 77-78, 122,
126, 128, 129, 138-
140, 172, 174-175, 178,
183, 187, 198-200,
216, 237, 240, 241,
253, 274, 276, 278,
282
Stapledon, Olaf, 23, 29,
92, 95
Staunton Military
Academy, 4, 11, 22,
29, 31, 239
Stead, Julian, 106-107, 111,
114, 123, 126, 129,
132, 134, 152, 178,
182, 196, 197, 198,
199, 208, 209, 233,
234, 239, 259, 260,
265, 274, 276, 283
Stead, William Force, 106,
259
Studio, the, 3, 105-108,
111, 114, 120, 148,
159, 177, 183, 187,
258-260, 262
Tao, the, 92, 96, 98, 99
Taylor, Jack, 227, 237
Teller, Gertrude, 148, 268
Tennyson, Alfred, 229,
278
Thomas, Cal, 207, 237
Time Magazine, 184-185
Tolkien, J. R. R., 1, 261.
Trimble, Bob, 46, 54
Trippet, Byron, 105, 128
Triumph TR-3 ("The
Jaybird"), 158, 163
Turner, John, 76, 128
Under the Mercy, 1, 111,

119, 135, 141, 151-
152, 163, 178, 206,
209-210, 237, 245-247,
249, 252, 269-278, 284
University Church of St.
Mary the Virgin, 90,
103, 148
U.S.S. Perry, 60-63, 251
Van Aken, Marinus, 12
Van Auken, Frank Buckle,
13-15, 246
Van Auken, Grace Merle
Hanselman, 14-16,
19, 21, 24-26, 30-32,
36-38, 59, 64, 250
Van Auken, Jacob, 12-13
Van Auken, Jean Palmer
Davis "Davy", 1-4, 6,
43-48, 50-56, 58-65,
67-71, 73-78, 81-85,
87-91, 97, 100, 103-
107, 111-115, 117-123,
125-129, 131-135, 139-
144, 146-150, 152-153,
155, 160-161, 174-177,
182-186, 190, 192-193,
196, 198, 203-207,
209, 212, 215-219,
223, 226, 228, 233,
237-238, 242, 248-
249, 254-257, 260-
266, 274-275.
Van Auken, Paul Slack,
16, 25, 31, 59, 83-85,
145, 170, 254
Van Auken, Robert
Glenn, 10, 13-16, 19,
21, 23-26, 30-33, 36,
38, 44, 47, 56, 64, 246,
250, 251, 252
Vancot, 2, 173, 182, 184,

187, 190, 193, 199, 207, 213, 236-237, 242
Vietnam War, 163-170, 191, 272, 273
Violins, 2, 47, 61, 74
Virgin Mary, 7, 107-108, 132, 198, 199
Virginia Military Institute, 22, 226
Wabash College, 11, 42-44, 46, 53-55, 71, 88, 105, 127-128, 131, 140, 145, 147, 182, 187, 210, 240, 245, 246, 247, 249, 250, 251, 252, 253, 256, 257, 258, 265, 266, 268, 283
Wade Collection (Wheaton College), 159, 176, 185, 241, 245, 246, 247, 256, 257, 261, 262, 265, 266, 267, 269, 270, 275, 276, 277, 283
Wake, Orville, 87, 128
War Between the States, 3, 22, 158, 212
Watson, Frank "Cap", 66-67
Wheaton College, 159, 176, 185, 187, 216, 217, 241, 245, 246, 247, 256, 257, 265, 266, 267, 275, 276, 277, 283
WIBC, 56, 60, 176
Williams, Charles, 91, 104, 111, 119, 134, 150, 171, 178, 209, 259, 264, 266, 267, 284
Wittenburg Door, 185, 189-191, 193, 275, 276
Wood, Maurice, 103, 129
Woodstock Flat, 88-91, 94, 97, 105
Wordsworth, William, 9, 137
World War I, 11, 16
World War II, 3, 56, 59-65, 75, 76, 103, 205, 250
Yachting, 66, 68, 80, 252, 253, 254, 283
Yale University, 43, 71-76, 78, 89, 97, 128, 255

Scripture Index

Psalm 116:6, 132
Ecclesiastes 3:11, v
Ecclesiastes 12:12, 203
Isaiah 35:10, 132
Isaiah 40:31, 132
Isaiah 41:10, 132-133
Matthew 16:18-19, 195
Mark 9:24, 100, 257
John 1:29, 263
John 9:1-3, 127
John 16:7, 270
Romans 1:26-27, 192
Romans 8:19-22, 232
Ephesians 5:22, 121
1 Timothy 3:15, 7

ABOUT THE AUTHOR

WILL VAUS

- was born in Sleepy Hollow, New York and grew up in La Jolla, California.
- is the son of Jim Vaus, former organized crime wiretapper who came to Christ through the ministry of Billy Graham in 1949.
- holds a Bachelor of Arts degree in drama from the University of California at San Diego and a Master of Divinity degree from Princeton Theological Seminary.
- has served as a pastor in California, South Carolina and Pennsylvania.
- is the president of Will Vaus Ministries, through which he has communicated the love of Christ around the world since 1988.
- is the author of *Mere Theology: A Guide to the Thought of C. S. Lewis, My Father Was a Gangster: The Jim Vaus Story, The Professor of Narnia: The C. S. Lewis Story, Speaking of Jack: A C. S. Lewis Discussion Guide, The Hidden Story of Narnia: A Book-by-Book Guide to Lewis' Spiritual Themes, Keys To Growth: Meditations on the Acts of the Apostles* and *Open Before Christmas: Devotional Thoughts for the Holiday Season*.
- and his wife, Becky, have been married since 1988 and have three sons: James, Jonathan and Joshua.
- has a website you can visit: www.willvaus.com

Other Titles of Interest

C. S. Lewis

C. S. Lewis: Views From Wake Forest - Essays on C. S. Lewis
Michael Travers, editor

Contains sixteen scholarly presentations from the international C. S. Lewis convention in Wake Forest, NC. Walter Hooper shares his important essay "Editing C. S. Lewis," a chronicle of publishing decisions after Lewis' death in 1963.

"Scholars from a variety of disciplines address a wide range of issues. The happy result is a fresh and expansive view of an author who well deserves this kind of thoughtful attention."
  Diana Pavlac Glyer, author of *The Company They Keep*

The Hidden Story of Narnia:
A Book-By-Book Guide to Lewis' Spiritual Themes
Will Vaus

A book of insightful commentary equally suited for teens or adults – Will Vaus points out connections between the *Narnia* books and spiritual/biblical themes, as well as between ideas in the *Narnia* books and C. S. Lewis' other books. Learn what Lewis himself said about the overarching and unifying thematic structure of the Narnia books. That is what this book explores; what C. S. Lewis called "the hidden story" of Narnia. Each chapter includes questions for individual use or small group discussion.

Why I Believe in Narnia:
33 Reviews and Essays on the Life and Work of C. S. Lewis
James Como

Chapters range from reviews of critical books, documentaries and movies to evaluations of Lewis' books to biographical analysis.

"A valuable, wide-ranging collection of essays by one of the best informed and most acute commentators on Lewis' work and ideas."
  Peter Schakel, author of *Imagination & the Arts in C. S. Lewis*

C. S. Lewis Goes to Heaven: A Reader's Guide to The Great Divorce
David G. Clark

This is the first book devoted solely to this often neglected book and the first to reveal several important secrets Lewis concealed within the story. Lewis felt his imaginary trip to Hell and Heaven was far better than his book *The Screwtape Letters*, which has become a classic. Clark is an ordained minister who has taught courses on Lewis for more than 30 years and is a New Testament and Greek scholar with a Doctor of Philosophy degree in Biblical Studies from the University of Notre Dame. Readers will discover the many literary and biblical influences Lewis utilized in writing his brilliant novel.

MORE INFORMATION AT WWW.WINGEDLIONPRESS.COM

C. S. Lewis & Philosophy as a Way of Life
Adam Barkman

C. S. Lewis is rarely thought of as a "philosopher" per se despite having both studied and taught philosophy for several years at Oxford. Lewis's long journey to Christianity was essentially philosophical – passing through seven different stages. This 624 page book is an invaluable reference for C. S. Lewis scholars and fans alike

C. S. Lewis: His Literary Achievement
Colin Manlove

"This is a positively brilliant book, written with splendor, elegance, profundity and evidencing an enormous amount of learning. This is probably not a book to give a first-time reader of Lewis. But for those who are more broadly read in the Lewis corpus this book is an absolute gold mine of information. The author gives us a magnificent overview of Lewis' many writings, tracing for us thoughts and ideas which recur throughout, and at the same time telling us how each book differs from the others. I think it is not extravagant to call C. S. Lewis: His Literary Achievement a tour de force."
    Robert Merchant, *St. Austin Review*, Book Review Editor

Mythopoeic Narnia:
Memory, Metaphor, and Metamorphoses in The Chronicles of Narnia
Salwa Khoddam

Dr. Khoddam, the founder of the C. S. Lewis and Inklings Society (2004), has been teaching university courses using Lewis' books for over 25 years. Her book offers a fresh approach to the Narnia books based on an inquiry into Lewis' readings and use of classical and Christian symbols. She explores the literary and intellectual contexts of these stories, the traditional myths and motifs, and places them in the company of the greatest Christian mythopoeic works of Western literature. In Lewis' imagination, memory and metaphor interact to advance his purpose – a Christian metamorphosis. *Mythopoeic Narnia* helps to open the door for readers into the magical world of the Western imagination.

Speaking of Jack: A C. S. Lewis Discussion Guide
Will Vaus

C. S. Lewis societies have been forming around the world since the first one started in New York City in 1969. Will Vaus has started and led three groups himself. *Speaking of Jack* is the result of Vaus' experience in leading those Lewis societies. Included here are introductions to most of Lewis' books as well as questions designed to stimulate discussion about Lewis' life and work. These materials have been "road-tested" with real groups made up of young and old, some very familiar with Lewis and some newcomers. *Speaking of Jack* may be used in an existing book discussion group, to start a C. S. Lewis society, or to guide your own exploration of Lewis' books.

George MacDonald

Diary of an Old Soul & The White Page Poems
George MacDonald and Betty Aberlin

The first edition of George MacDonald's book of daily poems included a blank page opposite each page of poems. Readers were invited to write their own reflections on the "white page." MacDonald wrote: "Let your white page be ground, my print be seed, growing to golden ears, that faith and hope may feed." Betty Aberlin responded to MacDonald's invitation with daily poems of her own.

"Betty Aberlin's close readings of George MacDonald's verses and her thoughtful responses to them speak clearly of her poetic gifts and spiritual intelligence."
    Luci Shaw, poet

George MacDonald: Literary Heritage and Heirs
Roderick McGillis, editor

This latest collection of 14 essays sets a new standard that will influence MacDonald studies for many more years. George MacDonald experts are increasingly evaluating his entire corpus within the nineteenth century context.

"This comprehensive collection represents the best of contemporary scholarship on George MacDonald."
    Rolland Hein, author of *George MacDonald: Victorian Mythmaker*

In the Near Loss of Everything: George MacDonald's Son in America
Dale Wayne Slusser

In the summer of 1887, George MacDonald's son Ronald, newly engaged to artist Louise Blandy, sailed from England to America to teach school. The next summer he returned to England to marry Louise and bring her back to America. On August 27, 1890, Louise died, leaving him with an infant daughter. Ronald once described losing a beloved spouse as "the near loss of everything." Dale Wayne Slusser unfolds this poignant story with unpublished letters and photos that give readers a glimpse into the close-knit MacDonald family.

A Novel Pulpit: Sermons From George MacDonald's Fiction
David L. Neuhouser

"In MacDonald's novels, the Christian teaching emerges out of the characters and story line, the narrator's comments, and inclusion of sermons given by the fictional preachers. The sermons in the novels are shorter than the ones in collections of MacDonald's sermons and so are perhaps more accessible for some. In any case, they are both stimulating and thought-provoking. This collection of sermons from ten novels serve to bring out the 'freshness and brilliance' of MacDonald's message."
    From the author's introduction

Behind the Back of the North Wind:
Critical Essays on George MacDonald's Classic Children's Book
John Pennington and Roderick McGillis, editors

The unique blend of fairy tale atmosphere and social realism in this novel laid the groundwork for modern fantasy literature. Sixteen essays by various authors are accompanied by an instructive introduction, extensive index, and beautiful illustrations.

Through the Year with George MacDonald: 366 Daily Readings
Rolland Hein, editor

These page-length excerpts from sermons, novels and letters are given an appropriate theme/heading and a complementary Scripture passage for daily reading. An inspiring introduction to the artistic soul and Christian vision of George MacDonald.

Christian Living

The Living Word of the Living God:
A Beginner's Guide to Reading and Understanding the Bible
Rev. Tom Furrer

This book is based on over 20 years experience of teaching the Bible to confirmation classes at Episcopal churches in Connecticut. Chapters from Genesis to Revelation.

Keys to Growth: Meditations on the Acts of the Apostles
Will Vaus

Every living things or person requires certain ingredients in order to grow, and if a thing or person is not growing, it is dying. *The Acts of the Apostles* is a book that is all about growth. Will Vaus has been meditating and preaching on *Acts* for the past 30 years. In this volume, he offers the reader forty-one keys from the entire book of Acts to unlock spiritual growth in everyday life.

Open Before Christmas: Devotional Thoughts For The Holiday Season
Will Vaus

Author Will Vaus seeks to deepen the reader's knowledge of Advent and Christmas leading up to Epiphany. Readers are provided with devotional thoughts for each day that help them to experience this part of the Church Year perhaps in a kore spiritually enriching way than ever before.

"Seasoned with inspiring, touching, and sometimes humorous illustrations .... I found his writing immediately engaging and, the more I read, the more I liked it. God has touched my heart by reading Open Before Christmas, and I believe he will touch your heart too."
The Rev. David Beckmann, Founder of The C.S. Lewis Society of Chattanooga

Called to Serve: Life as a Firefighter-Deacon
Deacon Anthony R. Surozenski

Called to Serve is the story of one man's dream to be a firefighter. But dreams have a way of taking detours – so Tony Surozenski became a teacher and eventually a volunteer firefighter. And when God enters the picture, Tony is faced with a choice. Will he give up firefighting to follow another call? After many years, Tony's two callings are finally united – in service as a fire chaplain at Ground Zero after the 9-11 attacks and in other ways he could not have imagined. Tony is Chief Chaplain's aid for the Massachusetts Corp of Fire Chaplains and Director for the Office of the Diaconate of the Diocese of Worcester, Massachusetts.

Harry Potter

The Order of Harry Potter: The Literary Skill of the Hogwarts Epic
Colin Manlove

Colin Manlove, a popular conference speaker and author of over a dozen books, has earned an international reputation as an expert on fantasy and children's literature. His book, *From Alice to Harry Potter*, is a survey of 400 English fantasy books. In *The Order of Harry Potter*, he compares and contrasts *Harry Potter* with works by "Inklings" writers J.R.R. Tolkien, C. S. Lewis and Charles Williams; he also examines Rowling's treatment of the topic of imagination; her skill in organization and the use of language; and the book's underlying motifs and themes.

Harry Potter & Imagination: The Way Between Two Worlds
Travis Prinzi

Imaginative literature places a reader between two worlds: the story world and the world of daily life, and challenges the reader to imagine and to act for a better world. Starting with discussion of Harry Potter's more important themes, *Harry Potter & Imagination* takes readers on a journey through the transformative power of those themes for both the individual and for culture by placing Rowling's series in its literary, historical, and cultural contexts.

Repotting Harry Potter: A Professor's Guide for the Serious Re-Reader
Rowling Revisited: Return Trips to Harry, Fantastic Beasts, Quidditch, & Beedle the Bard
James W. Thomas

In *Repotting Harry Potter* and his sequel book *Rowling Revisited*, Dr. James W. Thomas points out the humor, puns, foreshadowing and literary parallels in the Potter books. In *Rowling Revisited*, readers will especially find useful three extensive appendixes – "Fantastic Beasts and the Pages Where You'll Find Them," "Quidditch Through the Pages," and "The Books in the Potter Books." Dr. Thomas makes re-reading the Potter books even more rewarding and enjoyable.

The Deathly Hallows Lectures:
The Hogwarts Professor Explains Harry's Final Adventure
John Granger

In *The Deathly Hallows Lectures,* John Granger reveals the finale's brilliant details, themes, and meanings. *Harry Potter* fans will be surprised by and delighted with Granger's explanations of the three dimensions of meaning in *Deathly Hallows*. Ms. Rowling has said that alchemy sets the "parameters of magic" in the series; after reading the chapter-length explanation of *Deathly Hallows* as the final stage of the alchemical Great Work, the serious reader will understand how important literary alchemy is in understanding Rowling's artistry and accomplishment.

Sociology and Harry Potter: 22 Enchanting Essays on the Wizarding World
Jenn Simms, editor

Modeled on an Introduction to Sociology textbook. this books is not simply about the series, but also used the series to facilitate reader's understanding of the discipline of sociology and a development of a sociological approach to viewing social reality. It is a case of high quality academic scholarship written in a form and on a topic accessible to non-academics. As such, it is written to appeal to Harry Potter fans and the general reading public. Contributors include professional sociologists from eight countries.

Harry Potter, Still Recruiting:
An Inner Look at Harry Potter Fandom
Valerie Frankel, editor

The Harry Potter phenomenon has created a new world: one of Quidditch in the park, lightning earrings, endless parodies, a new genre of music, and fan conferences of epic proportions. This book attempts to document everything - exploring costuming, crafting, gaming, and more, with essays and interviews straight from the multitude of creators. From children to adults, fans are delighting the world with an explosion of captivating activities and experiences, all based on Rowling's delightful series.

Hog's Head Conversations: Essays on Harry Potter
Travis Prinzi, editor

Ten fascinating essays on Harry Potter are divided into five sections: Conversations on 1) Literary Value, 2) Eternal Truth, 3) Imagination, 4) Literary Criticism, and 5) Characters. Contributors include the following popular Potter writers and speakers: John Granger, James W. Thomas, Colin Manlove, and Travis Prinzi.

Fiction

The Iona Conspiracy (from The Remnant Chronicles book series)
Gary Gregg

Readers find themselves on a modern adventure through ancient Celtic myth and legend as thirteen year old Jacob uncovers his destiny within "the remnant" of the Sporrai Order. As the Iona Academy comes under the control of educational reformers and ideological scientists, Jacob finds himself on a dangerous mission to the sacred Scottish island of Iona and discovers how his life is wrapped up with the fate of the long lost cover of *The Book of Kells*. From its connections to Arthurian legend to references to real-life people, places, and historical mysteries, *Iona* is an adventure that speaks to eternal truths as well as the challenges of the modern world. A young adult novel, *Iona* can be enjoyed by the entire family.

Poets and Poetry

Remembering Roy Campbell: The Memoirs of his Daughters, Anna and Tess
Introduction by Judith Lütge Coullie, editor
Preface by Joseph Pearce

Anna and Teresa Campbell were the daughters of the handsome young South African poet and writer, Roy Campbell (1901-1957), and his beautiful English wife, Mary Garman. In their frank and moving memoirs, Anna and Tess recall the extraordinary, and often very difficult, lives they shared with their exceptional parents. The book includes over 50 photos, 344 footnotes, a timeline of Campbell's life, and a complete index.

In the Eye of the Beholder: How to See the World Like a Romantic Poet
Louis Markos

Born out of the French Revolution and its radical faith that a nation could be shaped and altered by the dreams and visions of its people, British Romantic Poetry was founded on a belief that the objects and realities of our world, whether natural or human, are not fixed in stone but can be molded and transformed by the visionary eye of the poet. Unlike many of the books written on Romanticism, which devote many pages to the poets and few pages to their poetry, the focus here is firmly on the poems themselves. The author thereby draws the reader intimately into the life of these poems. A separate bibliographical essay is provided for readers listing accessible biographies of each poet and critical studies of their work.

The Cat on the Catamaran: A Christmas Tale
John Martin

Here is a modern-day parable of a modern-day cat with modern-day attitudes. Riverboat Dan is a "cool" cat on a perpetual vacation from responsibility. He's *The Cat on the Catamaran* – sailing down the river of life. Dan keeps his guilty conscience from interfering with his fun until he runs into trouble. But will he have the courage to believe that it's never too late to change course? (For ages 10 to adult)

> "This book is a joy, and as companionable as a good-natured cat."
> Walter Hooper, author of *C. S. Lewis: Companion and Guide*

The Half Blood Poems
Inspired by the Stories of J.K. Rowling
Christine Lowther

Like Harry Potter, Christine's poetry can soar above the tragic to discover the heroic and beautiful in such poems as "Neville, Unlikely Rebel", "For Our Wide-Armed Mothers," and "A Boy's Hands." There are 71 poems divided into seven chapters that correspond to the seven books. Fans of Harry Potter will experience once again many of the emotions they felt reading the books – emotions presented most effectively through a poet's words.

Pop Culture

To Love Another Person: A Spiritual Journey Through Les Miserables
John Morrison

The powerful story of Jean Valjean's redemption is beloved by readers and theatergoers everywhere. In this companion and guide to Victor Hugo's masterpiece, author John Morrison unfolds the spiritual depth and breadth of this classic novel and broadway musical.

Through Common Things: Philosophical Reflections on Popular Culture
Adam Barkman

"*Barkman presents us with an amazingly wide-ranging collection of philosophical reflections grounded in the everyday things of popular culture – past and present, eastern and western, factual and fictional. This is an informative and entertaining book to read!*"
   Doug Bloomberg, Professor of Philosophy, Institute for Christian Studies

Above All Things: Essays on Christian Ethics and Popular Culture
Adam Barkman

"*Those who don't normally think of themselves as philosophically inclined will be surprised and delighted as Barkman rescues philosophy from dry classroom abstractions and reveals how it fills the glorious messiness of everyday life.*"
   Dr. Kevin Flatt, Assistant Professor of History, Redeemer University College

Spotlight:
A Close-up Look at the Artistry and Meaning of Stephenie Meyer's Twilight Novels
John Granger

Stephenie Meyer's *Twilight* saga has taken the world by storm. But is there more to *Twilight* than a love story for teen girls crossed with a cheesy vampire-werewolf drama? *Spotlight* reveals the literary backdrop, themes, artistry, and meaning of the four Bella Swan adventures. *Spotlight* is the perfect gift for serious *Twilight* readers.

Virtuous Worlds: The Video Gamer's Guide to Spiritual Truth
John Stanifer

Shows readers specific parallels between Christian faith and the content of their favorite games. Written with wry humor, this book will appeal to gamers and non-gamers alike. Those unfamiliar with video games may be pleasantly surprised to find that many elements in those "virtual worlds" also qualify them as "virtuous worlds."

The Many Faces of Katniss Everdeen: Exploring the Heroine of THE HUNGER GAMES
Valerie Estelle Frankel

Katniss is the heroine who's changed the world. She explodes across genres: She is a dystopian heroine, a warrior woman, a reality TV star, a rebellious adolescent. She's traveling the classic heroine's journey. As a child soldier, she faces trauma; as a growing teen, she battles through love triangles and the struggle to be good in a harsh world. This book explores all this and more, while taking a look at the series' symbolism. For all the curious fans who want to know who "Cinna" and "Plutarch" were historically, for all the kids confused about the trilogy's ending, for all the fascinated teachers and scholars, this book will be an invaluable resource.

www.ingramcontent.com/pod-product-compliance
Lightning Source LLC
Chambersburg PA
CBHW020356080526
44584CB00014B/1035